8 50

LENGER

PAREM

MWAHND PEIDAK

MWAHND PEIDI

SCALE

1 0 1 2 3 4 5 Km

UH

DEHPEHK

TAKAIU

N

NET

158° 23'

A RESIDENCE OF ELEVEN YEARS
IN NEW HOLLAND
AND THE CAROLINE ISLANDS

No. 4 of the Pacific History Series
General Editor: H. E. MAUDE
Literary Adviser: J. W. DAVIDSON

A Residence of Eleven Years
in New Holland
and the Caroline Islands

by

James F. O'Connell

Saul H. Riesenberg
Editor

THE UNIVERSITY PRESS OF HAWAII
Honolulu 1972

Library of Congress Catalog Card Number 72-82141
ISBN 0-8248-0219-5
Printed in Australia
Published in Australia by the Australian National University Press

To my wife, Mildred

The Pacific History Series of books provides an outlet for the publication of original manuscripts important to historians and others interested in the Pacific islands.

Works already published are:
1. *A Cruize in a Queensland Labour Vessel to the South Seas*, by W. E. Giles, edited by Deryck Scarr (1968)
2. *The Works of Ta'unga. Records of a Polynesian Traveller in the South Seas, 1833-1896*, by R. G. and Marjorie Crocombe (1968)
3. *The Trading Voyages of Andrew Cheyne, 1841-1844*, edited by Dorothy Shineberg (1971)

FOREWORD

PACIFIC historians and anthropologists alike are searching the
libraries and archives today for accounts of island societies at
or near the commencement of European contact: the former to
get as long a documentary time span as possible for their narratives, and the latter to obtain a baseline foundation on which to
build their studies of culture change.

The journals of the explorers are unfortunately of limited
value for these purposes, since the explorers were essentially
transients who, until Bougainville and Cook in the late 1760s,
were, in the absence of any means of verbal communication, only
able to record the material culture and external facets of island
life.

Hence arises the importance of the few accounts which, like
James F. O'Connell's *A Residence of Eleven Years in New Holland and the Caroline Islands*, have come down to us written
or dictated by the first Europeans to live ashore among the
islanders, sharing in their activities and conforming to their
customs. These were the so-called beachcombers who, like the
white trappers and hunters in North America, lived somewhat

precariously beyond the frontiers of European political, and even cultural, penetration.

There are some fourteen books 'emanating from beachcombers who spent months, and even years, among the islanders; people who were adopted into native families, usually married to native wives, who spoke the language of necessity and who wrote about customs and events in which they had participated and processes in which they had become proficient'.[1] Two of these works are still unpublished, while others are so scarce as to qualify for all practical purposes as manuscripts.

Three further 'beachcomber books' are considered of such significance and rarity that they are now being edited by specialists in the area they are concerned with for publication in the Pacific History Series; while two others await the finding of a suitable expert in the locality and period: no easy task if the high standards of scholarship hitherto set by the Series are to be maintained.

That competent editors are essential for books written on the islands prior to say the middle of the nineteenth century, and for many produced after that date, is shown clearly by Dr Saul H. Riesenberg's introduction and notes to O'Connell's text. Several of the classical English writers of the period considered it perfectly legitimate to intermix fact and fiction: George Borrow's *Lavengro* and *Romany Rye*, for example, 'are such a blend of romance and autobiography, that to say where literal truth ends and imaginative truth begins would have puzzled the author himself'.[2] Their Pacific counterparts were even more lacking in modern scholarly rectitude: Herman Melville, John Coulter, and Benjamin Morrell are among many authors who combined obvious fabrications with ethnographical and historical data of recognised value to researchers today.

Despite similar defects, however, O'Connell's work is essential reading for everyone interested in gaining a vivid picture of day-to-day life in a Pacific Island society at the dawn of European contact. But its value as a main ethnographical source on

[1] Maude, H. E., 'Beachcombers and Castaways', in *Of Islands and Men*, Melbourne, 1968, 168.

[2] Sampson, George, *The Concise Cambridge History of English Literature*, Cambridge, 1953, 839.

Micronesian culture is largely invalidated if it is accepted un-critically at its face value.

That most people in the past have done just this is admittedly not their fault, since they could scarcely be expected to possess Dr Riesenberg's unique knowledge of Ponapean society, gained as a result of a series of field-work visits to the island extending from 1947 to the present day, and supplemented by a study of everything that could be found published or in manuscript on the islanders.

Whether working at the University of Hawaii, as Staff An-thropologist to the High Commissioner of the United States Trust Territory of the Pacific Islands, or in his present position at the Smithsonian Institution at Washington, Dr Riesenberg has con-tinued his dominant research interest in Ponape and its people, as attested by numerous published papers culminating in his definitive book on *The Native Polity of Ponape*.[3] His exposé of Michelena y Rojas's account of Ponape, published in 1842, is a model of how textual criticism can aid in the clarification of early Pacific source material, while his interest in O'Connell himself and his narrative has already been shown in a study entitled 'The Tattooed Irishman'.[4]

As a result of Dr Riesenberg's researches we are now able to gain a far better appreciation of the strengths and weaknesses of O'Connell's book. As he suggests, the part relating to New South Wales appears to be, in everything relating to himself, a tissue of fabrications, in all probability designed to prevent his identification as an escaped convict, which would account for the fact that he never returned to England.

In the part relating to Ponape one has to remember that O'Connell was endeavouring to turn an honest penny by telling an exotic story of life as a castaway among savages on a remote and almost unknown island, and to have admitted that it was at the time a recognised centre of the Australian tortoiseshell trade, that there were other Europeans living ashore than his companions, and that it was visited by other ships during his

---

[3] Riesenberg, Saul H., *The Native Polity of Ponape,* Washington, D.C., 1968.

[4] Riesenberg, Saul H., 'A Pacific Voyager's Hoax', *Ethnohistory*, 6, 1959, 238-64; 'The Tattooed Irishman', *The Smithsonian Journal of History*, 3, 1968, 1-17.

period of residence would have detracted from the romance, and therefore the sales, of his book. It might have furthermore pointed the question as to why he did not leave on one of these ships from New South Wales, which was the last place an escaped convict would wish to return to.

But in his descriptions of native life on Ponape, which will be the particular interest of most readers, O'Connell provides us with invaluable material not otherwise obtainable, while his inaccuracies, now recorded by Dr Riesenberg, appear less serious and may perhaps be attributed to a shorter stay on the island than he admits, to his limited education and understanding, and to a not unnatural desire to make himself out to be a good deal more important and knowledgeable than in fact he was, rather than to any deliberate desire to conceal.

It is an appropriate coincidence that this Foreword is being written on the four hundred and fiftieth anniversary of the year in which the first Pacific Islanders were seen by a European. For the Chamorros discovered by Magellan in the Marianas in 1521 were also Micronesians and in touch with the people of the Caroline Islands to the south, who visited them in their long-distance sailing canoes for trade. One likes to think that there may well have been Ponapeans among the visitors to Magellan's ships on that fateful day.

H. E. Maude

Canberra, 1971

ACKNOWLEDGMENTS

THE editor's thanks are due to the Smithsonian Institution of Washington for permission to reproduce illustrations from his article 'The Tattooed Irishman' in the *Smithsonian Journal of History*, Vol. 3, No. 1 (Spring, 1968), pp. 1-18, and the map from his monograph *The Native Polity of Ponape*, published by them as Volume 10 of the Smithsonian Contributions to Anthropology in 1968.

CONTENTS

FIGURES

INTRODUCTION

COMPARED to other parts of the world, there is a paucity of first-hand accounts of the islands of Micronesia written in the days before the native cultures became influenced and altered by Western ways. Among the few descriptions we have, dating from the early nineteenth century and written by castaways, ship's deserters, and beachcombers, one of the most fascinating is the story of James F. O'Connell and his life on Ponape, in the Caroline Islands.

O'Connell's description of Ponape is not the first account of that island, but it is the first one based upon an extended visit. Loaysa in 1526 and Saavedra in 1528 may have sighted the island; the statements they give are meagre and inconclusive.[1] Quiros, who had taken command of the ill-fated Mendaña expedition after Mendaña's death, saw Ponape in 1595 and is to be regarded as the discoverer.[2] He did not land and the description is scanty; he

[1] Navarrete, Martin Fernandez de, *Coleccion de los Viages y Descubrimientos*, Madrid, 1837, Vol. 5, pp. 99-100, 468.

[2] Markham, Clements Robert, *The Voyages of Pedro Fernandez de Quiros, 1595 to 1606*, translated and edited by Sir Clements Markham, London, 1904.

only saw a few canoes and established no communication except by gesture. Nearly two centuries elapsed before the next known visitor, Captain Thomas Read of the American ship *Alliance*, in 1787.[3] This also was no more than a sighting. Later sightings, all uncertain, were by Musgrave in 1793, Ibargoita in 1801, and Dublon in 1814.[4] The East India Company's *Marquis of Wellington* passed the island in 1815.[5] Captain John Henry Rowe visited the island in 1825.[6] He also did not land; his vessel was chased by five canoes, this being his only contact with the natives. He gave the name John Bull's Island to what he regarded as his new discovery, after the name of his bark. Someone else, whose name is apparently unrecorded, must have been to Ponape some time before, because in a book on navigation published in 1824 the island's position is given correctly, with the name Ascension attached to it.[7] It was this name that got on the maps, beginning about 1828, and this is the name O'Connell used for it after he was rescued.

The first description of the island and natives of any length at all is by the Russian, Captain F. Lutké,[8] whose vessel, the *Senyavin*, gave its name to the group consisting of Ponape, Ant, and Pakin. He was at Ponape only a few days, 14-19 January 1828. His boats attempted to land but could not make the shore because of the throngs of canoes that pressed about them and the show of hostility. But natives came aboard, some trading occurred, a short word list was compiled, and a map was drawn. F. H. von Kittlitz, a member of the expedition, wrote a supplementary account.[9] The two reports, published

3 Manuscript copy of logbook in U.S. National Archives.
4 Hambruch, Paul, 'Ponape', *Ergebnisse der Südsee-Expedition 1908-1910*, ed. G. Thilenius, II. B. vii, 3 vols., Berlin, 1932-6, Vol. 1, p. 78.
5 Logbook, Microfilm M-105, Dept of Pacific History, Australian National University, 8 May 1815. (Original manuscript in India Office Library, London.)
6 *Sydney Gazette*, 15 June 1827; *Hobart Colonial Times*, 25 May 1827.
7 Riddle, Edward, *A Treatise on Navigation and Nautical Astronomy* . . ., London, 1824, Table XXXIII.
8 Lutké, Frédéric, *Voyage autour du monde exécuté par ordre de sa Majesté l'Empereur Nicolas Ier sur la corvette "Le Séniavine" dans les années 1826, 1827, 1828, et 1829*, 4 vols., Paris, 1835-6.
9 Kittlitz, F. H. von, *Denkwürdigkeiten einer Reise nach dem russischen Amerika, nach Mikronesien und durch Kamtschatka*, 2 vols., Gotha, 1858.

2

respectively in 1835-6 and 1858, together with others made by the scientific staff, provide the first real knowledge of Ponape.

But it is O'Connell who gives us the intimate sort of picture of the people that only residence among them could produce. The apparent value of his information was recognised at once. His book was published in 1836, and the next year, 1837, Horatio Hale, the philologist of the then preparing U.S. Exploring Expedition of 1838-42, under Captain Charles Wilkes, interviewed O'Connell. Says Hale, the book contains 'much valuable information . . . which has since been fully confirmed'.[10] Hale was not alone in his admiration. The German ethnologist Paul Hambruch, who worked on Ponape in 1910 and who in 1929 published a translation into German of O'Connell's book, heaps encomiums upon him. A free translation of his remarks is: Unburdened by preconceptions or knowledge O'Connell depicts a South Sea people and their reaction to whites, first seen in the form of six shipwrecked sailors who were admitted into their community. For this reason this book is so valuable. It provides information about customs, practices, and concepts that by 1910 had long belonged to the past. That he accomplished fundamental work is evident from his knowledge of the language, which at first impression appears to be sparse. He possessed an extraordinary memory. Even today one can follow his track on the basis of his description. . . The book is one of the most precious sources for knowledge of the Caroline Islands.[11]

To this may be added the judgment of the authors of the *Civil Affairs Handbook*, published by the U.S. Navy in 1944, that it is a 'valuable and fascinating account of Ponape',[12] and that of the American anthropologist John L. Fischer, who has done field work on Ponape, that it is a source of 'valuable historical information'.[13] But against this is the remark of Luther H.

[10] Hale, Horatio, *Ethnography and Philology* (United States Exploring Expedition, 1838-1842, under command of Charles Wilkes, U.S.N.) Philadelphia, 1846, Vol. 6, pp. 80-1.

[11] Hambruch, op. cit., p. 6.

[12] United States Navy Department, Office of Chief of Naval Operations, *East Caroline Islands*, Civil Affairs Handbook (OPNAV P22-5), Washington, 1944, p. 167.

[13] Fischer, John L., *The Eastern Carolines*, Behavior Science Monographs, Human Relations Area Files, New Haven, 1957, p. 249.

Fig. 1 Portrait of James F. O'Connell, from the cover of a pamphlet hawked at circuses in which he performed

Gulick, the medical missionary to Ponape in the 1850s, that 'so much of the irreconcilably and egregiously incorrect is mingled with O'Connell's narrative . . . concerning everything connected with the whole island . . .' that very little of what he says can be trusted.[14]

O'Connell's book was published in Boston in August 1836. As the title page states, it was actually edited from his verbal narration, the editor and the author of the preface signing himself

[14] Gulick, Luther H., 'The Ruins on Ponape, or Ascension Island', *Journal of the American Geographical and Statistical Society*, Vol. I, No. 5, 129-37, May 1859, p. 131.

4

only H.H.W. A search through biographical dictionaries produces only one H.H.W. who can be made to fit in place and time and who qualifies as the kind of literary figure the language and style of the preface suggest he must have been. This man is Horatio Hastings Weld, born in Boston in 1811, a printer, writer, and newspaper editor in several places. Later, in 1845, he took orders in the Protestant Episcopal church, but in his earlier years he published many sketches, tales, and poems. A number of these were brought together in a volume called *Corrected Proofs*, published in Boston in 1836, shortly before the O'Connell book. Many of the stories concern the sea and the life of a sailor, which probably has bearing on Weld's interest (if Weld is indeed H.H.W.) in O'Connell. One of these tales relates several incidents in the life of a fictitious sailor named Benjamin Fiferail and seems to be partially autobiographical. It is called 'In Callao Harbour', where the incidents occur, and where Weld apparently visited. There is a footnote in the O'Connell book in which H.H.W. states that he has been to Callao, which makes the identification of H.H.W. with Weld somewhat firmer.

In any case H.H.W. expends two paragraphs of his preface in anticipating the reader's scepticism and in protesting O'Connell's credibility in all respects, in terms like Hambruch's and very unlike Gulick's.

The truth must lie somewhere between these very different views of O'Connell and his book. From the first pages O'Connell leads us on an often exasperating chase through a maze of exaggerations, anachronisms, improbabilities, and outright fabrications, commingled with thoroughly accurate and original observations. To separate the truth from the falsehoods is no little task. Some of the misstatements are clumsy, some are hidden among unimpeachable facts. But what is the explanation of this deviousness, what is he concealing? We will return to this question, but one thing he conceals is evidently his true name. No trace of any historical James F. O'Connell can be found until after all the events of the book have taken place. The published narrative ends with his arrival in New York, and the man James F. O'Connell only then enters verifiable history, at the moment he embarks upon his new career in the theatre and circus. Before then the name appears nowhere.

He begins, like any picaresque adventurer, by telling us the

5

date and place of his birth. But 'an extensive search of the registers of baptism in all city churches in the vicinity of Thomas Street' in Dublin where he says he was born 'in an effort to trace the baptism of James F. O'Connell . . . has been fruitless'.[15] He may be in those registers, but if so it is under another name. As for his age, the only independent evidence of it is given in the New Orleans Port lists of disembarking passengers,[16] when he returns from Havana on 21 May 1853 after an unfortunate circus tour to that city. There he is stated to be 40, which would put his birth date in 1813 instead of 1808 as he gives it in the book. But to accept this date would make him far too young for the experiences he describes in the 1820s in Australia and as a member of the crews of two whaling vessels by 1830. We must assume that he was really born about 1808, though nothing about his story in Ireland and England is verifiable.

O'Connell says his residence in Australia was in the years 1820-6. He was eleven years old when he became a cabin-boy on the *Phoenix*, according to H.H.W., which would be about right if the birth date is really 10 November 1808 and if he did actually go to Australia in 1820. The six years in Australia, plus the five years he says he was on Ponape, would come to the 'residence of eleven years in New Holland and the Caroline Islands' of the title page of the book. But he also says that the *Spy*, which rescued him from Ponape, arrived at that island in November 1833. The captain of the *Spy*, John B. Knight, confirms that date in his journal,[17] saying that he picked up 'the Irishman' (he does not name him) on 27 November 1833. This would make it more like thirteen years, counting from 1820, and puts the actual date of arrival in question.

O'Connell names Macquarie as governor and F. A. Healey (Hely) as superintendent of convicts at the time of his arrival in Port Jackson. They, together with the quarantine physician,

15 Letter, Rev. Sean Murray, The Chancellery, Archbishop's House, Dublin, to Riesenberg, 23 October 1969.

16 U.S. National Archives, Passenger Lists of Vessels arriving at New Orleans, 1820-1902, Microcopy 259, Roll 38, No. 209, 26 April-30 November 1853.

17 Knights, John B., 'A Journal of a Voyage in the Brig "Spy", of Salem (1832-1834)', *The Sea, the Ship and the Sailor*, Publication No. 7 of the Marine Research Society, Salem, 1925, pp. 168-207.

supposedly inspected the convicts arriving on the *Phoenix* when they were landed at the dockyard. But to make Macquarie right the Irish boy must have arrived before November 1821, while Hely was not appointed superintendent of convicts until January 1823. They could not have served together. Moreover, no vessel named *Phoenix* arrived until 1822. Actually there were three convict transports called *Phoenix*, and one of them made two voyages. The first *Phoenix* landed 182 convicts from England at Hobart, in Tasmania, on 20 May 1822, and on her second voyage, to Sydney, arriving 14 July 1828, she disembarked 190 prisoners. The second *Phoenix* delivered 202 English prisoners at Hobart on 21 July 1824. The third vessel of this name, sailing from Dublin, arrived at Sydney on 25 December 1826 with 189 convicts.[18]

The convicts transported on all four of these voyages were male, while O'Connell says his *Phoenix* carried 200 females. Their commanders were, respectively, Captains Weatherhead, Cozens, White, and Anderson, while O'Connell gives the name of his captain as Salmon. He says his ship's doctor was named Walker, but the Surgeon Superintendents on the four *Phoenix* trips were respectively Evans, Carlyle, Queade, and Cook. There was only one Walker among the doctors who served on the convict ships in the 1820s. That was Hugh Walker, who sailed on the *Guildford* and the *Minstrel*, arriving in Port Jackson in 1820 and 1825 respectively.[19]

Yet if O'Connell came to Australia on any of these voyages it was most probably on the second *Phoenix*, under Captain Robert White. True, there are the discrepancies just mentioned, and others too. Some of the convicts on Captain White's vessel had been mutinous on the voyage and in consequence, after disembarking at Hobart, were sent to the special prison at Macquarie Harbour.[20] O'Connell makes no mention of this. And he says that his ship made no port during the five-month passage between Spithead and Sydney Cove, while the second *Phoenix*

[18] Rhodes, F., *Pageant of the Pacific, Being the Maritime History of Australasia*, Sydney, 1934-36, Vol. 1, pp. 207, 214; Mitchell Library 4/5198-99, Reports of Vessels Arriving, July 1826-1828.

[19] Mitchell Library, Adm. 101/59, ships' surgeons' logs; Bateson, Charles, *The Convict Ships, 1788-1868*, Glasgow, 1959.

[20] *Hobart Town Gazette*, 24 and 30 July 1824.

did touch at Teneriffe. But there are two curious parallels. Captain White's first officer was a David Salmon, which is the name given by O'Connell as the commander of his ship.[21] O'Connell says his *Phoenix* was declared unseaworthy upon arrival and was purchased by the government for a convict receiving hulk. Captain White's *Phoenix* suffered the same fate. After discharging her prisoners at Hobart she proceeded in August 1824 to Port Jackson. While in charge of the pilot she struck on the Sow and Pigs. In consequence, after being pulled off, she was condemned in September and purchased by the government early in 1825. She lay for many years in Lavender Bay, holding prisoners awaiting transportation to Moreton Bay, Norfolk Island, and other penal settlements.[22] It seems likely therefore that White's *Phoenix* and O'Connell's *Phoenix* are the same. If he did sail with White he arrived in Australia in 1824, when he would have been fifteen.

But it is also possible that he came on quite another ship. Suppose he arrived in 1825, after the government had moored the *Phoenix* at Lavender Bay, or even later. He would have seen the hulk where she lay in full view as his vessel sailed past her. He would have seen her many times again during his years of residence at Sydney and would have heard her name. If he was anxious to conceal his true story when he related the narrative to H.H.W. the name *Phoenix* could well have been the first to come to his mind. As for the name Salmon, the same thing could have happened; there was another connection between Salmon and O'Connell, as we will soon see. And if he did come on some other ship he would not have known that the *Phoenix* had gone first to Hobart and hence omitted that incident from his story; he would not have known Captain White's name, but if he later sailed with Salmon (as suggested below) when Salmon was a ship's captain and was told that he (Salmon) had come out on the *Phoenix* he might have thought that he had been captain of that vessel too; he would not have known the

21 The largest part of the information on Australian events and personalities in this and succeeding paragraphs was made available through the kindness of Mr H. E. Maude, Mrs Honoré Foster, and the late Miss Ida Leeson (letters of various dates), to all of whom a debt of gratitude is acknowledged.

22 Rhodes, op cit., pp. 217, 225.

sex of the convict cargo; and Walker, Macquarie, and Hely could be just names that he had heard and inserted into the story, unaware of the anachronisms.

According to O'Connell, after leaving the *Phoenix*, in 1820 by his account, he took service with a Mr Charles Smith, whom he describes as an ex-convict and an important contractor for the supply of meat to the government for the soldiers and prisoners. Smith was the first who succeeded in packing beef in Australia. He was also the owner of a livery stable, a sportsman, and a famous racehorse of the time, Boshee, belonged to him.

Now all of this information is in general correct. Charles Smith, a native of Shropshire, born in 1800, had been arrested at the age of fourteen for picking pockets and transported as a convict. He was given a ticket of leave and allowed to remain in Sydney on recommendation of the bench in 1827 and was granted a conditional pardon in 1830. When he died in 1845 he owned a prosperous butcher shop in Sydney, had many herds of high-bred cattle and horses, and was the possessor of several farms and stations. For ten years his racehorses had dominated the Australian turf. The name 'Boshee', however, does not appear in the records. Neither in 1820 nor in 1824 could Smith's interests have been so extensive as in O'Connell's description. Perhaps by 1830 it was a fair picture. O'Connell must have stayed in Australia until close to that year, if he is describing Smith's position from personal knowledge.

At some unspecified time (between 1820 and 1826, if we are to believe his dates) the young Irishman, we are told, made an exploration trip into the interior with the Surveyor-General, John Oxley. The trip lasted six months, and the party consisted of O'Connell, Oxley, and twelve or fourteen trusty convicts. This lad, somewhere between twelve and eighteen years old, with hardly more than cabin-boy experience, is supposed to have been second in command of one of Oxley's highly-organised and well-planned expeditions! The only place mentioned by name during this alleged exploration is Wellington Valley. Oxley was at Wellington Valley in his first expeditions, 1815-18, but this is much too early for O'Connell. Even Oxley's last expedition, of 1823, is probably too early, and in any case the party travelled up the coast from Sydney to the area around Moreton Bay and the Brisbane River and never penetrated far

9

inland. O'Connell's name does not appear among the participants listed for any of these trips. Between 1825 and his death in 1828 Oxley made surveys of the settled districts, and possibly O'Connell was attached to one of these parties, though there is no record of it.[23]

In 1822, O'Connell alleges, he shipped in the *Cape Packet*, under Captain Dillon, for a whaling voyage. He describes how the vessel foundered somewhere off the northern coast of Australia and how he saved himself, together with a Kanaka shipmate. Then, he says, he spent eight or nine months among the Aborigines while making his way to Port Macquarie. From there he was sent to Sydney as a runaway convict but he was able to clear himself of that charge.

The musters of vessels departing from Sydney during the period July 1821 to 1825 exist today in the Mitchell Library in Sydney.[24] There is no *Cape Packet* among the departures, and O'Connell's name is not on the muster of any vessel leaving in those years. In the last months of 1824, those immediately following the misadventure of the *Phoenix*, there appear on the musters the names of thirty-four seamen and officers who are noted as having been discharged from the stricken vessel. O'Connell says of the *Phoenix* that 'the ship's company, including the two extremes, officers and boys, numbered about thirty-five', so that just about all of them would be accounted for on the outgoing crew lists. Perhaps one of those names is his true name? Even if it is, he shipped out neither in 1822 nor on the *Cape Packet*. That vessel first came to Australia in 1826. If he signed on her that same year we must, as with the *Phoenix*, adjust his dates by four years. But if this is the famous Captain Peter Dillon who solved the mystery of the disappearance of La Perouse, the French explorer, he was never her captain, nor is any other Dillon known to have been. In 1826 Captain Laughton commanded the *Cape Packet*, and he was succeeded by Francis Dixon. The vessel was not a whaler until 1830, when the master's name was Hindson. She was making whaling voyages as late as 1838, when she was successively under Captains

[23] Favenc, Ernest, *The History of Australian Exploration from 1788 to 1888*, London and Sydney, 1888, pp. 50-74.

[24] Mitchell Library 4/4772-75, Ships' Musters of Departing Passengers and Crews, July 1821-1825.

Cape and Dixon. There is no record of a wreck of any vessel of that name. It looks as though James is indulging again in his habit of putting together isolated names and facts to make a convincing story.

For his eight or nine months of wandering about in Australia, while making his way from the north coast to Port Macquarie, O'Connell has remarkably few observations to make about the Aborigines. Indeed, some of those that he does make seem to be borrowed from published sources. The editor of the book, H.H.W., says in his preface that he acknowledges assistance from 'Cunningham's New South Wales' in the section on the 'natural history of New Holland'. In fact, he takes more than natural history from Cunningham, though the information in the book is given as though it comes from O'Connell himself. Thus James is made to say, 'At and about Port Macquarie, and to the north of that settlement . . . a large fire is built . . . to keep away Poloyan, the devil . . .'. Again, 'Koyan, God, or the Good Spirit is . . . seldom invoked'. Compare this with Cunningham, in describing the natives of Hunter's River, around Merton: 'They believe in a good spirit, which they call *Koyan*, and in an evil spirit named *Potoyan* . . . Potoyan strolls about after dark seeking for his prey, but is afraid to approach a fire, which serves as a protection against him . . .'. From O'Connell: 'instances of blacks promenading the streets of Sydney *in puris naturalibus* were not quite so rare as eclipses. Some would misappropriate garments given them, as, for instance, by buttoning the waistband of a pair of trowsers round the neck . . .'; and from Cunningham: many natives even 'at this day [may be seen] parading the streets of Sydney in *natural* costume, or with a pair of breeches dangling round their *necks* . . .'. Several other parallels might be cited.[25]

As for the incident O'Connell relates concerning his being sent from Port Macquarie to Sydney, where he cleared himself, the records of correspondence between the Colonial Secretary and the Port Macquarie commandant contain no reference to any incident resembling this.[26]

[25] Cunningham, Peter M., *Two Years in New South Wales*, 3rd ed., London, 1828, Vol. II, pp. 8, 34-5.

[26] Mitchell Library B40, Port Macquarie Order Books; Mitchell Library 4/3865, Colonial Secretary, letters to commandant of Port Macquarie.

At some time O'Connell 'belonged', he says, to the government ship *City of Edinburgh*, which transported 120 incorrigibles to Norfolk Island, six of them being killed in a riot. If O'Connell was really on this ship he was still in Australia in 1829, for the riot, as reported by the current *Sydney Gazette*, took place on 11 January of that year. The *City of Edinburgh*, which had been taken up by the government to transport 160 prisoners to Moreton Bay (not Norfolk Island) was lying in Sydney Cove when the rioting began, according to the *Gazette*, and the soldiers were finally forced to fire among the prisoners. Two jumped overboard but were captured, eight were wounded, and one died.[27]

The Irish sailor's final Australian note is as follows: 'In or about 1826, I shipped in the barque *John Bull*, whaler, Captain Barkus'. The vessel put in at Bay of Islands, in New Zealand, and after eight months, in a heavy storm and the captain being drunk, they struck on a reef and abandoned ship. O'Connell and five shipmates, in an open boat, made their way to Ponape in three days and four nights. Presumably the vessel would thus have been lost in 1827, possibly 1828. Horatio Hale evidently accepts the date 1827 when he says: 'Had the Russian navigator [Lutké, of the *Senyavin*, who was at Ponape in January 1828] been able to land, he would probably have had an opportunity of rescuing from captivity seven [*sic*] English seamen, who had shortly before reached the island in a boat, after their shipwreck . . .'.[28] Paul Hambruch also wonders why O'Connell nowhere refers to Lutké's visit.[29]

But the records show that the *John Bull* was still afloat in 1830. Captain Barkus's first (and only) command of her commenced when she sailed on 12 May 1830 for the sperm fishery. In August of that year the *Clarkstone* hailed her at the fishing grounds off Japan, when she had sixty barrels of oil on board.[30] A little later she seems to have been at Kusaie, in the Caroline Islands. On 31 October 1830, Captain Edward Cattlin of the whaler *Australian* reports, he spoke the *John Bull* near Ysabel, in the

[27] *Sydney Gazette*, 10, 13, and 24 January 1829.

[28] Hale, op. cit., p. 80.

[29] Hambruch, op. cit., p. 77.

[30] *Sydney Gazette*, 15 May and 3 November 1830.

Solomons.[31] The two vessels parted company the next day, the *John Bull* bearing up for Malaita. That, apparently, was the last seen of her.

There is a further curiosity, this one connected with David Salmon, the same Salmon, presumably, that O'Connell credits with having been in command of the *Phoenix* when the Irish boy first left England. When the *Phoenix* was abandoned on the Sow and Pigs in 1824, David Salmon, who had been first mate, signed on in the same capacity aboard another vessel. Which should that be but the *John Bull*! She thereupon sailed, under command of Captain Thomas Reibey, for China and Mauritius, on 13 November 1824. Aboard her, besides Salmon, were four other discharged members of the crew of the *Phoenix*, including one Thomas Lewsett, ship's boy.[32] (Would the *Phoenix* have had two boys, Lewsett and O'Connell?) Reibey, Salmon, and the *John Bull* were back in Sydney on 17 May 1825, and in the next few years Salmon made several voyages as captain of a schooner, the *Prince Regent*, to Batavia, Calcutta, and Manila. But on 19 October 1828, when the *John Bull* sailed for the sperm fishery, who should be in command of her but David Salmon! She returned to Sydney on 11 February 1830, with 162 tons of oil, was sold by her owners, Jones and Walker, to Lamb and Co., and sailed again on her last, fateful voyage under Captain Barkus on 12 May 1830.[33]

But there is still another coincidence. On an earlier voyage, when the *John Bull* was under the command of Captain John Henry Rowe, she passed by Ponape, on 10 September 1825, as already described. Rowe regarded himself as the discoverer and gave the island the name of John Bull's Island.

Could it have been on the voyage under Salmon that O'Connell sailed rather than the later one with Barkus? For O'Connell to describe Salmon as a ship's captain, as he incorrectly does in

[31] Mitchell Library MSS. 1800 (5-332C), logbook of the *Australian*, Captain Edward Cattlin, 1831-3.

[32] Mitchell Library 4/4775, Departing Passengers and Crews, 1824.

[33] *Sydney Gazette*, 18 November 1824; 19 May, 22 September 1825; 13 and 17 May, 12 July, 27 September, 18 November 1826; 3 October, 7 and 19 December 1827; 26 May 1828; 13 February, 11 March 1830. *Australian*, 22 September 1825; 13 May, 27 September 1826; 3 October 1827; 28 May 1828.

connection with the *Phoenix*, suggests that he knew him only in later years, when he was in command of either the *Prince Regent* or the *John Bull*, 1825 to 1830. If O'Connell was in the crew of the *John Bull* on the 1828-30 voyage and if Salmon took the bark to Ponape the Irish sailor might have deserted there, perhaps some time in 1829. Then, hearing later about the loss of the vessel under Barkus, he might have placed himself, in his narration to H.H.W., on that voyage instead. The description of the supposed shipwreck and the fate of the survivors, with all its circumstantial detail, suggests either that O'Connell had considerable imagination and inventiveness or else, if any part of it is true, that he is describing something that happened to another ship entirely.

The *John Bull* must have been lost late in 1830, soon after the *Australian* encountered her, or quite early the next year. The logbook of the *Australian* relates that when the two vessels met in the Solomons Captain Barkus and the ship's doctor came aboard. This was on 31 October 1830. Barkus told Captain Cattlin that ten members of his crew had absconded at Strong's Island (the modern Kusaie, 300 miles to the east of Ponape), where they had evidently stopped, though O'Connell does not mention it, some time between August on the Japan grounds and now in the Solomon Islands. (This was Captain Cattlin's first command. On his previous voyage he had been mate of another vessel, under a Captain Lewis, 18 August 1827 to 20 May 1828. It was—of course—the *John Bull*!)[34] Another ship, the *Albion*, arriving at Sydney on 30 January 1831, had also met the *John Bull* somewhere, and reported that Barkus had shipped a native crew, presumably Strong's Islanders, to replace the deserters.[35] Could this new crew have risen against Barkus and taken the vessel? If O'Connell was on this voyage with Barkus, was he one of the ten absconders, who subsequently made his way somehow to Ponape?

A newspaper years later suggests that the *John Bull* was lost about 1827 at McAskill (known today as Pingelap, lying between Ponape and Kusaie).[36] It attributes this information to

[34] Mitchell Library MSS. 1800 (5-332C), logbook of *John Bull*, Captain Lewis (logbook kept by mate Ed. Cattlin), 1827-8.

[35] *Sydney Gazette*, 1 February 1831.

[36] *The Friend*, May 1853, p. 8.

14

British Consul-General Miller of Honolulu. But there is much better evidence that the vessel met its fate neither at McAskill nor in the Solomons but at Pleasant Island (Nauru), 800 miles to the eastwards of Ponape. This place, in the 1830s and 1840s, and the many white deserters and beachcombers who lived there among the indigenes, had a thoroughly unwholesome reputation. Captain J. H. Eagleston refers to the 'white villains' ashore there in 1835, and George Cheever in the same year calls them 'a complete set of vagabonds'.[37] On 17 May 1837 the whaler *Duke of York* put in at Pleasant Island and there encountered what its captain, Robert C. Morgan, called some 'shockingly degraded' Europeans.[38] The next day, after putting out to sea, he discovered five stowaways aboard—three Englishmen, a Scotsman, and an American. These men, deserters from various ships that had called at Pleasant Island two to eight months before, said that they had fled the island through fear of the natives and of three or four white men (among some eight on shore) who controlled them. The remarks of the five men (Dennis Minney, Charles Bruce, George Campbell, Thomas Simpson, and William Burke) were of such a nature that Captain Morgan thought it advisable to take written statements, to submit to the authorities in Sydney. Three of the stowaways (Minney, Bruce, and Burke) were on 13 July put ashore, at their own request, at New Georgia, in the Solomons, and on 13 August the *Duke of York* was wrecked, but the crew got safely to Sydney and Captain Morgan gave the five statements to the editor of the *Sydney Herald*, where they were published in the issue of 7 September 1837. Their gist was as follows:

Among the ruffians living at Pleasant Island were two Irishmen that the stowaways were in particular dread of, Patrick Burke (or Cilo) and John Jones (or Dacy), convicts who had run away from the penal settlement at Norfolk Island and had killed others who had been in the boat with them *en route* to Pleasant Island. The island of Rotuma is also involved in one account. They had lived on Pleasant Island for several years.

---

[37] Eagleston and Cheever, both of the *Emerald*, at Nauru on 25 June 1835. Logbooks at Peabody Museum, Salem.

[38] Mitchell Library MSS. A 270, logbook of *Duke of York*, Captain Robert Clark Morgan, 1836-8.

There was frequent mention of the *John Bull* among the whites; Burke and Jones were said to have taken that vessel, but were also said to have endeavoured to throw the blame on the natives; it was dangerous to the other whites to appear to know anything about the whaler's fate; two men had fled Pleasant Island in a canoe because the two Irishmen suspected them of having such knowledge and would have murdered them. There were many ship's articles on the island, believed to have come from the *John Bull*. There was a white boy of 16 or 17 who lived among the natives, was not allowed to talk with strangers on the island, and had nearly lost his use of English. The newspaper, in its issue of 28 September 1837, concludes that 'there can be no doubt that the ill-fated *John Bull* whaler, with her master and crew, have been the victims of some Europeans and other savages residing at Pleasant Island . . .'.[39]

In spite of these published statements, the 'savages' remained undisturbed by any authorities. Yet they did meet a measure of retribution. When Captain Baker, on the *Gideon Howland*,[40] visited Pleasant Island on 26 September 1839 five white men came aboard, among them the infamous Jones. On Baker's next visit, 9 November 1841, he learned that the natives had massacred eight white men, possibly Burke among them, leaving only Jones and one other, Murphy, who soon left on another ship. Captain Baker took Jones on board his ship, apparently to save his life, together with his native wife, child, and property, and landed him at Ocean Island as a refugee. When the *Gypsy* was at Pleasant Island a few weeks later, on 23 December 1841, the same story of the massacre of all the white men was heard.[41]

The mysterious white boy, however, continued to live among the natives. In 1843 another visitor to Pleasant Island, Captain Simpson, was told that there was 'a white man on this island, who had been living there for many years; . . . is thought to be either one of the boys belonging to the *John Bull* or *Princess Charlotte*, both which vessels were supposed to be lost or cut

[39] *Sydney Herald*, 4, 17, and 28 September 1837.

[40] Logbook in Nicholson Collection, Public Library, Providence, R.I.

[41] Logbook, Microfilm M-198, Dept of Pacific History, Australian National University.

out near this island, and he is thought to be either a lad named Backs or LeBurn'.[42]

These evidences of nefarious doings hardly accord with O'Connell's version of the fate of the *John Bull*. Was he a participant in these affairs at Pleasant Island and did he later make his way to Ponape by some other vessel? Or did he in fact desert the *John Bull* on her previous voyage, when she was under Captain Salmon, as suggested earlier? The missionary Albert Sturges, writing in the early 1850s, reports that he met one of O'Connell's fellow 'castaways' who was still on Ponape and says flatly that the Irish sailor deserted a ship, which was lying off the southern shore of the island by swimming ashore, and that his story about shipwreck is all 'stuff'.[43] Yet it is a question whether information given to Sturges 25 years afterwards would be reliable. If O'Connell assumed that name only after he got to the United States, as seems likely from the failure to find any record whatsoever of him in Australia, how could his alleged comrade have known to whom Sturges's questions referred?

In the lifeboat with himself and his five shipmates, escaping from the foundering *John Bull*, O'Connell's story places the wife and daughter of a missionary, the family having been put aboard the vessel at Bay of Islands by Bishop Marsden. They were intended for Kusaie, the easternmost of the Caroline Islands. As Captain Cattlin tells us, the *John Bull* did actually go to Kusaie on this voyage of Barkus's, losing ten deserters there, but James says nothing about this. The two women supposedly died before the lifeboat reached Ponape, and other boats, containing the missionary and other sailors, were never heard of again.

Now Marsden made seven visits to New Zealand between 1814 and 1837. Two of these visits are of dates possibly coinciding with O'Connell's time; they are 5-10 April 1827 and 8 March-27 May 1830. But Salmon's voyage with the *John Bull*, 19 October 1828 to 11 February 1830, fits neither of them. Nor does the previous voyage of that vessel under Captain Lewis, 18

[42] Simpson, T. Beckford, 'Pacific Navigation and British Seamen', *The Nautical Magazine and Naval Chronicle*, London, 1844, pp. 99-103.

[43] Sturges, Albert, Records of the American Board of Commissioners for Foreign Missions, Vol. III, No. 268, p. 3, Houghton Library, Harvard University.

August 1827 to 20 May 1828. The last voyage, under Barkus, does overlap slightly, since the ship left Sydney on 12 May 1830, but there is hardly time to get to New Zealand in that period even if she went straight there. If the Irish sailor did encounter Marsden in New Zealand he must have been on some other vessel. But in any event, there is nothing in Marsden's published statements to support O'Connell's story, and there is no mention of any missionary being sent to Kusaie, although each stay in New Zealand is described in detail.[44] The first missionaries to go to Kusaie went there in 1852, and then it was the Boston-based American Board of Commissioners for Foreign Missions that sent them.

Now followed more than five years of life on Ponape, if we are to believe James. He was adopted by a native chief, became a chief himself, married his benefactor's daughter, sired two children, made an enemy, and was tattooed in native fashion, the tattooing to become the basis for his circus career after his rescue from Ponape. As will be seen from the footnotes that accompany the text, O'Connell's observations about the native life are often accurate and discerning. Most valuable to ethnography is his recording of customs and habits that were soon to vanish in the years immediately following his rescue, which took place in November 1833. Between then and 1840 some forty-seven American and English whalers and other vessels visited Ponape. By 1835 there were forty foreigners living ashore, increasing in number to 150 by 1850. Already in 1835 Ponapeans had signed on as members of the crews of visiting ships and had been to Hawaii and Sydney.[45] Under these influences Ponapean culture changed rapidly, and O'Connell's description, coming just ahead of these changes, provides us with an exceedingly valuable ethnographic account of an as yet undisturbed culture—providing always that one sifts O'Connell's information through a screen of personal familiarity with the island and its people.

But some of O'Connell's remarks are anything but discerning. Some are so flagrantly incorrect that we wonder if they were not concocted. Up to the point of our Irish sailor's arrival

[44] Marsden, J. B., *Memoir of the Life and Labours of Samuel Marsden*, London, 1858; Johnstone, S.M., *Samuel Marsden*, Sydney, 1932.

[45] Riesenberg, S. H., *The Native Polity of Ponape*, Smithsonian Contributions to Anthropology, Vol. 10, Washington, 1968.

at Ponape we have been spun a web of truths and lies so tangled together that it has been impossible always to know which is which. What he seems to have done is taken isolated names, events, facts, experiences of other people, shuffled them about and put them together again, with himself as the chief actor, to make a tale coherent enough to satisfy H.H.W.'s doubts. It is the sort of thing a man might do if he wanted to cover his tracks, divert a pursuer, and conceal his identity. And he seems to have done all that successfully. The man James F. O'Connell appears no-where in Australian documents, nowhere in the convict records, in none of the Australian census lists.[46] The most logical assumption we can make is that he was an escaped convict. If not that, he had something else unsavoury to hide. To spin such a tale as he told H.H.W., while hiding his real name, even in the safety of Boston, must mean that the truth would have been pretty damning.

But this does not explain the apparent falsehoods in the description of Ponape and its people. What harm would it do O'Connell to be truthful in those matters? He inflates his father-in-law's position outrageously, making him the highest chief on Ponape when actually his title was a lowly one—but perhaps this exaggeration was only in order to enhance his esteem in the eyes of H.H.W. He refers to experiencing the use of bows and arrows in warfare, which no reporter in the years immediately following mentions and which modern Ponapeans deny the existence of except for sport and as toys. His insistence upon calling place after place, all on the mainland of Ponape, 'islands' seems inexplicable. His description of the ruins of Nan Madol is so far from reality that one might wonder if he did not suffer from some visual disability. A glance through the footnotes which accompany the text in this book will provide many other examples of seemingly pointless fabrications.

At one point O'Connell and his shipmate and constant companion, George Keenan, spent, he says, six months away from Ponape on Wellington Island, whose native name he gives as

<hr/>

[46] Admiralty Papers 6/418/21, Convicts with Particulars 1819-34; Colonial Office Papers 207/1-2, Lists of Convicts with Particulars 1788-1825; Home Office Papers 10/16-18, Persons Convicted in London, 1821; H.O. 10/19-20, New South Wales Muster, 1825; H.O. 10/21-28, New South Wales Census 1828; H.O. 11/3-7, Convict Transportation Registers, 1818-30.

Pokeen and which he says is 60 miles distant, getting there in a canoe belonging to natives from that island who had come to visit Ponape. Now Wellington is on charts of the time as the name for modern Mokil, just as Ponape is shown as Ascension Island. Yet it is highly doubtful that Mokil was the place he visited. That atoll by O'Connell's time had suffered a disastrous typhoon which destroyed most of the original inhabitants and had been repopulated from the Marshall Islands, so that its culture was by no means as like that of Ponape as O'Connell would have it. He must have made the identification of 'Pokeen' as Wellington from a chart, perhaps one that H.H.W. showed him and which he misread. It seems obvious that the place he visited was Pakin, whose people were identical to those of Ponape. 'Outside the reef which bounds Bonabee are two islands, one called by the natives, Hand, about twenty miles distant, the other Pokeen, about sixty miles distant.' These are the two atolls, Ant and Pakin, which together with Ponape comprise the Senyavin group. But Ant actually lies about 8 miles southwest of Ponape and Pakin is 18 miles to the west-northwest, while Mokil is 88 miles to the east. Here is confusion piled upon confusion! Yet the issue is not settled, for O'Connell's description of 'Pokeen' as made up of three islands, only one of which was inhabited, applies better to Mokil than to Pakin.

These and other confusions and errors are elaborated upon more fully later, and we need go no further into them here. The most reasonable explanation is probably that James's residence on Ponape was briefer than the five years that he claimed and that the shortcomings of his descriptions and of his knowledge of the language are due to that. As for deliberate untruths, we may assume that when he could not answer a question put to him by H.H.W. and when confession of ignorance might have caused suspicion he simply concocted an answer.

With reference to the matter of O'Connell's facility in the speech of the island, Horatio Hale writes: 'In 1837 I became acquainted with him, and saw him frequently, for the purpose of taking down such a vocabulary of the language as he could furnish,—which, notwithstanding his long residence, and his general intelligence, was very scanty. He was one of those who seem to have a natural incapacity for acquiring foreign languages . . .'.[47]

[47] Hale, op. cit., p. 81.

Paul Hambruch also speaks of O'Connell's 'Sprachkenntnisse, die allerdings zunächst spärlich zu sein scheinen . . .' but apologises for him on the ground that it was three years after his departure from Ponape before he had opportunity to have his experiences set down on paper.[48] But even with the most meagre linguistic ability, a lapse of three years (actually it was somewhat less) seems hardly long enough to allow one to forget a language learned over a period of five years, a language learned while living with wife and father-in-law in a completely native household and community, and while seeing only one other speaker of English most of the time. Moreover, it is not just a question of being a poor learner as Hale suggests, or of forgetting as Hambruch implies. The vocabulary at the end of the book is studded, as a glance will reveal, with question-marks inserted by the present editor wherever O'Connell's Ponapean words cannot be stretched to resemble in any way those of modern Ponapean. It is as though he has coined a whole new language.

The reader might ask whether some of the vocabulary could not have changed in the years between O'Connell's time and now. Fortunately there is another early visitor with whom we can compare O'Connell. This is the trader, Andrew Cheyne, who spent a total of 7 or 8 months on Ponape during several visits in 1842 and 1843, only a decade after our Irish sailor left the island. During those visits he compiled a vocabulary of 238 items.[49] Ten of these items are loan-words from English, introduced to Ponape between 1833 and 1842. Of the other 228, though several are in a kind of pidgin Ponapean, only two are not recognisable, another two being obsolete but still known. In comparison to this, in O'Connell's word list, even with the widest liberality in accepting faint similarities, there are 50 items out of a total of 171 that cannot be recognised as Ponapean. (Two others are obsolete but known.) That is to say, 30 per cent of his vocabulary appears either to belong to some other language or to be invented. A comparison of these 50 items with the languages of Kusaie and Nauru, suggested by the possibility (discussed elsewhere), that O'Connell may have lived on those islands at one time, reveals no similarities at all. Two of the 50

---

[48] Hambruch, op. cit., p. 6.

[49] Cheyne, Andrew, *A Description of the Islands in the Western Pacific Ocean, north and south of the Equator*, London, 1852.

are obviously English (the words he gives for 'banana' and 'plantain') and one is pretty surely Spanish ('milk').

The explanation may be that O'Connell simply said whatever popped into his mind whenever H.H.W. asked him for a word he did not know, inventing most of them on the spot. This is said in spite of H.H.W.'s remark that O'Connell himself wrote the word list and that he tested him on it some days later. Having in his narrative to H.H.W. said that he had lived at Ponape for five years, it would have seemed odd to admit that he was ignorant of common words in the native language, hence the need to make them up. (Strangest of all, the words one would suppose would be learned among the first, those for the parts of the body, are the very ones that O'Connell seems to know least. Twenty-two parts of the body are listed by him, and nineteen of them are unrecognisable as Ponapean.) The conclusion one must draw is that James lived on Ponape for a much briefer period of time than he says he did. Perhaps he needed to make the claim of five years in order to account for time spent in some other place in circumstances that he did not wish to make known.

Leaving further discussion of Ponape itself to the footnotes, let us proceed to O'Connell's rescue from that island. This came about by a trading brig, the *Spy* of Salem. This vessel, built in 1823 at Medford, Massachusetts, was of 98 tons burden. In the Ship Enrolments at the National Archives in Washington she is described as a schooner having one deck and two masts, with a square stern and no galleries.[50] This little vessel, 74 feet long, 22 wide, and 7 deep, left Salem on a trading voyage to the Pacific on 8 August 1832 with a crew of thirteen under Captain John Buttolph Knight, as he is called in the Salem vital records and by O'Connell, or Knights, as the consular records of Manila and his own journal spell it. This was his first and only command; otherwise he is described as a merchant, born in 1803 and dead by suicide in 1846.

What we know of Knight comes mostly from his journal and from O'Connell's account of his own deliverance from Ponape. The two stories are in close accord in their description of events while the *Spy* stopped at the island and in the remainder of their brief association. So close are they that it is clear that here, at

---

50 U.S. National Archives, 1823 Enrolments, No. 181; 1828 Enrolments, No. 33; 1823 Register, No. 304; 1824 Register, No. 126.

least, O'Connell's apologies for a defective memory are quite superfluous. Indeed his lapses in other matters are the more suspect.

The *Spy* arrived at the island on 17 November 1833. (Knight says 27 November, but this is clearly an error, as three days later he gives the date as 20 November. O'Connell says only that it was early in November.) She lay off the northern shore for several days, seeking to find an entrance through the reef. The natives came out in canoes to trade, the *Spy* hovering off what is aparently Net. Then O'Connell came out and piloted the vessel to a harbour in Madolenihmw, on the eastern side of the island. The natives were soon trying to pull the guard irons out from under the chains. Knight grew apprehensive, fearing that they would try to take the vessel. Soon there was an attack, with slingstones and spears, and the crew returned the fire. The second officer was laid senseless by a slingstone and several natives were killed. Trading resumed, then a thief entered Knight's cabin at night and was shot dead. Intermittent fighting continued, alternating with trading. A canoe had been purchased as a curiosity and fastened to the stern. Two hours later some natives stole it back and made off with it. Knight sent men in a boat in pursuit, firing at the natives, but with no success.

Attempting to beat out of the passage through the reef the vessel nearly got on the rocks. From daybreak till afternoon she laboured, while wave after wave of canoes attacked her. Finally she reached deep water. This would have been 23 or 24 November.

Once at sea Knight and O'Connell soon quarrelled. On 7 December, at Guam, Knight attempted to put the Irishman ashore, but the Spanish authorities would not allow it. On 20 December, in the San Bernardino Straits, between Luzon and Samar, Knight put O'Connell into a boat with his friend George Keenan, who had also signed on to work his passage, and instructed the crew to put both men ashore. James and George, however, refused to leave the boat and were not forced to do so, but were returned to the *Spy*, much to the captain's mortification. Finally, in Manila, on 22 December, Knight had the two men clapped into jail as mutineers, the *Spy* was sold as an unfit vessel, and in January Knight took passage for New York.

Thus far the two accounts agree in essential detail, save that each narrator makes the other to be the villain in the piece. But in certain important matters there are differences. James relates that when he descried the *Spy* he persuaded his father-in-law and his wife to let him go out to her, promising solemnly to return. On his first attempt his canoe was swamped but the next day he, George Keenan, and two natives succeeded in getting to her. Several canoes were already there, trading yams and breadfruit. Knight let him and George aboard and asked him to pilot the *Spy* to a safe anchorage.

As Knight has it, 'the Irishman', whom he never names and of whom he was highly suspicious, himself offered to show him a good harbour, which he was allowed to do after being assured 'that his life should be the immediate forfeit if he led me into any trap'.[51] Knight states that the first canoes that came out to him brought tortoiseshell to barter, and in the harbour they brought him more of it. There is every indication here that the natives were familiar with commerce and knew of the demand for tortoiseshell by the ships then plying the Pacific. As O'Connell has it, the *Spy* was the first vessel he had seen in the five years he was on Ponape, but Knight says that 'the white man [meaning O'Connell] told me that a Botany Bay ship left the coast only ten days before, after obtaining upwards of seven hundred pounds of shell and in consequence I should find it much scarcer than usual'.[52] The last three words bespeak a commercial history and, indeed, make O'Connell sound like an established trader. Knight states that when he was at Bay of Islands, earlier in 1833, he inquired of various English whaling captains as to where was the best place to trade for shell; 'one and all were united in saying that Ascension was the best island for shell in the Pacific'.[53] Such a reputation could not have been acquired without at least an occasional visit to Ponape, and it would not have been possible for O'Connell to remain ignorant of such an event. Further to this point, O'Connell says that no important chiefs came out to the ship, nor were any natives allowed to board her. But Knight says that 'the King' did go aboard and immediately asked for rum, an item with which he seemed already perfectly familiar. This would have been the Nahnmwarki of Madolenihmw, or

[51] Knights, op. cit., p. 200.

[52] Ibid.

[53] Knight, John B., letter to S. C. Phillips, 18 January 1834, at Peabody Museum, Salem.

24

Matalaleme as O'Connell spells it, this place being the harbour where the Irishman had piloted the vessel. (This same 'King' was soon, in 1836, to be shot and his brother hanged by the survivors of the *Falcon* and other white sailors in revenge for the burning of that vessel and the killing of her captain and some of her crew by a party of natives.) That Knight calls him 'the King' as he and his successors were called until the time of 'King Paul' of Madolenihmw in the 1890s suggests that he was following a tradition already established before him, by earlier visitors.

O'Connell makes no mention of any whites on Ponape other than Keenan and the four other shipmates from the *John Bull* cast away with him. Of these men he says he saw nothing during the visit of the *Spy*. But, says Knight, 'a lot of whites came off with a quantity of shell which I purchased. These fellows had been put into canoes of the natives by the Botany Bay whalers as they passed the island and undoubtedly were convicts who had hid away on board before the ships sailed, which is often the case . . . I . . . agreed with them to cut my wood and fill the water casks . . .'.[54]

Even more curious is O'Connell's complete silence on the subject of the Sydney bark *Nimrod*. This vessel, a whaler, then under a Captain Joseph White, had anchored at Kiti in November 1832. In the same month another Sydney whaler, the *Albion*, Captain John Evans, also stopped at Kiti.[55] The *Nimrod* was now back at Ponape, a year after her previous visit. Knight first saw her—much, as he says, to his relief and pleasure—on the day before the *Spy* got out of Madolenihmw harbour. As Knight tells it her master, McColliff, had been killed, along with two of his crew, three days before, at McAskill Island (Pingelap), about 220 miles east of Ponape. Newspaper accounts give additional details:[56] on 19 or 20 November the captain (here named McAuliffe) had put ashore two boats' crews at McAskill to obtain produce. The natives at first appeared friendly but suddenly the captain was knocked down by a club and killed; Thomas Cox,

[54] Knights, op. cit. pp. 200-1.

[55] Gulick, L. H., 'The Climate and Production of Ponape or Ascension Island, one of the Carolines, in the Pacific Ocean', *American Journal of Science and Arts*, Ser. 2, Vol. 26, pp. 34-49.

[56] *Sydney Gazette*, 8 April, 8 May, 26 November 1834; *Sydney Herald*, 8 May 1834.

a passenger from Kusaie, was also killed; the three officers and five of the crew were wounded, and five of the natives killed. The survivors retreated to the bark, which then made for Ponape.

The *Nimrod* must have been at Ponape a day or two before Knight saw her, to allow time for the events which the new captain, whose name is not given, reported to him. This captain told Knight that one of the whites on Ponape, who had come aboard the *Nimrod* while drunk, had boasted that he and the others were about to join the natives in taking 'the damned Yankee' and the *Spy*. Knight questioned their power, but the captain answered that he himself had left at Ponape nine whites who had come off from Pingelap and assisted him against the natives there; all of them had muskets and would without doubt join the others.

Such an attack by the whites, if it was really intended, never came off. The *Spy* succeeded in getting through the reef in time the next day, and we are left with the mystery of who the nine men were and how they had got to the remote atoll of Pingelap, as well as who the other whites were that brought tortoiseshell out to sell. But the interesting point is that O'Connell says not a word about any of this. Why in his narration he should conceal the fact that other whites were on shore is difficult to understand. Possibly it was because he himself had a hand in the conspiracy.

Knight says further: 'The cook and a black sailor, who were both sick, wished to be discharged here and as they were useless fellows I paid them off and took a fellow from shore who had been cook before and also two others who begged hard to be allowed to work their passages to Manela'.[57] Later, in connection with the abortive attempt to put O'Connell and Keenan off at San Bernardino Straits, he refers to O'Connell's boon companion thus: 'Another fellow who had shipped as cook swore he would go too [in the boat which had been lowered to put James ashore] so he went along', thus identifying the unnamed cook as Keenan.[58] But of the third man mentioned by Knight James says nothing. And though he refers to a ship's cook, whose place Knight says Keenan took, being discharged at Ponape, he does not mention the black sailor.

Regarding the disagreement between O'Connell and Knight,

[57] Knights, op. cit., p. 203.
[58] Ibid, p. 206.

which caused the attempt at marooning, O'Connell claims that he was sick and one night, when he had the watch, lay down on the forecastle in pain. Knight found him there, kicked him, the two men struggled, Knight threatened to shoot him, and the next day tried to set 'the two Irish villains' ashore. But Knight's version is that one of his Portuguese sailors reported to him that O'Connell had proposed to the crew to take the vessel and that he was therefore keeping a close watch on him; that on the night referred to O'Connell was making a loud racket and would not desist when ordered to. Instead he insulted Knight, and it was this that decided him to take the course of action that he took.

From James's account we gain an impression of Knight as a fearful, yet injudicious man. He is described as nervous, agitated, beside himself for fear of treachery, but foolishly indiscreet. To be fair to Knight, his suspicions and trepidations had plenty to feed upon. He had just learned about the *Nimrod*'s misadventure at Pingelap and feared to suffer the same fate. Indeed, earlier on this same voyage, while in Fiji, the *Spy* was narrowly saved from being taken by the natives only through exposure of the plot by David Whippy, a Nantucket man who had taken up residence in these islands. (Whippy had performed a similar good deed for another vessel, the *Glide*, in 1831.) But his timorous qualities must have played a part in the events at Ponape, as O'Connell says.

The owner of the *Spy*, Stephen C. Phillips of Salem, who had sent Knight on this voyage, seems to have been aware of his shortcomings. In a letter of 23 October 1833 to his agent in Manila, J. W. Peele, he writes, 'I now think Capt. Knight has gone through the worst part of his voyage and has acquired sufficient experience to make him feel easy on the score of navigation'. A few days later he writes again, 'I now fear he may be compelled from want of provisions to terminate his voyage prematurely . . . If he gains nothing else by his first voyage, Capt. Knight must have acquired sufficient nautical experience to qualify him to proceed wherever you may choose to send him upon a second . . . [so that] the success of his second attempt [might] fully compensate for the failure of the first'.[59]

Knight's experiences at Fiji are also told by Captain John H.

[59] S. C. Phillips letter-book, at Essex Institute, Salem. Phillips to Peele, No. 1600, 23 October 1833; No. 1606, 27 October 1833.

Eagleston in 1834, in the logbook of the ship *Emerald*. On his previous voyage Eagleston had commanded the bark *Peru*, which the *Spy* was supposed to rendezvous with early in 1833 at Fiji. This vessel was also owned by Stephen Phillips. Knight was supposed to bring Eagleston trading materials and provisions, and in turn had hoped to get extra hands and an interpreter from Eagleston. Phillips's instructions to Knight were to meet Eagleston, 'whom you can hardly fail to find at the Feejee Islands', and to work with him to load the *Peru* with bêche de mer to take to Manila.[60] The *Peru* was then to return at least once for bêche de mer and the *Spy* was to make short excursions for shell during her absences. The *Spy*, however, did not arrive in the Fijis until May 1833, owing, says Knight, to 'misfortunes' of his voyage and the poor behaviour of his vessel. He missed the *Peru* which had departed for Manila two or three months before. On the trip to Fiji in the *Emerald* the following year Eagleston writes: 'Capt. Knight was no seaman and but little qualified to take charge of a ship for a Feejee voyage, he was easly [*sic*] frightened and while at the Islands he was never on deck when his vessel was underway. The cause of this was the sight of Rocks made him sick and if she went on shore, he did not wish to be on deck at the time. He was underway but little, and when he was his mate and some of the men at the Island had charge of her until brought to anchor again'.[61] Eagleston's criticism and annoyance is understandable, since he had exhausted his supplies and had barely enough provisions to take him to Manila, but what he says seems to confirm O'Connell's estimate of Knight.

Peele did not send Knight on a second voyage, as Phillips had hoped. Instead the *Spy* was sold in Manila in January 1834 as, in Knight's words, 'totally unfit for the business for which she was intended', though she had sailed well enough under other captains to make several successful voyages to East Africa between 1823, when she was built, and 1833. When Knight left Manila as a passenger to New York he must have been thoroughly relieved to be done with a captain's life.[62]

[60] Ibid., Phillips to Knight, No. 1054, 6 August 1832.
[61] Eagleston, *Emerald*, op. cit.
[62] U.S. National Archives, Records of American Consul at Manila, Consular Statement of Fees, 1 July-31 December 1833; Letter, 25 January 1834, Consul Edwards to Louis McLane, U.S. Secretary of Treasury; Knights, op. cit., p. 207.

Knight sailed for America on 28 January 1834, leaving O'Connell and Keenan in the Manila jail, and bewailing the fact that 'the government would not try them and they [would] probably . . . get imposed as honest men on someone else . . .'.[63] He arrived in New York on 20 May 1834,[64] married the next year, and by 1836, the year O'Connell's book appeared, was well established in business at Derby Wharf in Salem, as his newspaper advertisements for the next ten years reveal. These advertisements, appearing in almost every issue of the *Salem Gazette*, and a miniature of him by an unknown artist, preserved at the Essex Institute, suggest a picture of a conventional, respectable merchant, devoted to the selling of coffee, soap, salt, brandy, cigars, and ship's guns, among other things. He was an owner of warehouses and a rigging loft. For four years he was Deputy Collector at the Salem Custom House. He died by his own hand on 7 June 1846, leaving to his only daughter what was described as a substantial fortune. It seems hardly credible that he made no answer to O'Connell's devastating attack on him, which could hardly have failed to come to his notice, but none can be found in the Salem or Boston newspapers of the time. One wonders whether that attack, plus Captain Eagleston's frank contempt and owner Stephen Phillips's more charitable allowances for his ineptitude, did not contribute to the despair that must have preceded his suicide.[65]

The two Irishmen were indeed never brought to trial. Upon their release from prison they were, according to James's account, sent to Macao and thence to Canton; there they agreed to join a caravan which was to go to Constantinople from Peking, but on arriving at the latter city they changed their minds and returned to Canton.

If the story about going to Macao on a Spanish vessel is true,

[63] Knights, op. cit., p. 207.

[64] U.S. National Archives, Passenger Lists of Vessels Arriving at New York, 1820-1897, Microcopy 237, Roll 22, No. 303, 14 February-20 May 1834.

[65] Essex Institute, *Vital Records of Salem, Mass., to End of Year 1849*, Salem, 1925, Vol. 5, p. 382; Essex Institute, 'Catalogue of Portraits in the Essex Institute, Salem, Mass.', *Historical Collections*, 1935, Vol. 71, p. 247; Knight's will, at Essex County Courthouse, gives his fortune as worth $23,000 (Docket No. 44659).

it must have been in March of 1834, and the prison confinement was therefore no longer than three months. Only three Spanish vessels arrived in Macao from Manila in 1834, all of them in March. The same vessels made other visits to Macao later in the year, but by then O'Connell and Keenan were on the high seas again, *en route* to Halifax. But the authenticity of the whole Chinese adventure is open to doubt. If the two men made the stir in Macao and Canton that James says they did, no one thought to make a note of it in any published source of the time, nor is there any record of it in the official documentary files of the Leal Senado at Macao.[66] O'Connell refers to his debt of gratitude to the English consul at Macao for his kind treatment, but there was no such official in Macao, or Canton either, until about 1844. True, he may have been referring to the Superintendent of Trade. But it is quite impossible that Europeans would have been allowed to visit Peking at this time, or that caravans would have travelled thence to Constantinople. Westerners were permitted residence only at Macao and Canton and could not travel elsewhere. A few did travel to the interior in disguise, but none got anywhere near the capital except for members of a Russian mission who were granted residence at Peking under terms of a treaty of 1689. The open assembling of six Europeans and their encampment outside the city, as O'Connell describes, would never have been allowed.

Furthermore, to go by a junk from Canton to Peking in ten days, as James says he and George did, is likewise impossible. The difficulties of sailing in the shoal waters and narrow channels along the China coast are impressive. Much shorter distances took longer than ten days. It took the fastest of horses, by relay, at least twenty days and nights to make the journey from Canton to Peking.[67]

About all we can accept as probably not questionable in this Chinese episode is that the two men were in Canton after their release from prison. According to the narrative they signed on, in that port, on the *Elizabeth*, Captain Rudkin, and arrived in

---

[66] Letter, Major António Herculano de Miranda Dias, Chief of Cabinet, Macao, to Riesenberg, 23 February 1960.

[67] Letters: Earl H. Pritchard to Riesenberg, 3 February and 25 April 1960; Gordon K. Harrington to Riesenberg, 10 February 1960; Chaoying Fang to Mrs Chang-su Swanson, 11 October 1967.

Halifax in September 1835. Here the cholera was raging and the two men made their way on foot to St John, New Brunswick. George, becoming sick, was left behind there, while James shipped on an American schooner, landing in New York late in the fall of 1835.

In one of the condensed versions of his book which appeared in pamphlet form in later years, to be hawked at theatres where he performed (*Life of Ja's. F. O'Connell, The Pacific Adventurer,* New York, 1853) James sails from Canton not in the *Elizabeth* but in the clipper ship *Flying Cloud,* the captain's name again being Rudkin. This vessel is made to arrive in New York in September 1835, and there is no mention of Halifax or St John.

Regarding the *Elizabeth,* O'Connell's dates again seem to be out. A Singapore newspaper reports the passage of that vessel through the Straits of Sunda from Canton, for North America, early in April 1834 (the exact date, a one-digit number, is blurred).[68] Her captain's name is given as Redkin. It must therefore have been some time in 1834, not September 1835, when she would have arrived in Halifax. As for the cholera epidemic, the chronology needs adjustment here too. Cholera broke out in eastern Canada in July of 1834. It appeared in Halifax by 5 August. In the week ending 3 September there were 115 dead in that city and in the following week 268 more. Despite the quarantine established in St John, a quarantine O'Connell knew of and tried to circumvent, as he describes, the disease reached St John by 25 September. It carried off fifty victims before it terminated in November. James's description of the activities in both cities connected with the epidemic is convincing enough to put him there in September, as is also the schedule of the *Elizabeth,* but a year earlier than he says.[69]

However charitable we may feel towards a possibly unreliable memory, it is impossible not to accuse O'Connell of lying in this last matter. It will be remembered that the book's preface is signed H.H.W., Boston, August, 1836. Let us suppose that by some miracle of efficiency it was possible to publish the book as little as a month after O'Connell's narrative was recited to

[68] *Singapore Chronicle and Commercial Register,* 22 May 1834.

[69] Raddall, Thomas H., *Halifax, Warden of the North,* New York, 1965, pp. 176, 178; Jack, D. R., *History of the City and County of St. John,* St John, 1883, p. 119.

H.H.W., which would put that recital in July at latest. Can anyone's memory be so poor that he thinks he has been in a foreign country only ten months, possibly less, when he has really been there a year and ten months?

No trace of O'Connell or Keenan can be found in the archives at St John in the New Brunswick Museum. Their names do not appear in the shipping files. If George Keenan, left behind sick at St John, entered the Alms House Hospital, which was opened to take care of the victims of the epidemic, there is no record of it. If he died at St John, neither of the two graveyards of the time record his name. If any part of the story is true the two men must have been using other names.[70]

The St John newspaper of 20 September 1834 reports an incident of a few days before which tantalisingly parallels the description O'Connell gives of his own experience in Canada. Because of the epidemic the local Board of Health had established a *cordon sanitaire*. 'Kenneth McKenzie and Robert Cameron, shipwrights, while crossing the ferry to the western side of the harbor, having stated in the hearing of the ferryman that they were only three days from Halifax, he immediately gave information . . . measures [were] immediately taken for the apprehension of McKenzie and Cameron. The officers who were despatched in pursuit succeeded . . . in tracing and arresting the supposed law-breakers, when it was found that they were not so recently from Halifax as they had stated, but His Worship the Mayor . . . very properly determined to punish them for such reprehensible conduct, and directed that they should be conveyed to Partridge Island, there to undergo the usual fumigations, and await the further orders of the board'.[71]

There is no more about these men in later issues of the newspaper. Were they our friends O'Connell and Keenan? This is the only case of violation of the *cordon sanitaire* reported in the newspaper during the epidemic at St John. Is it a coincidence that the two Irishmen were also in violation of the quarantine, as O'Connell tells us? But if they were the same, would they not have given Irish names rather than Scots ones? Captain Knight refers to them as 'the Irishmen', as though their origins were

[70] Letter, Eileen C. Cushing to Riesenberg, 5 December 1969.

[71] Quoted in *St. John Globe* of 2 February 1907 from a St John newspaper of 20 September 1834, the name of which is not given.

altogether obvious, perhaps too obvious to attempt to conceal under a Scots pseudonym.

As for the story Jim tells of shipping to New York from St John in an American schooner, the passenger lists of vessels arriving at New York in those years, in the U.S. National Archives, show only one arrival named James O'Connell. He landed in New York on 7 November 1835 from Liverpool and cannot, therefore, be our man. Nor does anyone of that name appear on the passenger lists for Boston or for those labelled Miscellaneous Ports. There is no mention of Keenan anywhere. Nor did any *Flying Cloud* arrive in New York in 1834 or 1835. Jim must still have been going under a different name.[72]

The first time the name James F. O'Connell is on record is when he began to perform with the Lion Circus, in 1835.[73] His true name, if it is not O'Connell, ought to be found in the Manila prison records. Unfortunately, inquiry at the Philippine National Archives has been fruitless. And the pertinent records of the American consul in Manila, whom O'Connell mentions, do not exist for this period in the U.S. National Archives. Very likely the name was assumed when he joined the Lion Circus, where he apparently began the career with which the rest of his history is connected. O'Connell may have been the first tattooed man to be exhibited in an American circus.[74] Of the Lion Circus we are told, 'the lecturer had a rare story about this man, of the torture inflicted by savages doing the work of tattooing'.[75] The next year O'Connell must have been in Boston, for his amanuensis signs the preface 'H.H.W., Boston, August, 1836'. In 1837, according to the circus historian Glenroy's recollections, O'Connell, already billed as 'the great tattooed man', joined Palmer's new company. This was toward the end of April 1837, and on 5 May they sailed

---

[72] U.S. National Archives, Passenger Lists of Vessels Arriving at New York, 1820-1897; Index to Passenger Lists of Vessels Arriving at New York, 1820-1846; Passenger Lists of Vessels Arriving at Boston 1820-1891; Passenger Lists of Vessels arriving at Miscellaneous Ports 1820-1873.

[73] O'Brien, Esse Forrester, *Circus: Cinders to Sawdust*, San Antonio, 1959, p. 211; letter, Leonard V. Farley to Riesenberg, 20 February 1959.

[74] Parry, Albert, *Tattoo*, New York, 1933, p. 59.

[75] O'Brien, op. cit., p. 211.

from Charleston for Havana.[76] Their stay in that city must have been remarkably brief, for a handbill (reproduced in fig. 4) bearing a Buffalo, New York, printer's imprint and dated 15 June 1837 advertises O'Connell's performance that night at an establishment called simply the 'Theatre', presumably in Buffalo.

We next hear of O'Connell when he joined Welch and Bartlett's Broadway Circus at Hudson, New York, which was touring after playing in New York until March 1840. Glenroy, who was in the same circus, says he was 'the first man I ever saw do clog dancing', and according to Lambert it was 'Jimmy O'Connel [sic] who first introduced clog dancing into this country at the old Chatham Theater in Chatham Square, New York City'.[77] On 24 August 1840 the Chatham Theater advertised that O'Connell, 'the Tattooed Man, will go through the drum exercise, executing the single, double, and treble Drags in perfect time'.[78] On 2 November the American Museum, at Broadway and Ann Streets, billed a dual attraction, O'Connell, the tattooed man, and Theresa Clemence, Dancer.[79]

We hear nothing of him in 1841 but on 19 February 1842 he was again at the Chatham, which announced that after the play *The Provost of Bruges* was ended 'Mr. O'Connell will perform his wonderful foot race for a bet of six hundred dollars'. What this race was like we are not told, but again he danced. Through most of November he and two others, Winchell and Booth, were what came later to be called 'headliners' at P. T. Barnum's American Museum. In the same month he appeared at the Circus, and to the end of the same year the Franklin, a variety house, carried O'Connell, Winchell, and Emmett. (Dan Emmett, banjo player, was later the composer of the famous song 'Dixie'.) On 16 January 1843 R. D. Dinneford advertised that he was lessee of Little Drury—The Franklin Theater, and listed O'Connell, 'with his savage pranks', for two weeks. On 6 March there was the last performance at the Park of Welch's Olympic Circus, a benefit for Rufus Welch, with whom O'Connell had

[76] Glenroy, John H., *Ins and Outs of Circus Life*, Boston, 1885, p. 14.

[77] Ibid., p. 32; Lambert, William, *Show Life in America*, East Point, Georgia, 1925, p. 202.

[78] Odell, George C. D., *Annals of the New York Stage*, New York, 1928-31, Vol. 4, p. 392.

[79] Ibid., p. 512.

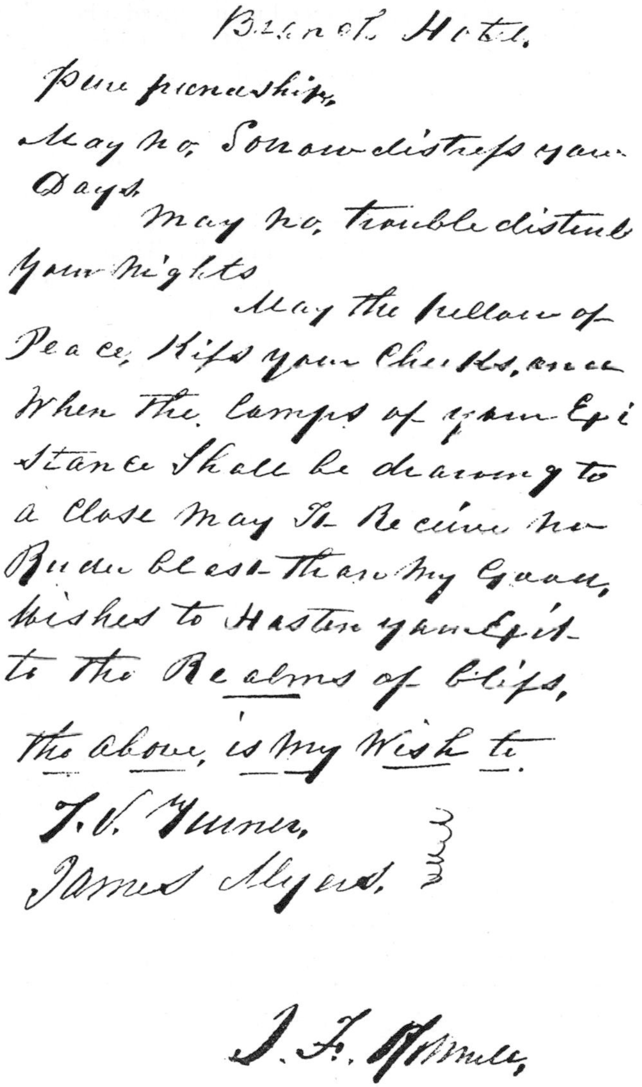
Branch Hotel.
Pure friendship,
May no Sorrow distress your Days
May no trouble disturb your Nights
May the pillow of Peace; Kiss your Cheeks, once When the lamps of your Existance Shall be drawing to a Close May It Receive no Ruder blast than my Good wishes to Hasten your Exit to the Realms of bliss,
the above, is my Wish &c.
T. V. Turner,
James Myers.

J. F. O'Connell

Fig. 2 Front fly leaf of a copy of the 1841 edition of O'Connell's book, now in the Enoch Pratt Free Library, Baltimore. O'Connell's signature appears, and he gives it in 'pure friendship' to the Messrs Turner and Myers whose names are shown.

been the previous year. The tattooed man danced a hornpipe and 'the Devouring Ogre ended all'. On 8 March and on 13 April he appeared at benefit performances at the Bowery Amphitheater, and at some time during the year he was with Nathan Howes.[80]

James then drops out of sight until 1849, except that he was with S. P. Stickney in 1847.[81] It is a mystery, what he did in those years. Perhaps there was a recession in show business and he turned to some other occupation. But on 21 October 1849 we learn that 'The manager of the Franklin Theater, Chatham Square, has at an enormous expense engaged Mr. J. F. O'Connell, the "Wonderful Tattooed Man," who will go through a variety of performances peculiar to himself and perfectly original'.[82]

In these years theatre and circus celebrities, Bohemian characters, and sporting men of New York mainly patronised two hotels, the North American and the Branch, both in the Bowery. References of the time to the Branch Hotel often used the adjective 'notorious' preceding the name. The two hotels were the scene of many turbulent embroilments. The Branch Hotel was run by Tom Hyer, who in 1849 fought and beat 'Yankee Sullivan', an escaped convict from Australia, and thus became America's first heavyweight boxing champion.[83] It was in this hotel that James O'Connell lived at some time or at various times between 1841 and 1850, as figs. 2 and 3 indicate. These figures are the front and back fly leaves of a copy of the 1841 edition of O'Connell's book, covered with his own handwriting and signed by him. Since other evidence indicates that this copy of the book belonged to someone else in 1850, it must have been in the 1840s that he was a resident at the Branch. Incidentally, the doggerel on the fly leaf (fig. 3) and that at the top of the theatre handbill (fig. 4) obviously have the same inspiration. One hopes that O'Connell's dancing genius was more felicitous.

In October 1850 Jim joined Dan Rice's circus at Buffalo. Rice, born in New York in 1823, had had a most varied career, beginning as a jockey before he was nine, becoming a riverboat card shark at seventeen, then a livery stable operator, circus

---

[80] Ibid., pp. 566, 615, 665, 667, 673; Farley, op. cit.

[81] Farley, op. cit.

[82] *New York Herald*, 21 October 1849.

[83] Williamson, Jefferson, *The American Hotel*, New York and London, 1930, pp. 139-40.

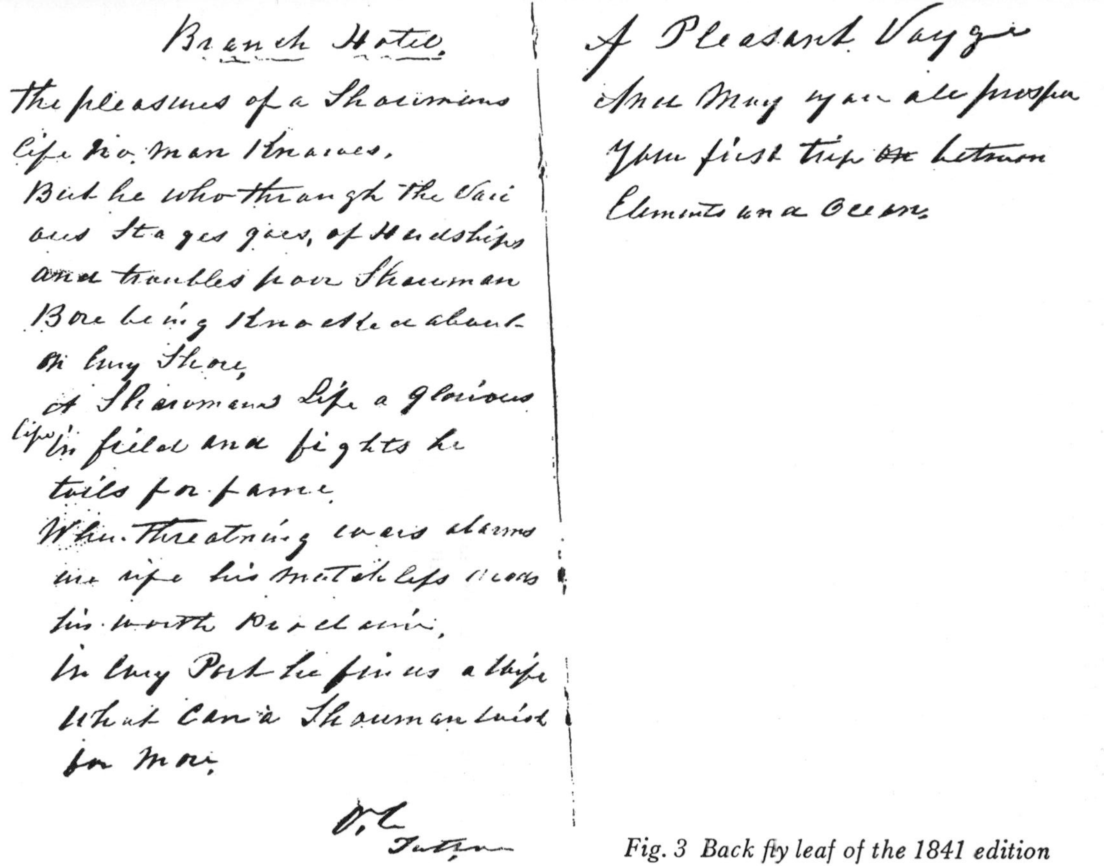

Branch Hotel

the pleasures of a Showmans
Life no man knows.
But he who through the vari
ous Stages goes, of Hardships
and troubles poor Showman
Bore being knocked about
on Evry Shore,
A Showmans Life a glorious
Life in field and fights he
toils for fame.
When threatning wars alarms
are rife his matchless deeds
his worth proclaim,
In Evry Port he finds a Wife
What Can a Showman wish
for more.

A Pleasant Voyage
And May you all prosper
Your first trip ~~on~~ between
Elements and Ocean.

Fig. 3 Back fly leaf of the 1841 edition

clown, partner in an educated pig act, strong man, Mormon missionary, finally in 1848 proprietor of his own circus, which he won at cards. After O'Connell joined it the show travelled by canal boat to Pittsburgh and Cincinnati, where the sheriff attached the horses. Thereupon all the members of the troupe deserted, save for O'Connell and Jean Lafitte Johnson, a twelve-year-old grandson of the buccaneer, Jean Lafitte, and now an equestrian and tightrope performer. Jean became James's faithful friend and companion of his last years. In the Rice shows James would relate the story of his life on Ponape and his escape; he would exhibit his tattooing, dance the hornpipe with Johnson, and perform the Egg Dance—this last was done blindfolded, hands behind the back, while leaping about and weaving back and forth between rows of eggs set on the floor.[84]

Rice's show continued down-river to New Orleans at the end of 1850, exhibiting at a number of towns *en route*. On 26 January 1851 in New Orleans O'Connell, Dan Emmett, and Rice appeared 'in a grand Ethiopian Melange, consisting of Melodies, Breakdowns, Burlesque Dances, etc . . .'. On 1 February there was a benefit for O'Connell, 'the Great Irish Dancer', and among the 'rich variety of exciting performances' were 'several interesting Nautical Acts' by O'Connell. The foregoing is from a newspaper advertisement; in the same issue of the paper appeared an article: 'J. F. O'Connell, the far-famed dancer, whose exploits among the South Sea Islands have made him so famous, takes a benefit tonight; an excellent and novel bill of entertainment will be produced, which, independently of his own claims upon the sympathy of the public, whom he has so often amused, ought to insure him a crowd of patrons'.[85]

Then followed the up-river tour, with Jim performing in Cincinnati in June of 1851,[86] and then Pittsburgh. The show was at Albany in September.[87] On 30 October 1851 an article in a Memphis newspaper describes the performances given by the

[84] Kunzog, John C., *The One-Horse Show*, Jamestown, N.Y., 1962, pp. 79 *et seq.*

[85] *New Orleans Daily Picayune*, 26 January, 1 February 1851.

[86] *Cincinnati Enquirer* in June 1851 per letter from John Mullane, Librarian of Public Library, Cincinnati and Hamilton County, 21 September 1970.

[87] Kunzog, op. cit.

Dan Rice Circus the night before and refers to 'J. F. O'Connell, the celebrated tattooed man and Irish dancer'.[88] In 1852 the show was again at Memphis and New Orleans. O'Connell left Rice in the spring of 1852 and was with the Star State Circus in Mobile later that year.[89] An advertisement by that circus in New Orleans lists among its performers, 18-22 September 1852 'Jas. F. O'Connell, The Tattooed Man'.[90] In November and December he and his friend Jean Johnson, among others, performed in H. M. Whitbeck's troupe at the New Orleans Amphitheatre.[91] Whitbeck formed a new company in January of 1853 which James joined and set sail for Havana from New Orleans. At Havana most of the company fell prey to yellow fever and apparently disbanded.[92] Among the twenty-five passengers disembarking from the *Empire City* at New Orleans on 21 May 1853, after her passage back from Havana, three are listed as having the occupation of actor: Whitbeck, Jean Johnson, and J. F. O'Connell.[93]

When Dan Rice opened his winter season in New Orleans in December of that year, at a new building called Dan Rice's Amphitheater, O'Connell was again with him, as was also his friend Jean L. Johnson. Here James gave his last performances, and here, on 29 January 1854, he died. His death notice in the local newspaper reads only: 'On Sunday night, 29th inst., James F. O'Connell, the "Tattooed Man"',[94] thus continuing to the end to give prominence to his principal article of showmanship, acquired at Ponape.

Even in death O'Connell eludes us. A search of the records of Orleans parish, in the New Orleans City Hall, produces no O'Connell among the vital statistics of 1854. The explanation is that he may have died outside the parish; unfortunately, records as early as this of surrounding parishes and of the State of Louisiana no longer exist.

[88] *Memphis Commercial*, 30 October 1851.

[89] Glenroy, op. cit., p. 91; Kunzog, op. cit., p. 93; Farley, op. cit.

[90] *New Orleans Daily Picayune*, 18-22 September 1852.

[91] Ibid., 17 November-6 December 1852.

[92] Glenroy, op. cit., pp. 87, 91, 99, 101; Kunzog, op. cit., pp. 102-4.

[93] New Orleans Passenger Lists, op. cit.

[94] *New Orleans Daily Picayune*, 31 January 1854.

THEATRE.

The pleasures of being Tattooed no man knows,
But he who through the operation goes;
The hardships and troubles poor sailors bore
By being cast away on a savage shore,
Where nothing but wretchedness the Mariners find,
Too late they sigh for comforts left behind.

Third night of the engagement of

JAMES F. O'CONNELL

THE CELEBRATED TATTOOED MAN,

Who was, for a period of six years, living amongst the natives of the Island of Ascension.

Thursday Evening, June 15, 1837.

First night of a Dramatic sketch in two parts, consisting of Pantomime and dialogue, interspersed with Music, Dances, &c, founded on the adventures of the hero of the piece, entitled the

SAILOR OF THE

S O U T H   S E A,

Or the Adventures of James F. O'Connell. As played in Boston with great success.

James F. O'Connell, (the Sailor of the South Seas,) James F. O'Connell,
George Reeman, (his companion,) Mr. Wiaans,
Ahoundel, (chief of the Island of Nutt,) Koro,
Namudow, (an inferior chief) Burton,
CREW OF THE SHIP.
Tom Taffrail, Merryfield. Sailors, Natives, &c. &c.
Lawoni, (Ahoundels daughter married to O'Connell,) Mrs Kove,
George Keennans Wife, (also a native,)
The Scene of the piece lies in the Caroline Islands. A space of six years is supposed to intervene between the 1st. and 2d. parts.
Scene 1. Represents a Bay in one of the Caroline Islands called the Island of Nutt.

A Terrific Storm.

The ship John Bull appears tossing on the waves; Ahoundel, the Chief, and a body of natives are seen viewing the ship with marked astonishment; she fires guns of distress; alarm of the natives. Thunder Bolt;

Ship is Wrecked;

O'Connell and Keenan seen in a boat, which is dashed against the rocks, Ahoundel and Namadow plunge from a high rock into the sea; O'Connel and Reenan are saftely landed; Surprise of the natives at seeing White Men for the first time their alarm at Fire Arms; the Islanders instigated by Namaduro, are about to slay the European.

O'CONNELL DANCES

AN IRISH JIG.

Scene 2. Namadow attempts the life of O'Connell; Lawoni preserves him.
PART THE SECOND. Six years are supposed to have elapsed since O'Connells arrival; O'Connell is now a chief and has been Tattooed; Scene 1. Outside of O'Connells Hut; Congugal felicity; George Reenans fiddle and the fate of the Looking Glass; The American Schooner Spy comes in sight; Crew land; a general Dance; Tableau, Curtain.

Paul Hambruch, in the introduction to his German translation of O'Connell's book,[95] makes the astonishing remark that O'Connell died in July 1904, when he would have been 96, just 50 years longer than he actually lived. How Hambruch came to assert such a completely erroneous piece of information is of interest. He had done ethnographic work at Ponape with the Hamburg South Seas Expedition of 1908-10, but to his great regret, he says, he did not know of O'Connell or his book until his return to Germany. Then, he says, he searched all the libraries of Europe for a copy, but in vain. He became convinced that the British had supressed the book because their interest lay in concealing the facts concerning the penal colony. (It is unnecessary to spend any time in refuting this absurd contention, save to say that the government was publishing parliamentary reports of select committees dealing with convicts and transportation as early as 1812. In any case, a copy of the book existed at least at the British Museum.) Finally a friend in the United States got permission for him to borrow a copy from the Library of Congress. Hambruch refers to this as the only existing copy; actually there were others in the collections of at least the Peabody Museum in Salem, the University of California Library, and the Enoch Pratt Free Library of Baltimore. (On the fly leaves of the last of these O'Connell's handwriting and signature appear and are reproduced in figs. 2 and 3.) The title page of the Library of Congress copy has, unfortunately, now been lost, but it was in place at late as 1960. On it was the pencil notation 'm.m. July 1904'. Librarians say that this note could have been

---

[95] Hambruch, Paul, *Elf Jahre in Australien und auf der Insel Ponape, Erlebnisse eines irischen Matrosen in den Jahren 1822 bis 1833, von James F. O'Connell*, Berlin, 1929.

Fig. 4 Part of a theatre handbill advertising the third night of a four-night appearance by James O'Connell, presumably in Buffalo. O'Connell is shown being tattooed on Ponape. He is here represented to have been on the island six years instead of the five he claims in his book, the John Bull *is wrecked on Ponape itself instead of four days distant, and other liberties are taken with the original story. The type setter can hardly be accused of being finical. O'Connell's native wife, Laowni, is here Lawoni, Ahoundel (his father-in-law in the book) is also given as Ashoundel, his enemy Namadow becomes Namudow and Namadoro, and his friend George Keenan is capriciously Reeman, Keenman, Keehan, and Reenan. Photograph by courtesy of the Buffalo and Erie County Library.*

Fig. 5 Above *O'Connell dancing on stage. The tattooing pattern
which can be seen on his arms is in fairly authentic Ponapean style,
but not that on his chest.* Below *Typical tattooing on the hand
and arm of a male Ponapean, done before 1910. From Paul
Hambruch,'Ponape',* Ergebnisse der Südsee-Expedition, 1908-10
(ed. G. Thilenius, IIB, Vol. VII, 3 vols., Hamburg, 1936, Fig. 51.)

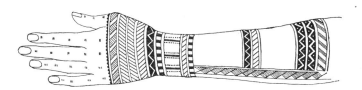

made by any library worker and would have meaning only to him; it might refer to some stage of the cataloguing process. But Hambruch apparently took it to stand for *Memento Mori*, 'remember that you must die', and assumed that this and the date referred to O'Connell's death.

According to witnesses of his performances, O'Connell exhibited his tattooing, his chief claim to fame, stripped to the waist. Old men of Ponape today, if so attired, would have nothing to show in the way of tattooing except that on their arms and hands, if their legs were covered. According to Lutké and Kittlitz of the *Senyavin* expedition, which was at Ponape in January 1828, before O'Connell, about 500 people were seen; and tattooing on the men is described as being limited to the arms and legs.[96] But O'Connell says that his back was also tattooed. There is fuller discussion of this matter in the footnotes accompanying O'Connell's description, but this is one subject in which he could hardly have hoped to deceive H.H.W., since the patterns on the back, shoulders, and breast which Jim describes but which are not traditional were subject to verification. He does not mention facial tattooing, yet it is reported that on the streets women and children screamed in horror when they met him, and ministers inveighed from the pulpit that unborn children would bear his markings if pregnant women viewed them. The descriptions of O'Connell's face, arms, and chest by circus goers of the time are of blue-black and red welts, caused by producing incisions with sea shells and filling them with a mixture of charcoal and berry juice.[97] None of this is Ponapean. The operation that O'Connell describes, quite accurately, is altogether different. If red designs were seen, and if any of them were on the chest, possibly the descriptions are of another man who performed under O'Connell's name, as was sometimes the case in those days among rival circuses, when a successful act would be imitated and the name taken as well. But it could also mean that James might have thought it necessary to enhance his exhibition value by improving on the Ponapean style.

A great-granddaughter of Dan Rice, recalling her grandmother's stories, has described James to John Kunzog as having a repulsive appearance because of his tattooing. He was moody

[96] Lutké, op. cit., Vol. 2, p. 24; Kittlitz, op. cit., Vol. 2, p. 72.
[97] Letter, John C. Kunzog to Riesenberg, 23 March 1959.

43

and inclined to bemusement. But in the ring he was jolly and took delight in performing his dance. After his act, during which he would recount his story, he would be besieged by people who wanted more particulars.[98]

Dan Rice, in a warning against the use of electric lights, says: 'In 1852 a member of the celebrated Rosel family . . . traveled with me on my steamboat on the Ohio and Mississippi Rivers . . . and got up the electric light to light up my circus tent . . . He in a short time died from the effects of the chemicals that he created the light with. Many of my troupers took sick and one member, James O'Connel, who had weak lungs, died in a short space of time . . .'.[99]

The final, undated note we have is by Maria Ward Brown, a relative of Rice. This lady, who took a rather sceptical view of James's veracity, writes: 'James O'Connell, known as the tattooed man . . . professed to have the same distinguishing embellishments upon his cutaneous coats as the Fiji [sic] Islanders, although it is doubtful if his acquaintance with that geographical part of the globe had any closer relation than in his imagination'.

Of his last days Mrs Brown says: 'While traveling with the show, he was taken sick and unable to perform, but he was kindly looked after by Dan Rice and the few members that comprised the company . . . His malady increased and his condition became hopeless. Finding the closing hour approaching, he made a characteristic request which was finally carried out. When committed to the earth the band played a lively tune and Jean Johnson danced a hornpipe over the grave. Poor O'Connell thought . . . that the transition from a life of privation and suffering was more appropriately celebrated by music and mirth than grief and lamentation'.[1]

[98] Ibid., 26 October 1963.

[99] May, Earl Chapin, *The Circus from Rome to Ringling*, 2nd ed., New York, 1963, p. 241.

[1] Brown, Maria Ward, *The Life of Dan Rice*, Long Branch, New Jersey, 1901, p. 276.

EDITOR'S PREFACE

TO THE FIRST EDITION

The narrations of travellers, sailors, and adventurers, have always been sought for, and always have possessed a peculiar interest in the ears and eyes of those whom circumstances have debarred from participating in the pleasure of witnessing varying scenes, or whose quiet lives have allowed them excitement only in listening to the hairbreadth 'scapes of people of a more nervous temperament. A reciprocal interest is conceived between the narrator and the listener; sometimes it is something more than mere interest. Othello says of Desdemona—

> *She loved me for the dangers I had passed,*
> *And I loved her, that she did pity them.*

The more simple and nearer nature the character of a people, the higher are those persons among them esteemed who can draw upon their memory or invention for the wonderful and strange. The ancient and fascinating Arabian tales of the thousand and one nights partake largely of the relations of travellers. Among the uncivilized, but not always barbarous, inhabitants of Oceanica; in the depths of the deserts, mental and

45

A

RESIDENCE

OF

ELEVEN YEARS

IN

New Holland and the Caroline Islands:

BEING THE

ADVENTURES OF JAMES F. O'CONNELL.

EDITED FROM HIS VERBAL NARRATION.

"All which I saw, and part of which I was."

BOSTON:

PUBLISHED BY B. B. MUSSEY.

1836.

Fig. 6 Title page of the 1836 edition of O'Connell's book

natural, of Africa; in the tents of the Nomades of Asia; in the wilds of Siberia; and among the snows of Greenland, Iceland, and the land of the Esquimaux; the white stranger purchases comparative ease, (when his acquaintance with the language will permit it,) by his history of the character and habits of his countrymen. A charm is thrown upon the sitters round the council-fires of our own aborigines by the relation of the tales of the traveller; his spell rests upon the Patagonian of high southern latitudes; and the "ponderous strength" of the lasso-swinging arm of the Brazilian and Peruvian Indian is relaxed while he "leans to hear."

This love of the marvellous is a purely natural feeling. It is unrestrained in the savage, and all the caution, incredulity, and experience of civilization, while they have robbed it of its wildest features, and shorn it of its principal charm, implicit belief, can never entirely eradicate it with the civilized. Although the palmy days of the traveller have passed, when Lope de Vega, Columbus, Americus Vespucius, Magellan, La Perouse, Cabot, Cook, Wallace, Van Couver, Willoughby, Belzoni, Brydone, Humboldt, and Mungo Park, and hosts of others, were winter evening classics;—although the wand of the Wizard of the North, the pencil of Irving, the humor of Paulding, the novels of Cooper, the prose-poetry of Bulwer, the graphic sea scenes of Marryatt, and the thousands of other lights, quite as brilliant, in polite literature, have supplanted Capt. Cook and Prince Lee Boo;—although the lighter magazine literature, and the severer studies, libraries of useful knowledge, scientific magazines, and lectures, prompted by the utilitarian spirit of the day, have in a measure superseded books of voyages whose chief recommendation is novelty;—still there is in the public mind a fondness for the narratives of those who have travelled and suffered much.

That rivalry does not always prompt to excellence, is proved by its operation upon this species of literature. Driven, in a measure, from the library and the drawing-room by their comparatively modern rival, romance, the writers of adventures in "far countries" began to cater for a taste less intellectual. They substitute for highly-finished narratives bare personal sketches; and instead of informing their readers upon the customs and history of the people the traveller has seen, they make his book a monodrama, in which he is the only character, and the *acts* are the mere operation of circumstances upon the narrator,—a

47

character in whom the reader must concentrate all his interest, inasmuch as there is an omnipresent *I* from title-page to finis. Still, the insurance of a rapid sale has always been found in furnishing abundance of *distress*, that being the most efficient agent for creating that interest in the narrator, which, as we have seen, is the principal point relied on for the popularity of a book of voyages. "Disaster" or "shipwreck" will arrest the eye quicker than the announcement of the discovery of a new continent. *Distress* is so indispensable an ingredient in the compilation of modern books of voyages, that a newspaper paragraph will suffice for the most important voyage of discovery, unattended with that agreeable stimulant to the curiosity of the reader—misery.

Parry, Ross, Back, were nine-days' lions each; but who reads accounts of their voyages if he can find a copy of any of the popular works of fiction of the day? We repeat it, the palmy day of the voyager has passed. While one cause is found in the gratification of curiosity, and the satiety produced long since, another and more surely acting cause exists in the catchpenny manner in which "narratives" have of late years been got up. We intend not to say, in recommendation of our own book, that it is to restore the days of Lee Boo or Robinson Crusoe—far less that it will command an attention which the works of the great modern voyagers have not. But we do say, that time and care have been taken in compiling and arranging it, and that if it succeed it will not be because it gratifies a morbid taste for the horrible and the disgusting. Care has been taken to dwell as little as possible upon gloomy passages. The narrator is made to occupy the place of an artist in a land scape print, as he is introduced from time to time only to show from what point each view was taken. His personal adventures are introduced only so far as appeared to the editor necessary to give the work the character of a narrative. Had it been the mere object of the narrator to make himself famous, the editor had in his story a succession of adventures at which a De Foe might have leaped for joy—never had book-wright a better subject. Mr. O'Connell has experienced varieties of fortune and situation, rare and varied opportunities for observation, such as seldom have fallen to the lot of an individual. A brief programme of the events of his life will give the reader a view of what the work *should* be; and whether it does him justice, it is the reader's province to decide.

Left, by an inconsiderate uncle and temporary guardian, un-watched in the living wilderness of London, at about eleven years of age chance led him among the sailors about Deptford and Wapping; thence he found his way on ship-board, as cabin-boy, and went in a convict ship to Port Jackson. A two or three years' residence in New Holland, during which he accompanied the English government surveyor, Mr. Oxley, on a six-months' ex-ploring expedition, acquainted him not only with the history of the colony, discipline of the convicts, punishments and rewards, but gave him opportunity to learn the character of the aborigines, —an opportunity repeated by his being cast away in a whaler on the north of the continent, and spending nine months in working his way, by land, back to Sydney. Shipwrecked, in a subsequent voyage, among the Caroline group; living over five years there, during which time he was indelibly stamped with the native patent of nobility, tattooing; marrying, and having children born to him; taken off by the American schooner Spy, of Salem; thrown into prison at Manilla as a pirate [!] or a run-away from New South Wales; discharged, because there was no shadow of proof against him, while his ingenuous story carried truth upon its face; sent to Canton; thence over land to Pekin, to join the caravan there; leaving it before he joined it, and feeling his way back;—we ask whether there is not in such adventure abundant material for an interesting book?

If it be uninteresting, the fault is the editor's. "But do you believe it all?" Religiously, dear reader. When he was first intro-duced to us, the incredulity which is, sooner or later, the gift of connection with the world, induced us to be very suspicious; but continued and frequent conversations with him, in which, assisted by others, we repeated trivial questions, and invariably received the same answers, soon disarmed us of all suspicion. We say *trivial* questions, because, in a system of imposture, while it would be quite possible to be uniform on important matters, it would be next to impossible not to be betrayed by trifles. Add to this his rapidity of answering out-of-the-way questions, which permitted no time for invention; and another circumstance, more wonderful than either, supposing him an impostor, but not at all surprising if his truth be admitted; and the proof of his veracity is unquestioned—at least, in our opinion. The circumstance to which we allude is this: he amused himself one day by writing a list of a couple of hundred words in the language of the

Carolines, and their English signification. We preserved the paper, and, some days afterward, questioned him from it. His answers were invariably correct, evincing such a knowledge of the language as could only have been acquired by a long residence. If he be an impostor, he is superior to all who have appeared since Mahomet. The Mormon leaders are children to him.

Mr. O'Connell kept no notes, and had, to assist his relation, no aid but a retentive memory. Under such circumstances, confusion in dates, should there prove to be any, will be excused. The avoidance of errors is impossible, even to professed tourists who take notes at every step of their progress, and burden memory only with the distance of the next stage. So far as we have had opportunity to compare Mr. O'Connell's story with published geographical works and travels, we have found him correct. Much of the matter in the book, however, is unlike any heretofore published. That part of the narrative referring to the Carolines, or, rather, to the particular group upon which he resided, treats of an island of which there is no other history extant. Indeed, if we except the early works of the Jesuits, and the volumes which have appeared upon the Sandwich and Society Islands, this will be the first published, circumstantial history of a community of Oceanic Indians.

Acknowledging assistance from "Cunningham's New South Wales" in giving the natural history of New Holland, we have few more remarks to make before dismissing the reader from the preface to the book. Events are placed in the order in which they occurred, without attempts exactly to fix dates to all. Truth has been adhered to; and it has also been the aim of the editor to make the work amusing, as well as authentic. Repeating his conviction of the credibility of the witness whose voice is here raised in vindication of the character of one nation of the much-abused South Sea Islanders, the editor is willing to submit the work to the test of examination; errors inseparable from the manner of its compilation always excepted.

H. H. W.

Boston, August, 1836.

CHAPTER I

Parentage.—Birthplace.—Meeting with parents.—Journey to London.—Neglect of guardian.—Petted by sailors.—Ships in the Phoenix.—Embarkation of passengers for Botany Bay.—Their appearance and deportment.—Visits of friends.—Three cheers for Botany Bay.—Sea-sickness.—Discipline of passengers on board.—Food.—Agreeable anticipations.—Punishments.—Land ho!—Royal visit.—Royal insignia.—Flash.—Quarantine.—Old friends.—Debarkation.

My father was neither an Irish peer, a resident, nor an absentee landholder; neither a squireen nor a bog-trotter. Though his name speaks him an O'Connell, his relationship with the agitator is so many moves removed, that it was never found worth his while to trace it. In Dublin, it were something important, perhaps, to prove my birthplace; here, it is nobody's business that, on the 10th November, 1808, James O'Connell first saw light in the chambers over one Jones' book-bindery, Thomas street, Dublin, directly opposite a warehouse where brogues are or were sold by the hamper.

E

The first thing I remember of childhood, is, being an inmate of a school at Monaster Evean, about forty miles from Dublin; whence myself and two sisters were, one day, forwarded to Dublin, and shipped to Liverpool, consigned to the landlord of my father's boarding-house. We arrived in the evening, and he carried us to the circus. I can recollect, as distinctly as though it were yesterday, my childish astonishment at what appeared to me the magnificence of the building, the glare of light, the gorgeous tinsel ornaments, and, more than all, the superhuman feats of the ring. The drolleries of the clown filled me with a childish delight, which nothing in after years has paralleled. I thought the riders the most remarkable and enviable beings I had ever happened upon. Did I inherit this passion, or not? When I was told that one of the troupe was my mother, and a person sparkling with *jewels* was pointed out to me as that mother, I would not have exchanged my parentage with the son of a duke. I could hardly refrain from throwing myself into the ring, to assert, before the audience, my claim to a portion of their applause, as the son of the person they were so loudly cheering. All these feelings I could not, perhaps, so well have expressed; but I felt them, nevertheless.

Our first meeting with our parents, after a five years' separation, took place in my mother's dressing-room. She stifled our expressions of wonder at her princely vocation, by maternal caresses, more tender and repeated than gentle. There was a feeling of wounded vanity mingled with my joy at meeting;— shame that the son of such a princess, a man full ten years of age, should be so be-babyfied; but who can check a mother's fondness? I could not conceive, either, why it was that she cared so little to converse upon a profession which I thought so glorious.

My father was costumer to M'Kean, an equestrian, then of some note, at least in my prejudiced eyes. His name never rung so wide as that of Ducrow, but still he was a famous man among his admirers. My mother, and her brother, John Noonan, also an equestrian of some reputation, and a posture-master and tumbler, made the round of the provincial towns with M'Kean, occasionally appearing in Liverpool and Dublin, but never, as a company, venturing near the metropolis. With my parents I spent about a year, and then, with their permission, went to the "big wen" of Cobbett, London, with my equestrian uncle, who had an engagement at Astley's. Mr. Noonan did not keep a very strict watch upon his troublesome little charge; and when he did assume authority, it was put on in a manner more *spirited* than conciliatory. Taking advantage of his inattention, I spent my time in lounging about Deptford and Wapping; and was, from my antics, learned in the purlieus of a circus, an acceptable visitor to John Tar, who is ever fond of physical precosity and agility. Acquaintance with sailors led me frequently on ship-board. I practised climbing about the shrouds and rigging, and learned to fancy that, next to that of an equestrian, the life of a sailor was the most wonderful and noble in the world. At length Capt. Salmon, of the ship Phœnix, took a fancy to me, and, without the knowledge or consent of any of my friends, I shipped as cabin-boy on board his vessel.

A short time after I joined her at Deptford, she moved down to Woolwich, to take in live freight; being chartered by Government, for the transportation of female convicts to Botany Bay. The ship's surgeon superintendent was Dr. Walker, who officiated in the double capacity of physician to soul and body, reading the Episcopal Church service on Sabbath afternoons, and prescribing for the bodily ailments of the convicts at all times. It is my impression that this officer draws his salary by a premium on the head of every convict who reaches Port Jackson in good health: this may be correct, or it may be a sailor's yarn. The ship's company, including the two extremes, officers and boys, numbered about thirty-five. Her precise tonnage[1] I cannot recollect, but her passengers were rising two hundred in number. A small amount of baggage was allowed to each, and each, upon coming on board, had two purser's suits served out to her.

No crime or worthlessness of character can destroy all feeling of pity, on the part of the philanthropist, for such unfortunates as render themselves amenable to the laws of their country. Indeed, as the worst conduct calls down the severest punishment, perhaps the vilest characters command more pity than those who are less guilty, and, consequently, liable to punishment less severe. But pity for women embarking for Port Jackson seems a waste of sympathy, as, just taken from jail, they seem rather giddily to rejoice in the anticipation of a change of scene, than to feel sorrow at the prospect of punishment. Taken from the

---

[1] *Phoenix* I was of 493 tons, *Phoenix* II 589 tons, *Phoenix* III 500 tons.

very lowest haunts of vice and misery, generally entirely destitute of self-respect, and apparently careless of every thing but mere bodily comfort and ease; incapable, by habit, of appreciating any thing but pleasures of the senses, they wore the outward seeming of careless indifference or thoughtless merriment. Occasionally, among the crowd, there was a face the index of remorse, and a consciousness of degradation; or, perchance, of the remembrance of friends, and bitter grief at the loss of respectable standing. Such, however, were rare; in the chatter of the convicts, flash, obscenity, and profanity were the principal features. In dress they varied from the beggars' rags of St. Giles', to the tawdry finery of the aristocracy in vice: and there was not wanting even an occasional neat dress, which bespoke the wearer not all degraded. Over the faces of the whole there was more or less of the "prison aspect," a wanness, the effect of trial and confinement.

After receiving her passengers, the Phœnix laid three or four days at Woolwich. The acquaintances and connections of the convicts were on board in crowds, bidding farewell, and bringing trifles to minister to the comfort of their erring friends during a long passage. This affectionate solicitude looks beautifully upon paper; but in too many cases the unconvicted differed only from the sentenced in the circumstance that they were as yet legally undetected. Indeed, I heard, more than once, the *probability* of meeting again at Botany Bay spoken of between parting friends. The utmost vigilance was necessary to prevent the conveyance of liquor on board; and in view of the whole scene, pity, disgust, and a sort of mirth, struggled for mastery in the mind of the spectator. Weeping, embracing, hysteric laughter, snatches of flash songs, ribaldry, affected mirth, and unaffected despondence, soon took the place of the general appearance of cheerfulness with which the convicts came from their places of confinement.

The anchor is weighed, and the steamboat takes us in tow down the river. Handkerchiefs of all complexions are waving to the people who swarm in boats in our wake;—"Hip—hip—hip—hurra!"—three cheers for Botany Bay from the convicts, and a response from the watermen and the banks of the river. In a few hours the steamer left us; we were in the channel. Two hundred female convicts, a little million to appearance in the snug quarters of the vessel, are not missed from among the swarms of the vile in modern Babylon. They are as a bucket from the ocean; and

54

yet every one of these despised beings has friends; low, and probably vicious, but still affectionate. Feelings and sensibility they have too; blunted it may be, but still human. Their disappearance may be unnoticed by the spectator of the mass, but each of them leaves a void in the circle in which she has moved, though that may have been none of the purest. Weeping eyes follow the departure of the convict ship; aching hearts yearn after the guilty beings whom it is bearing to a distant and degrading place of exile.

American steamboats are floating palaces; so are the splendid packet ships between the old world and the new. Even in the steerages of the latter, there is much attention to comfort. The reader will probably draw his conceptions of the horrors of sea-sickness from the situation of passengers under all advantages which a sea passage will admit,—comforted by attention, and cheered by the sympathy of friends. Even then it is horrid, prostrating to mind and body. Judge, then, if the situation of two hundred women, unfitted by previous habits and vicious education for any thing like patience; consoled with next to no attendance, because, were such treatment compatible with the purposes of punishment, their numbers would preclude its possibility; suffering the gnawings of conscience, and the bitter reflections attendant upon their reminiscences and future prospects;—imagine all this, and judge of the situation of a female convict ship, three or four days out! Sea-sickness is a disease at which those who have not suffered it, and those who have, are wont to laugh; the former because they know nothing about it, and the latter from the selfish pleasure we are too apt to feel in the misery of those who are undergoing a *seasoning* that we have passed through. Consequently, the miseries of sea-sickness are not duly commiserated. Even with it before them, the *exempts* laugh; but its severity on board the Phœnix made it a point of duty, as well as of expediency, to put in at Spithead, and give the passengers a respite, after the (to them) boisterous passage from the Nore. At Spithead we lay two days, and on the third weighed again; and made no harbor, till at the end of a five months' passage we came to, in Sydney Cove.

The convicts were divided into three general divisions, according to their sentences;—the sentenced for seven years, those for fourteen, and those for life. The crew of the vessel lived in the steerage, the short sentenced convicts under the main hatch, the "lifers" forward; and forward of them, in what is, on board of merchant ships, the forecastle, is the "sick bay," or hospital. The berths, in tiers at the sides, accommodated six persons each; and the inmates of each berth formed a mess. The women were all compelled to muster, in divisions, on deck, at least once a day, in tolerable weather, one division at a time; and to ensure this airing, necessary to health, female "boatswains" were appointed. It was the duty of these petticoat officers to compel cleanliness also. The provisions were similar in quality and kind to those furnished vessels of the navy. In lieu of "grog" a cheap wine was served out, which the prisoners were obliged to drink at the tub, to prevent hoarding, or selling to one another. The usual punishment for minor offences was cutting off this allowance of wine; for the more refractory, a machine was contrived, similar in operation to the stocks, but more resembling a very straight sentry box. The offender was locked into it, standing erect, and when it was closed upon her she could hardly move a limb.

The passengers, after the first fortnight, were generally healthy, and, notwithstanding they were sentenced convicts, happy. The majority of them had been in England as poor as vicious; no change could, with them, have been for the worse, and the temperate and regular manner of living, attention to cleanliness, and relief from squalid poverty, made them happy even under what are usually thought the privations of the vessel. Judicious change of food, and judicious treatment on the part of Dr. Walker, secured them from disease, and they came out, at the end of the passage, renovated in health, and in possession of a buoyancy of spirits new to them. It may be matter of surprise to those who have heard only of Botany Bay as a sort of penitentiary, but the passengers looked forward to the day of their arrival with impatience. Botany Bay was the burden of their songs; for there is *poetry* even in the flash of St. Giles'—*unwritten* poetry. And as all poets have been wont to sing the future, it may well be imagined that those whose future is usually so well defined, the end of whose course is seen, "not through a glass darkly," but distinctly through the grates of Newgate, do not forget it in their songs.

Land ho! from the fore-top-gallant yard, land ho! on deck, and land ho! the hearts of two hundred women responded. Hearts! Most assuredly; at least at Botany Bay it would not do to doubt it: women have hearts, and men too, however apparently degraded. The policy of Old England for regenerating the vile, has succeeded in opening a field for improvement where the subjects upon whom the system operates cannot be frowned back into the place from which they have just stepped, by the rigidly righteous, the unreflecting, and those whose habitual contempt for poor fallible human nature leads them to the opinion, that once debased, man can never rise above the self-inflicted degradation.

It was four or five days after making the land before we could fetch the harbor. The first joy at the sight of land had changed, on the part of the women, to impatience, and from impatience to a sort of careless, half despair, which did not a whit abate at sight of the rocky heads of Sydney Cove. When the headland was doubled, and the romantic situations of gentlemen's country seats, and then the settlement at Sydney, was spread before them, hope and expectation were awake again, and there was nothing in their deportment to remind the observer that they were unwilling emigrants. The pilot boarded us outside the Heads; the next visitor was a much more interesting and august personage,— no less than KING BUNGAREE, of flash memory, by descent, ratified by permission of H. B. M.'s government, chief of the Sydney Cove blacks, boarding officer, and official welcomer and usher of new comers to Botany Bay. He paddled alongside of us in a whale-boat, for his safety in which, all riddled as it was, he had the sufficient guaranty that the boat "carried Cæsar." His Bungaree Majesty's coat was of approved texture and quality, inasmuch as it had served a long apprenticeship to an English corporal, before falling into his hands. Upon his neck was suspended the order and insignia of his nobility,—a plate which might have been gold, but was brass, bearing the inscription,

"BUNGAREE,
KING OF SYDNEY COVE."

Bungaree, like the ancient Pharaoh of the Egyptians, is the hereditary title of the royal family. His Majesty's pantaloons were of similar extraction with his coat; and as for shoes or sandals, it was sacrilege to suppose that the royal feet of the House of Bungaree need such plebeian defences. His head was surmounted with a cocked hat of magnificent dimensions, in which waved, and swam, and flaunted in air, a martial plume; the de-

pendent feather's feathers of which kissed his sable cheeks, giving
and receiving lustre. The brightness of darkness of his face, who
shall describe? and who in fitting colors paint the glory of his
suite, the tribe of Bungaree? The fair representatives of St. Giles,
Wapping, St. Catherine's Lane, Ratcliffe High Way, Winnifield
Bay, and St. George's Fields, entertaining high ideas of royalty,
stood all abashed at the magnificence of the monarch, of whose
fame the gossip of a five months' passage had possessed them. In
silver tones, their queries and comments rose in exquisite confusion, as they crowded round his Majesty of Port Jackson. "The
rum cove of this vile is up to lushing max, like a Billingsgate fish-
monger."* "The cove's kicksies† is rayther seedy." "His kelp‡
and his tug,§ stewed down, would fill the doctor's coppers¶ with
soup;" with thousands of other observations, more various than
edifying. King Bungaree, who is indeed better entitled to his
rank than the English to his land, deigned no notice of the gad-
ding women, but proceeded aft, to announce himself to the
officers, and demand of them, in addition to the "max," which
he had received of course, the customary tribute. Even royalty
must submit to disagreeables, and King Bungaree was ordered
away, upon the arrival on board of Dr. Bowman, quarantine
physician, and F. A. Healey, Esq., superintendent.

Vessels which have sickness on board are ordered to the quarantine ground; those which, as was our case, have no apparent
sickness, other than the usual effects of a long passage, ride out
a half quarantine outside the usual range of anchorage. People
are not allowed to come on board, but all communication is by
no means cut off, as boats are continually alongside, selling fresh
provisions, bread, &c. to the convicts. It may be well here to remark, that if a convict is discovered to have money to any considerable amount, it is taken from him or her, and deposited in a
Savings Institution at Sydney, where it accumulates till the time
of sentence expires. The conversations of the passengers with the
boats alongside are peculiar, and have a character which no
greetings away from New South Wales can resemble. "Lord
lov'ee, Sal! is that you? and how long are ye lagged for?" "Only
for seven years." An Irish girl among our passengers was hailed
by her mother, who had preceded her to this land of promise

---

* *The king of this place drinks gin, &c.*

† *Trowsers.* ‡ *Hat.* § *Coat.* ¶ *Cook's kettles.*

about two years. "Och, Mary!" cried the parent, "is it here I see you? and how long are ye lagged for?" "Only eighty-four months, mother." "Och, my child, avourneen machree! It's glad I am that you're not lagged for seven years. I tould ye at home, that the mornin' snake 'ud bring the avenin' boult upon your fate."* "An' where did ye lave Jemmy, my son?" "He's hanged, mother, the assize before they lagged me. An thin we brought him to St. Giles', an a beauthiful corpse he made, ounly he had the black stroke roun his neck." As many as can make themselves heard, are singing out at once: "Where is one-eyed Suke of St. Giles'?" "Oh, she's aboard for a seven yearser." "Oh well, she need n't grunt—it's a long run she had before the pigs† brought her to the scratch." "Did you see Tom Brown in Newgate?" "Ay, he stood his patter last assizes, and has got a bellowser."‡

But enough of flash. In about ten days after our arrival, the convicts were landed at the dockyard, where they were inspected by Gov. Macquaurie, F. A. Healey, Esq., and Dr. Bowman. Upon the arrival of a convict ship at Port Jackson, it is usual for such free residents as need domestics to make application at the super-intendent's office for them. These applications are first answered, then the unappropriated residue are sent to the factory at Parra-matta, if females, if males, to the prisoners' barracks.

---

* *I told you that stealing in the morning would put your feet in irons at night.*

† *Constables.*

‡ *He was tried last assizes and sentenced for life.*

CHAPTER II

Legitimacy.—Phoenix condemned.—Mr. Charles Smith.—His business, character, standing, &c.—Botany Bay greetings.—Tomlinsonian philosophy.—Mr. Samuel Terry.—Mr. Thomas Cooper. —Whiskey.—Mr. Haynes, and others.—Capt. Rossi.—Theatre.— Richard Third.—Impromptu performance of the "pigs."—Ventriloquial imitations.—Tragic end of a tragic tragedy.—"Home, Sweet Home."—Police.—Theatre at Emu Plains.—Hunt, the murderer of Ware.

Legitimacy, in all other parts of the world a coveted qualification, is in New Holland a term of reproach,—or, perhaps we should say, the denial of the fact that one is a *legitimate settler*, is the boast of voluntary emigrants, government officers, and discharged seamen, after their return home. In New Holland it is of less consequence; but as this work is not prepared for the New South Wales market, the reader will at once perceive the reason and propriety of the detail of circumstances in the commencement, which might otherwise appear of no consequence to the reader. The veracity of this narrative is not so questionable as it might be, were he left to the presumption that the narrator was a *legitimate, legal,* or *sentenced* visiter of Botany Bay.

The Phœnix was condemned at Port Jackson, as unseaworthy, purchased by Government, and made a receiving ship for double convicts, sentenced to penal settlements. This discharged the crew, and I was taken into the employment of Mr. Charles Smith, with whom I remained about a year. Mr. Smith's history was that of many of the free residents in New South Wales. Originally,

"He left his country for that country's good."

Correct behaviour procured him, at the end of three years, a "ticket of leave," and at the end of his sentence he had collected a pretty little capital to commence the world with anew. Enterprise, shrewdness and industry, made him one of the wealthiest men in the colony. He was a large contractor for the supply of butcher's meat to the government, for the soldiers and prisoners, and was one of the first, if not the very first, who succeeded in packing beef in New Holland; the climate, prior to his giving proof to the contrary, having been supposed an insuperable objection. Mr. Smith had large tracts of land under cultivation, beside many acres of grazing land. He had also a livery stable, which was much frequented by bloods connected with the government offices, both as patrons, and as horse fanciers, who found in Smith a kindred spirit. His attachment to horses was not entirely a pecuniary arrangement;—Mr. Smith was a sportsman, and the owner of *Boshee,* then a famous horse on the Colonial turf. My employment was ostensibly and nominally that of a clerk, and, being a lively little Irish lad, full of fun, frolic, and flash, learned in my year's attendance on the circus, I soon became the pet of Mr. Smith's callers. I accompanied Mr. Smith in his excursions into the country for the purchase of cattle, wore my demi-sailor rig (all the go in New Holland) with a jaunty air, and was just at the age, and in the possession of spirits, to note carefully what passed around me. Mr. Smith's intercourse, as contractor, with the convicts, gave me unusual advantages for becoming acquainted with their discipline and situation, and, besides these, there were not wanting excellent opportunities of observing the general character of the colony.

There cannot be a better place than this to introduce notices of some other of the freed-men of the colony, who at the time of my residence there, 1820 to 1826, were prominent members of society. Their history was as common as the Gazette, and being only orally preserved, my relation may be inaccurate, but is sufficiently correct to be depended upon in the main. No secret is attempted to be made of the cause of one's sojourn at Sydney. If two strangers meet in any situation where conversation seems necessary, almost the first question exchanged is, "Are you free, or a transport?" The next may be, "What were you lagged for, and for how long?" Freemen are sometimes foolish enough to take offence at a Botany Bay greeting. I was at first, but soon learned the folly of permitting any such sensitiveness to appear, and becoming acclimated, I ceased to feel it. It purchases no good by squeamishness to say, "I am better than thou!" for the philosophy of the Botany Bay school is so nearly that of Bulwer's Augustus Tomlinson, that the eminently moral novel in which Tomlinson figures, Paul Clifford, is undoubtedly a popular work in New South Wales. Crime *detected* is misfortune; sentence and transportation are *events*, inconvenient, at first, it is true, but they lose much of their particular stigma in the atmosphere of Australia, and become mere circumstances, convenient for reference in fixing dates.

Mr. Samuel Terry paid a pig for his passage from England to Sydney,—that is to say, the pig purchased his passage. It is to be presumed however that the simple feat of "going a whole pig," though reported as the ostensible cause of his transportation, could not have been the whole cause. Previous convictions and character must have affected his sentence, as it was, in flash phraseology, a *winder*. Nor did his acquisitive propensities cease upon his arrival, as it is in the memory of some of the colonists that the rich Samuel Terry has been whipped for stealing poultry. Growing, however, after a while, to see the evil of his ways, he obtained by good conduct a ticket of leave; put his acquisitiveness under restraint, and by legal cultivation of that organ, became one of the wealthiest men in the colony. There was upon him the nominal restraint of a convict, but with his ticket of leave, and ticket of exemption, he was in effect free excepting the single condition of remaining in Australia. To this however he had a stronger tie than government restriction, the proprietorship of one of the largest estates in the possession of any individual. He married, and sons and daughters were born unto him. Although his children may not be particularly anxious to perpetuate the family history, and care nothing about heraldry, they are not a whit the less respectable in Sydney from the slight circumstance that their father is a *winder*. Mr. Terry is, or was, also connected with the whale fishery.

Mr. Thomas Cooper was a sort of aristocrat among convicts. He was transported for fourteen years, his crime being "standing a fence," that is to say, purchasing stolen goods. The articles upon which he was convicted were stolen from the wardrobe of the Prince of Wales. Upon gaining a ticket of leave, he commenced the manufacture of a sort of gin from Indian corn, and his name is identified with the grocer's vocabulary, "Cooper's best" being as readily understood as Cogniac or Jamaica. The stock-keepers, and other inland settlers, are however the principal consumers of the article.

Mr. Haynes, a proprietor of whale ships, a principal stay of the Methodist Church, and a local preacher, was a convict. Among others, doing a heavy and profitable business, were Cooper and Levi, Thomas Straits, Alexander Long, William Hutchinson, and —— Lyons, whose names may be found, with those of many other prosperous citizens of Sydney, in the criminal records of their own country.

There were two newspapers in Sydney, one of which, the Monitor, an opposition paper, edited by Edward Smith Hall, used to abound in police reports, more remarkable for their witty libels upon the police magistrate, Capt. Rossi, than for their truth. Indeed, Hall has been more than once imprisoned for his libels upon this dignitary, whose broken and unintelligible Corsican English, bench law, and despotic sentences, made him a fair mark for satire. He was one of the witnesses upon the trial of Queen Caroline, and probably held his office at Sydney as a reward for services there rendered. The abundant use of alcoholic liquors, and the infractions of the rules imposed upon convicts, supplied the captain with busy daily morning occupation. To the drama the Corsican was an especial foe.

While I was at Sydney there was no regular theatre, but a large hall in a building in George's street, belonging to Mr. Levi, was used sometimes by amateurs. The upper story was a flour mill, the sails—for it was carried by wind—being on a tower in the centre of the roof. Admission to the pit was a dollar and a half. Seats in the music gallery across one end of the hall were called box seats, and sold at two dollars. Queer scenes sometimes

63

occurred there, the directions for which were not laid down in the prompt book.

One Palmer, a nice little fellow belonging to the prisoners' barracks, obtained leave of absence one play night, till nine o'clock. It was not known at the barracks what use he purposed to make of his time, and the officers were astonished when from the front they recognised in the voice which began the soliloquy,

"Now is the winter of our discontent,"

the convict Palmer's.

"By Gar, I shall make it a one dam sauvage season!" growled Capt. Rossi, astonished at seeing such an offence to his dignity. But there was no help for it,—King Richard was on liberty. A warrant was made out, however, in readiness for the hunchback tyrant, should he overstay his time. Meanwhile, the play went on briskly. Richard stormed, wooed, murdered his way through, drawing down peal upon peal of applause, till at length came the tent scene. The index of Capt. Rossi's watch began to near the point at which he so impatiently wished it. The bell commenced ringing—

"Do hear it, Richard! for it is a knell
That summons thee to—"

the barracks! No, no; he is too busy in the tent scene with the ghosts of Buckingham, and Rivers, and Anne, and the young princes; but the noses of less airy torments are peeping in at the side scenes. Squirming, after the most approved spasmodic fashion, Richard bounds from his couch, comes down to the footlights on his bended knee, and tries the temper of his sword, *a la Kean*, by raising his weight upon it. But why are the plaudits of the house all at once changed to hisses and swinish grunts? Why is the tender language of the delicate pig, the manly base of the reverend father of pork, and the angry rock-ok-ok-ok of the matron swine, imitated in all sorts of voices by flash ventriloquists? Alas, to the question, "Who's there?" no Shakespeare murdering amateur answered—

" 'Tis I, my lord, the early village cock,"

but the *pigs** have nabbed the royal dreamer! "Let him alone!"

* *Constables.*

"Don't stop the piece!" hisses, grunts, and all sorts of pig music were of no avail. Richard was hardly allowed to doff his stage habiliments, before he was walked to the barracks. Divers of the audience were also snaked out, as having trespassed by overstaying their time.

Nor did the amateur performances of the constables cease here. Between the play and the farce was a song, to be sung "by a lady." Capt. Rossi's eyes dilated, when a *bellowser,** a *flash blowen*, entered, simpering and smiling to the audience, waited very engagingly till the prelude to the song was played, and then began to warble "Home, Sweet Home!" Again the *pigs* ran upon the stage, and the cantatrice was not allowed to finish even the first stanza, before she was ingloriously dragged off, to remain in custody till the next morning, when Capt. Rossi would dispose of her.

Upon the next day Rossi had his hands full of employment in which he delighted. The theatre offenders were summarily disposed of. "You shall play Richard de tree times, hey? By Gar, so you shall vingt-et-un, twenty-one, twenty-eight days, by Gar! You shall ride de treadmill for one horse!" Mrs. Chambers, the vocalist, was sent to the factory. "Ha! miladi! you shall sing 'Sweet Home,' hey? So shall you wid you head shave-ee, by Gar! Home! hey! you shall find home in the factory tree, yes, twelve monts, by Gar!"

There was also a theatre at Emu plains, about thirty miles from Sydney, on the Bathurst road. There had once been a penal settlement there, but at the time I knew the place its character had changed, as the sending double convicted prisoners there had ceased. The theatre at Emu was in its exterior much less promising than that at Sydney, being a log hut, unplastered; and the interior corresponded. At Sydney the magistrates discouraged theatricals, and Capt. Rossi in particular, bent all his artillery against them; but at Emu, the company were all convicts, and played one night a week by the permission, and in a manner, under the patronage of Gov. Brisbane, the superintendent of the settlement. Sir John Jamieson, Mr. M'Henry, and others, magistrates, the officers of the army, and other persons connected with the government, often made the "fashionable" part of these log-hut theatrical audiences. Here I first heard Hunt sing. Hunt was

* *Person under life sentence.*

transported as a confederate of Thurtle in the murder of Ware; a crime which was perpetrated in England about the year 1823. The three persons were gamblers, if I recollect, and Ware was one night the winner, under circumstances more creditable to his art than to his honesty. Hunt and Thurtle murdered him, concealing the body in a well or a lake. The murder was discovered, Thurtle was convicted and executed, and Hunt by turning king's evidence had his punishment commuted to transportation. There used to be current a flash conundrum, "Why is Thurtle like an old coat?"—"Because he is the worse for Ware," (wear.) Hunt's sentence was the most severe one ever known in the colony. It was for his natural life, without any of the convict's usual privileges. Sentence of death was recorded against him, and he was sentenced perpetually to a chain-gang. He was an excellent ballad singer, and this accomplishment procured him the temporary alleviation of his sentence enjoyed while singing songs and ballads upon the stage. I believe, however, this was but temporary; as when, by the interest of the Sydney theatre-goers with the Bathurst authorities, Hunt was permitted to "star it" in Sydney, the papers took the authorities so severely to task for permitting it, that Hunt was remanded to the chain-gang, after his first appearance.

CHAPTER III

Paramatta factory, situate about fourteen miles from Sydney, is the depôt for female convicts before they are assigned as servants, and the place to which assigned servants are sentenced for punishment for light offences, upon complaint of their masters; and wives upon complaint of their husbands. The manufacture of the cloth which makes the uniform of the convicts, male and female, and the making of it up into garments, supplies the convicts at Parramatta with employment. The factory is about two

F

miles from the town of Paramatta. The most laborious work upon the native wool from which the cloth is made, is done in the town by the male convicts; no unassigned females being employed except at the factory.

The convicts in the factory are divided into three classes; arranged, not with reference to their crimes before transportation, but to their conduct in the factory. All convicts, upon entering, are placed in the first class, in which their employment is needlework, and other comparatively light occupations. Infraction of the rules, or disobedience and disrespect to the government of the factory, degrades the convict to the next class. Here she is employed in carding, weaving, and other laborious employment, usually given to male convicts at Parramatta, but imposed upon females as punishment. No agency of water or other power is used in any part of the process of the manufacture of Paramatta cloth; the first object being, not the production of the cloth, but the employment of the convicts; and the fabric is coarse and blankety in its appearance, and undressed. When convicts are degraded from the second to the third class, employment suited to their sex ceases; their heads are shaved, and they are set to breaking stone, wheeling earth, and cultivating the grounds about the factory.

The government of the convicts at this institution is intrusted principally to a female, whose title is "The Matron." The matron must be a free woman; not a freed transport, but a person whose character has never been endorsed by a judicial tribunal. She selects, from each class, convicts as monitresses. No males are employed about the institution, except two or three superannuated old men as sentinels or porters. The sway of the matron is not despotic; she cannot even degrade a convict to a lower class without preferring a formal complaint to the magistrate at Paramatta. When a *lady* (these women always speak of each other as "*ladies*") is, in the third class, incorrigible, solitary confinement in a cell, or a visit to the dancing school, *alias* treadmill, is imposed as a punishment. Freed women, married *ladies*, and assigned servants, when recommitted to the factory, are placed in either class, as their offences merit.

Spirits and tobacco are forbidden the convicts in the factory. Wine, allowed as a cordial on the passage out, is also withdrawn, but the food is wholesome and abundant. Indian corn meal stirred in boiling water, called in America hasty pudding, or mush, in Australia hominy, makes the breakfast. At dinner they

68

have animal food and vegetables, and at supper "Scotch coffee," i. e. burned corn.

Convicts are discharged from the factory by three methods—tickets of leave at the expiration of half their time of sentence, tickets of exemption upon the arrival of their husbands in the colony, and tickets of exemption upon the application of a suitor, who must marry, forthwith, the damsel whose liberty he seeks. Sailors who have conceived a penchant for lady passengers on the voyage out, and are also, upon their arrival in the country, so in love with it as to wish to remain; and *legitimate* settlers who have served out their sentences and taken grants of land, are usually the applicants for wives at the factory. Applications are often made by persons who come without any particular damsel in view; and obtaining a wife is pretty easy, from among a set of women who are ready to take any thing for a husband, rather than remain at the factory. The exchange, on the part of the woman, is however, only the exchange of a mild government for a despotic, as the husband can at any time turn her back to the factory by preferring a complaint. Consequently, the most frequent result of matches formed by a mere freak, or love not the most refined, on the one part, and the acceptance of any offer, rather than remaining in durance, on the other, is the remanding of the bride back to the factory and a shaved head. The advantage is altogether on the side of the husband, the wife's sentence to the colony being standing evidence against her to corroborate his testimony. Gray-bearded old settlers, who have served out their sentences, and are ready to recommence the world on an Australian farm, need a wife to take care of the homestead. Debarred by character, ill personal appearance, and other disagreeables, from obtaining an assigned or freed woman to wife, these gentry seek in the factory a wife who will shut her eyes to the defects of a husband, be they ever so glaring, when by marriage she can again obtain "a home of her own." Quarrels soon follow the tying of the nuptial knot, and a large proportion of the police cases are complaints preferred by husbands against wives, who have too soon let the motives of their marriage become apparent by their conduct.

The process of a factory courtship is worth describing. Let us suppose the suitor an old "stringy-bark," such being the soubriquet in which inland settlers rejoice. He has no particular maid in view, but has obtained of Bishop Marsden permission to visit the factory and seek a wife, and a letter to the matron certifying his intent. The girls are paraded in each room as the Cœlebs enters it, that is, the marriageable ones of the first and second classes, and the visiter scans them as a Turk would Georgians in a slave-market. I have been myself present at two or three of these negotiations, as they usually take place upon visiting days, when the friends of the convicts are allowed to enter the factory. I would not be understood that *I* had friends there; Mr. Smith could always make some pretext to enter, and we visited them from curiosity. The girls, all agog for a husband, would show various faces upon the examination. Some, all sheepish smiles and blushes, would look as foolish as all young ladies are supposed to, when a third person happens in upon an interview at which the question has just been popped. Others would avert their faces in a sort of indifference; as, although a refusal is seldom met by an applicant, still these seekers for help-meets are not all of such an appearance as to tempt a woman half way. A third set would most prudishly frown upon a proceeding which pays so little respect to the prescriptive rights of the ladies; while, as if purposely set in contrast to these fastidious ones, others would make attempts, not always successful, or with the best grace, to appear as amiable and pretty as possible, spite of the Paramatta frock and petticoat, of which they were evidently heartily tired. It requires the face of a Turk to come on such an open and acknowledged errand; so the case is, that the inspector is usually at as much of a nonplus as the inspected. The matron accompanies him, and answers his questions respecting the particular lady or ladies who attract his eye, giving each the best possible character. It is a regular frolic, after the first few moments, in each room. The matron cannot suppress a half laugh at the farcical scene, the Cœlebs begins to be dashed, and the girls break out into jokes upon his personal appearance, particularly if he happens to have passed the meridian. The chance is, that his quizzical reception by the first class, and the confusion of faces hindering his choice, will send him to the second, and a preconceived and natural prejudice against No. 2 will send him back to No. 1 again. Upon his return, all pretence to reserve is thrown aside. "Ha! old boy, could n't you find a moll to suit? Is there never a blowen in the lot good enough for an old stringy-bark settler like you?" Flash is pattered at him with all a woman's volubility, and the old blowens* who have been so often turned back to the factory for drunkenness or other faults that their case is past redemption, commence quizzing the wife-hunter. "There, there's a new chum, just come out!" pointing to some uninviting looking maiden; "she's the girl for you!" "There! there!" by a dozen bidders; or, "You'd better take one of your age!" from some old toothless Jezebel. The matron and monitresses wink at these irregularities as things of course, and impossible of prevention. The choice at length made, spite of all the discouragements thrown in his way, the settler is seldom obliged to apply to more than one, and after uttering the awkward "yes," the bride elect flies round to her pals, bidding hasty adieus, and the bridegroom leads her out. "I'll give you three months before you're returned!" cries one, and "It's a *bargain* you've got, old stringy-bark!" cries another. Hubbub and confusion mark the exit of the couple, and the bride's character is immediately picked to pieces by the neglected, as soon as her back is turned, and the appearance of her husband elect most scientifically blasted, after the usual manner of decrying sour grapes. The clothes of the convict are returned to her, and, dressed again like a free woman, she hies with her suitor of an hour to the church. Government gives her a "ticket of exemption" as a dower, and she steps into her husband's carriage to go to his farm.

Such a carriage! In it is previously deposited something hardly less beloved by the planter than his wife—a five-gallon keg of Cooper's gin. The harness is bark cordage, the body may be slabs, or bark, save the bottom, and as for springs, they are an unnecessary luxury. The beast is oftener a bullock, or a brace of bullocks, than a horse. The sixty or seventy miles' journey nearly achieved, the bride begins to look anxiously for the farm, picturing to herself such a house and homestead as she had been used to in England. Perhaps a bark cottage heaves in sight—"Is that your house?" "No!" and she breathes again. But the end of the journey reveals nothing better. Bark or log, perhaps plastered, and perhaps not—surrounded by stumps with black tops, and half burned trees—the whole scene conveying to the new comer the idea of discomfort and desolation, rather than the home feeling of a farm; Mrs., the new made bride, indignantly refuses the

* *Byron spells it 'blowing'; but the Botany Bay orthography is unquestionably best.*

hand which her attentive husband offers to help her from the chariot. "Help yourself then, if you like it!" and while the husband proceeds to unharness the bullocks, she makes one jump to the ground, careless of concealing either her angry disappointment or her legs. The interior of the house over which she has come to preside, contains full room to chase a cat round, if puss would take the precaution to double up her tail. The bed is the everlasting stringy-bark, which the reader has heard before as the settler's soubriquet; the furniture, a broken stool or two, and a table; the cooking utensils, a broken spider for frying, and a royal George, *alias* a big kettle, for boiling, with a few corresponding articles. The first feeling of disappointment over, she concludes even this preferable, with liberty, to Paramatta and the dingy white frock; and by the time her husband enters with the five-gallon keg, and other town-purchased merchandise under his arm, she has found her tongue.

Then comes the wedding party. Neighboring settlers, if there be any, with their wives, and stock-keepers who have charge of the cattle grazing in the interior, knowing when to expect the bridegroom, come unbidden to welcome him home with his better half. The royal George is slung over the fire, and in such a teapot is the beverage fresh from Paramatta concocted. The "damper," a wheaten cake of hugeous dimensions, is clapped flat on the clay hearth, and buried in hot ashes. Less adheres to the cake than one would imagine; so little that a very little use accustoms the settler to it. The damper baked, the royal George is set in the middle of the floor, into which the guests dive with their pannikins, diluting the tea with an abundance of fresh milk, it having been sweetened in the pot. The damper is laid upon the table, flanked with a firkin of butter, and all hands fall to without other preparation, assisting the bread with a slice of cold meat. The dishes are rounds of logs, sawed off thin. The damper finished, the table is cleared, and the keg of Cooper's best set upon it, duly guarded round the bung with a leather tongue. The pannikins which had just served for tea-cups now act as drinking-glasses, and the liquor is taken *neat*, that is to say, without the enervating introduction of water. Pipes and tobacco are produced, and an edifying conversation commences between the new wife and her female visitors—an exchange of experiences, in which each details how cruelly she was "lagged" on suspicion; all innocent as the fifteenth generation yet to be born, of the crime

72

for which the magistrates had the tyranny to convict her; the dirty vagabonds of witnesses cruelly swearing her life away!

If the party separates without a row, one is next to inevitable between the new-married couple. The husband drunk—wife do.—mad, crazy, from her first regular "tuck-out," probably, for a year. Such is the first lesson of the married convict, the burden of whose punishment government has shifted to her husband. She may run away to the bush within a week, she may stay a fortnight before she elopes, she may remain till her husband complains of her at Paramatta, or she may, by the last possibility, remain "till death do them part," as the liturgy hath it. The above is a faithful picture of too many "factory weddings." When an assigned servant woman is married, the consent of her master or mistress is first to be obtained. The form of proclaiming the bans in church is also, in such matches, adhered to. They are in every way more respectable, as the parties know each other some *weeks* at least. In such matches, the husband has also the right of turning his wife into the factory again; but in all cases he is bound to take her out when her term of punishment has expired. If he does not, her board is charged to him.

CHAPTER IV

Of a female convict ship I have spoken from observation. The ships used for the transportation of males are managed in like manner, except the additional precautions necessary for restraining men. The usual number of females conveyed in one ship is about ninety; why an exception was made in the case of the

Phœnix, I have forgotten.[2] Male convicts are usually ironed, or a majority of them, on the passage. At night a strong grating separates each berth from the centre of the hold, and a guard of about thirty men are always on duty. I believe the only instance on record of the capture of a convict ship, is that of the Jane Shore. That vessel carried female convicts who instigated the sailors to rise upon the officers. They took the vessel into Monte Video, but the usual fate of mutineers and runaways overtook them there.

In addition to the security afforded by the presence of soldiers and other precautions, on board a male convict ship, the appointment of boatswains or captains to each mess, from among the convicts, is a farther assurance of safety. The jealousy thus created prevents concert among the prisoners; the performance of his duty makes the convict officer unpopular, and the creation of such a state of feud begets a jealousy which renders him vigilant. The food allowed the prisoners is good and abundant; lime juice, vinegar, and three or four gills of Spanish wine per week, are allowed for the prevention of scurvy. Under good officers, amusements are permitted as preventives of disease; sometimes *private theatricals*, and more frequently dancing.

The convicts upon landing are marched to the prisoners' barracks. There, such as are not immediately assigned to answer applications for servants or laborers, don the livery,—a Paramatta suit, adorned with the initials "P.B." and the broad arrow. There were at Sydney two sets of barracks, one called Hyde Park, for adults, the other Carter's, for male children and youth. At Carter's barracks was a school, the teachers of which were taken from among the better sort of transports; and a workshop in which young men were apprenticed to trades.

Some mischief was formerly the result of permitting applications to be made for particular convicts as servants, as coalitions or contracts, subversive of the purposes of government, arose from such a liberty; and it was found necessary to make the appli-

[2] Earlier O'Connell has told us that the *Phoenix* carried 200 female convicts. But of the 52 vessels that disembarked female convicts at Sydney and Hobart between the years 1801 and 1826, the largest number on any vessel was 136. The average number was only 93. After 1826 there was one vessel, in 1827, that carried 161 women; one in 1828 with 194 female convicts; one in 1829 with 177; and finally one vessel, in 1830, carried 200 women.

cations specify in general terms only the character of the labor required, leaving the choice of the particular person to the superintendent of the barracks. The prisoners in direct custody of the government are employed about trades, if they are fortunate enough to have them, if not, in road gangs, and in breaking stone. Saturday is allowed to each prisoner to keep his person and clothing in order, and to earn money for himself, if he chooses to labor. Upon this day the weekly rations are served out; articles which bear keeping, sufficient for the next week, and tickets to obtain butcher's meat and other perishable necessaries, at the stores of the contractors.

At Wellington Valley, about a hundred and fifty miles from Sydney, is a station to which are sent convicts from the better classes of society; well educated men, convicted of such offences as forgery, genteel swindling, or a single departure from rectitude, sufficient, indeed, to transport them, but not to sink them to a level with the representatives of St. Giles and Ratcliffe High Way. They are employed in agriculture, till such time as they have given evidence of reformation, or proof of the fact that the crime for which they were transported was an exception to their habitual mode of life. As opportunities offer, they are placed at the head of schools, and employed as clerks in the government offices. Thus are those who are supposed to possess some self-respect, allowed, as far as is compatible with punishment, to retain it; instead of being degraded to the standing of those who are known to be utterly vile. Appointment to schools, or secretary-ships, makes them in a manner their own masters, and is a re-posal of confidence which appeals to, while it nourishes their self-respect. Should one, however, despite these favourable circumstances, transgress by inebriation, theft, or other crime, all the respect at first paid to their circumstances is forfeited. They are more rigorously punished than common convicts, as they are supposed to sin against superior light and knowledge. Of the low rogues transgression is expected, and they are treated as if constant oversight and rigorous discipline was necessary as a thing of course; lighter peccadilloes being winked at. The favoured prisoners who abuse the privileges extended to them are punished for ingratitude, as well as the bare infraction of the law. They get longer sentences to the treadmill, to the iron gang, and to the penal settlements, than more ignoble offenders, while their previous habits of life render any sentence to severe labor a double punishment. Labor on the road, which to a common convict is considered no extra punishment, is such to them.

No system of human invention is without its defects. The reader will perceive that to carry out all the machinery of the colony and the discipline of prisoners, a very large number of sub-overseers are necessary. These were at one time provided from a regiment of soldiers called "Saffron Miners," all of whom were mechanics. The exact meaning of this phrase I never could discover. The *Saffron Miners* possessed very little other qualification for overseers than their knowledge of trades, and their inefficiency as overseers was apparent in their unwillingness to *compel* the convicts to labor; they were not stern enough, and the amount of work turned out did not answer the expectations of the authorities. The plan was thrown up, and the old system revived. This was the making of tyrants from slaves; the appointment of convicts, correct in conduct, to the oversight of their comrades. Wherever the experiment has been tried, it has been found that promoted bondsmen make cruel task-masters. The tyranny of these sub-agents of power overdoes the purposes of punishment, rendering men desperate, and driving them to attempt elopement, or, in the country phrase, to "take to the bush."

The first steps in an escape are by no means difficult, except to members of a chain gang, as these, in addition to their irons, are watched by soldiers. Goaded by the arrogance and cruelty of their overseers, two or three prisoners, or more, concert an escape. There are constables' lodges outside the town, which the fugitives avoid by avoiding the high road.

This first difficulty surmounted, the runaways meet at an appointed rendezvous, and the first move is burglary. They surprise the house of some settler or stock-keeper, and plunder it of such movables as can be most conveniently carried off; always taking care, if possible, to seize fire-arms. When armed, the fugitives organize themselves with others who have preceded, or who follow them to the bush, into banditti, robbing the market carts for food, and finding the little shelter which the climate renders necessary in caves and bark huts, like the natives. Some probably have method and wisdom enough to betake themselves into unfrequented parts of the interior, where they make clearings, build more substantial houses, and till the earth, upon which very little labor is necessary to produce sufficient for subsistence, and remain undiscovered. During my residence in New Holland, I once accompanied the government surveyor, Mr. Oxley, on an exploring expedition into the interior, a trip which occupied about six months. Our party was made up of Mr. Oxley, myself, and twelve or fourteen trusty convicts. Beside the instruments and provision, a surveyor's baggage is so light that "a surveyor's kit, a quart pot and blanket," has passed to a proverb. It is unnecessary to attempt any thing like a regular journal of this jaunt, as the details would not be interesting to the reader, because, while they might be minute enough to tire, they would not preserve the scientific and geographical objects gained by the excursion; which it cannot be supposed that, without any memoranda, I can at this distance of time remember. The adventures of interest will be introduced in appropriate places, and the observations made introduced in my general account of the aborigines. The object in introducing the excursion here, is to speak of an establishment which we encountered after three weeks' journey from Wellington Valley into the interior. There were two comfortable bark houses, and several acres of ground under cultivation, stocked with horses, bullocks, sheep, swine, poultry, and all the et ceteras of a well appointed farm. We were directed to it by some natives, who gave us to understand by signs that there were people like us living in a direction to which they pointed. The first person we saw was a man dressed in opossum skins, who started back, and without uttering a word ran into the house. Mr. Oxley and I followed, and found a woman and a family of children. The other house was similarly tenanted, and the poor people confessed at once that they were runaways; mistaking us for a party sent expressly to apprehend them. Never were visitors so unwelcome; the women wept, the men stood, too proud to weep, but despair personified, and the children, who had never before seen white men except their parents, looked at us in pained curiosity, as they clung to the garments of father and mother. They had been there six or seven years, and in all that time had been unmolested. Their farm, stock and tools were, it is true, stolen in the first instance, but they lived too far from any settlement to continue the usual predatory habits of bushrangers. To this circumstance they were indebted for their security; and the absence of alcoholic liquors, necessary from their non-intercourse, conduced to their quiet and happiness. It seemed, indeed, almost a sin to break up a settle-

78

ment so strictly pastoral; and while Mr. Oxley's duty compelled him to do so, he pledged his word that his interest should be exerted to prevent farther punishment than their removal back to Sydney. He also engaged to make a favorable report of their conduct and circumstances at Sydney. In all these particulars he redeemed his word; but it was punishment enough to compel the party to abandon a spot endeared to them by so many circumstances and recollections. They were, however, in a measure reconciled to their fate, by the commiseration and promises of Mr. Oxley, and after the first hour of meeting, stood to us rather in the light of hosts than prisoners. A sheep was killed, and we produced, on our part, various little articles, which to them were rarities after their long hermitage. In the morning, taking away their horses and some corn, the two families turned their backs upon their home, abandoning stock and grain enough to make any English or American farmer wealthy.

The above is the only instance of the detection of runaways so comfortably situated, which occurred during my residence in New Holland. But, as before remarked, it is highly probable that there are other families of "squatters" in similar circumstances. I doubt whether government, unless compelled by an accidental encounter with them, like that of Mr. Oxley, or by too great publicity of the fact that such a retreat existed, would disturb it. It certainly is humane policy, after the fugitives have encountered and weathered all the harassing dangers of an escape, and are living in innocence, to disturb them. With the population of Sydney the arrest of these people, who had long before been considered dead, was the most interesting event connected with Mr. Oxley's tour. The children were sent to the charity school at Paramatta, the men to the barracks, and the women to the factory; but no proceedings were instituted against them as runaways.

To return to the more usual fate of fugitives. In order to secure their apprehension, it is a standing rule that the apprehension, or the giving of information which shall lead to the apprehension, of four runaways, entitles a seven years' convict to a ticket of leave; six entitles a fourteen years', and eight, a life transport to the same reward. In some cases a handbill is issued, offering a ticket of leave, or a gratuity in money, to the person who shall bring in a notorious highwayman, burglar, or murderer, *dead or alive*. The reward is of course adapted to the situation of the person who apprehends the culprit, as a ticket of leave could not be given a free man. Sometimes a free pardon and passage to England is held out as an inducement. Bushrangers cannot, by delivering up comrades, avail themselves of these offers, unless a specific proclamation is issued to that effect. Neither bushrangers or barrack prisoners, however, often betray runaways, and when they do, those betrayed are usually persons whose crimes on the road have become too revolting even to convicts.

Trusty natives are created "bush constables." These are about the only blacks who have guns and ammunition. The majority of the natives are incapable of using them, and as they have no articles to offer in traffic, they could not obtain arms if they wished. The guns of the black constables are given them by government, and they wear a brass plate, on which is inscribed the name of the wearer, the tribe he belongs to, and the certificate of his office. These fellows pretend to follow a man by the scent, like a dog, and I have known several circumstances which would seem to prove their possession of some such faculty. The capture of a prisoner, and the surrender of him at the barracks, creates the black captor a bush constable, and he is presented his musket and brass plate. They get also a gratuity of some sort for each prisoner surrendered.

Still another method of arresting runaways is, to disguise soldiers, and send them, in such squads as not to alarm suspicion, into the interior. It is however dangerous service. Bushrangers who have plundered a house, or a market cart, are burglars or highway robbers, and of course liable, upon conviction to death. Murder of their pursuers can subject them to no worse punishment, and may procure their escape. The sale or gift of arms or ammunition to a bushranger is punishable by transportation to a penal settlement, or other heavy penalty; yet the fugitives provide themselves in some way with arms, and encounters with them are by no means trifles, after they have been absent long enough to become desperate. The dead bodies of fugitives who fall in defending themselves are frequently brought into Sydney to be identified.

Where a prisoner is retaken, if no robbery or murder is proved against him upon trial, and no attempt at forcible escape by the use of deadly weapons, he gets a sentence to a penal settlement, for the crime of running away. After this sentence is completed, he is returned to the barracks, on his original sentence, and serves out that; the time spent in the woods and in the penal settlement counting him nothing. If he has resisted the soldiers or officers with weapons, or if he be proved to have committed burglary or highway robbery, he is hung. Executions are frequent, and are done on the condemned in the jail-yard. The jail at Sydney is at the "Rocks," or rather in front of that district. The roofs and windows of the houses in the rear are crowded with spectators. The yard is thrown open, and is also crowded with spectators. Very few penitent speeches are made, it appearing rather to be the intent of the malefactor to die game. What few words are said are generally exculpatory of their conduct, on the plea of the cruelty of the overseers. There was one instance where the malefactor suddenly thrust a knife, of which he had by some means obtained possession, at the hangman, inflicting a slight wound, and throwing him from the platform. The man's elbows were pinioned behind him, and it was necessary to throw the blow with his whole body. Another hangman was substituted for the regular Jack Ketch, who was disabled by the fall. That dignitary, a hangman before his transportation, protested that in all his experience he had never before met such a game customer as the one who attempted his death.

CHAPTER V

Tickets of leave.—Privileges and restrictions of leave-men.—Challenges of police.—Tickets of exemption.—Husbands and wives.—Servants returned to the barracks.—Magistrates.—Punishments.—Payment for convict labor.—Sentences at quarter sessions.—Iron gangs.—Road gangs.—Penal settlements.—Norfolk Island.—State of prisoners there.—Mutiny on board City of Edinburgh.—Port Macquarrie.—Cape Packet whaler.—Advantages of ground for Botany Bay whalers.—Squall.—Capsizing.—Escape of Mr. O'Connell.—Fixtures of a whaleboat.—Distress for water.—Death of companions in boat.—Four days' exposure.—Temptation to cannibalism.—Landing.

The "ticket of leave" frequently referred to in the preceding pages, is a conditional pardon, granted to convicts after a series of years of good behavior in the colony. Those sentenced originally for seven years, if convicted of no crime in New Holland, receive a ticket of leave at the end of three years; fourteen years' transports at the end of six; and *lifers* at the end of eight or ten. Sometimes these tickets give the possessor the liberty of the whole continent, but more generally, only particular towns or districts. Unconditional pardon, or emancipation, seldom precedes the expiration of the sentence. Ticket of leave men are permitted to employ their time as they please, and are exempted from the spotted livery, as also are assigned servants. Drunkenness, idleness, theft, or other misconduct, forfeits to the offender his ticket of leave, and subjects him of course to such farther punishment as his offence merits. No ticket of leave man may be legally in the street after eight in the evening, and innholders who permit any except freemen to remain in their premises after that hour, forfeit their licenses. The police arrest all with whose faces they are unacquainted, and the inquiry follows, "Who are you?" If the answer be "a freed-man," the person arrested is required to produce his certificate of freedom; if he be a ticket of leave man or an assigned servant, he is turned into the barracks till morning; if a barrack prisoner, his dress saves the trouble of inquiry.

A "ticket of exemption" may be obtained by a male convict after two years of good behavior. This allows the receiver, if a barrack prisoner, to live out of the barracks with his wife. No extra ration is allowed him for her support, but only four days in the week are required of him for labor, the day extra being supposed, with his wife's industry, sufficient for her support. Facilities are afforded for the passage out of husbands or wives whose consorts are separated from them by the inconvenient edicts of the law, but never in the same ship. Where a couple are sentenced to transportation, good behavior on both sides will procure them the privilege of living together; the husband still subject to barrack rules, or to the will of his master, while the wife's liberty is unconditional, till abridged by her husband's complaint at the police. Masters must relinquish the services of females upon the arrival of their husbands, *free*, from the mother country, but are not bound to free an unmarried woman who wishes to wed. Servants must be returned to the barracks or to the factory, when their terms of service cease; and mere nominal service is guarded against, by strict watchfulness on the part of government, as instances have been detected, in which the master stood, in effect, between the criminal and punishment.

In the discipline and punishment of convicts, the intervention of a magistrate is always customary. Complaint must be preferred to the police authorities, particularly in the case of assigned servants. One magistrate may inflict fifty lashes; a bench of two

83

or more punish at discretion, by lashes or the stocks, or the treadmill. Crimes of a character meriting severer penalties, go before the higher court at the quarter sessions for final trial and sentence. Without the assistance of the civil authorities, masters, particularly inland settlers, could not control their servants; as there is quite a hamlet of convict laborers about the residence of an Australian farmer. Payment for their labor is at the option of their master, he being bound only to feed and clothe them; but experience having demonstrated that to work well, men must be fed well, their provisions are abundant.

For the offences which come before the quarter sessions, the convicts are sentenced to iron gangs, to penal settlements, and to death. The sentences to penal settlements are, like the original sentences to the colony, for seven, fourteen years, and for life. Iron gangs labor under heavy guards of soldiers in clearing tracts of land in the interior, all wearing gyves, proportioned in weight to their crimes. Theirs is the first and most laborious labor of clearing, and the work is finished by gangs of laborers, without irons, who are thus employed as no extra punishment.

"Penal settlements," to which frequent allusion has been made, are the places to which criminals are sent after conviction, before a colonial court, of offences which degrade them even below the Botany Bay standard. The life-sentenced double convicts are usually sent to Norfolk Island. This island has no harbor, and the residents upon it are allowed no communication with the world, except such as is afforded by the arrival of new exiles. A strong guard prevents the landing of boats from any vessel, except those of the government. There is not even anchorage near this surf-bound isle; and while vessels are landing convicts or stores, they lay on and off. In one place only is it accessible to boats; so that it is a complete natural prison. The boats used by government vessels for landing here are built expressly for that service. Prisoners sent here are, with few exceptions, sentenced to a perpetual and irremediable exile from the world; tickets of leave and other indulgences are unknown, and I verily believe that many of the prisoners brought to Sydney from penal settlements for trial, commit crime to obtain that deliverance which is only reached by the gallows. What I know of Norfolk Island, I learned while belonging to a government ship called "The City of Edinburgh." She transported to Norfolk Island, at one trip, one hundred and fourteen reckless incorrigibles. The orig-

84

inal number was one hundred and twenty, but before leaving Port Jackson, some symptoms of disturbance were effectually quelled by a discharge of musketry down the hatchway, which sent six of the convicts to their long home.

The employment of the prisoners at penal settlements is calculated exclusively for punishment. Most of the males labor with irons on their legs. Indeed, the discipline of iron-gangs and of settlers at penal stations differs only in name, and in the duration of the punishment. Port Macquarrie, situated on the eastern coast of New Holland, some hundreds of miles above Sydney, was the principal penal station. Here was a garrison too strong to permit even the symptoms of a rise among the prisoners. In the course of my adventures, after a misfortune which I shall shortly relate, I visited Port Macquarrie, and had ocular proof of the severity with which the prisoners were treated. The government of the colony is entirely in the hands of the military officers, and offences which do not require a removal to Sydney for trial, are visited with summary and severe corporal punishment. The recklessness of the incorrigibles, inducing disrespect, and perhaps, in despair, open contumely toward their military masters, does not a whit abate the rigor of their treatment. The soldiers seemed to think that the attempt to manage by any thing like mild measures was folly; and that the convicts were too far below the scale of humanity to be sensible even of corporeal suffering. As to degradation, that is part of a double-convict's existence. The reader will smile incredulously, when I tell him that the heads of the convicts were once reshaved at Port Macquarrie, during my six weeks' stay there, to mix with lime to plaster a house belonging to one of the officers!

There have been several cases of runaway convicts anticipating their sentence, by straying to a penal settlement, in ignorance of the country! Such fugitives enjoy a termination to their journey, the anticipation of which would have prevented its commencement.

To step back to the relation of the event by which I was introduced to Port Macquarrie. In 1822, I shipped in a vessel called the Cape Packet, Capt. Dillon, originally what her name purported, but at that time a whaler. She was a half-rigged brig or schooner, of between one and two hundred tons,* and her

* *The editor of this work has seen in Callao a Sydney whaler of scarcely heavier tonnage.*

owner was the Mr. Haynes mentioned in a preceding chapter. At that period the Sydney whalers were in almost exclusive possession of a certain cruising ground to the north of the continent of New Holland, since improved by American and English whalers. The limited operations of the Sydney whalers were gloriously repaid, until the entrance of vessels of other nations reduced this field to the present precarious standard of all whaling grounds. Notwithstanding that Sydney was a rendezvous for whalers, particularly English, the Sydney trade managed for a long time to preserve a monopoly. The Kanakas (South Sea Islanders) discharged from American and English whalers, at Sydney, supply the Sydney whalers with half their crews. In the Cape Packet, out of sixteen hands, seven at least were Kanakas.

The *modus operandi* of taking whales is so familiar to all those whose reading taste would lead them to take up a book like this, that I shall not here introduce a description, farther than is necessary to make my story intelligible. We had been five months upon the ground, and were cutting in the last fish necessary to complete our cargo. The purchase for hoisting in was from the main-stay, and the tackle fall led to the windlass, where all hands of our small crew were at work. The operation, with the head and fluke ropes, gave the schooner something of a heel; and while we were all intent upon the work, a white squall, which had been gathering unperceived, combing and frothing along on the surface of the water, in a N. N. W. direction, struck us, and threw the little craft upon her beam-ends. All was confusion; she lay for a moment, her keel out of water, struggling and working like a living thing against the power of the elements. Another moment and the topsail and jib, under which she was laying to, went to tatters—her light spars snapped and fell to leeward—the first fury of the squall was over—the resistance of our vessel to the wind was lessened—and she righted, quivering and trembling. A steadier gale, accompanied by terrific thunder and lightning, followed; but, in all the horror and confusion of the scene, our hearts leaped to heaven with a momentary feeling of security. It was, however, but momentary; for the appalling fact was almost immediately ascertained, that, racked and riven by the tempest, in her peculiarly exposed situation, our vessel was rapidly filling. Before we could clear the stern and quarter boats from the davit tackles, their keels were in the water, and our utmost exertion was necessary to prevent their being swamped under the davit heads. Each consulted his own safety; we stripped the harness cask of its contents, and shoved away from alongside in haste, to escape the vortex which we supposed would be caused by her sinking. We might, however, have been more deliberate, as, even after she was water-logged, we could, while daylight lasted, see the stumps of her masts. There may be question whether, with her cargo, she sank at all; but no traces of her were ever afterward discovered, though a vessel was despatched from Sydney Cove to look for her.

In the boat with myself were five of the Kanakas. We put into the boat from the vessel only some pork and beef from the harness cask; but every whale-boat is kept supplied with a compass, a tinder box, and a water keg, in addition to the apparatus for destroying fish. The water keg, however, was nearly empty through carelessness, and the excitement of danger and escape produced such a thirst on the part of the Kanakas, that their repeated draughts soon consumed what water was in the boat, even before I had any inclination to drink. Upon applying to the keg, I found it entirely empty. Still this did not cause me much more than a little vexation at the disappointment, as, knowing we were probably only about fifty miles from land, and having a compass in the boat, I expected to make it that afternoon or night; the squall having struck us about noon. The boat was, however, over four days in reaching the land! During that time four of my Kanaka companions died from thirst and exhaustion. The surviving Kanaka was sorely tempted as the fourth of his countrymen died before his eyes, and hesitatingly proposed to me to eat of him. I shuddered at the proposal and discouraged it with disgust, and my companion gave it over. Even then we were in sight of land, but so completely exhausted from hunger, fatigue, and want of sleep, that we could no longer make any exertion to reach it. My wrists were swollen and weak—my feet, where they had been in the water in the bottom of the boat, shrivelled and raw. With a feeling of careless despair we resigned our boat to the mercy of the wave, careless whither we were driven. The wind had gone down, and the spot to which we providentially drifted was a level, sandy beach. Hosts of the natives, who had long discerned our boat as it slowly drifted to the shore, waded out, took it by the head, and hauled it up. Some of them immediately stepped into it and plundered it of every thing movable—oars, irons, lances, tubs, &c. The question will naturally occur to the reader, why they did not put off to us in their canoes; the answer is, that the aborigines of New Holland have no canoes in which they venture upon the sea at all; as their boats are the rudest known—inefficient and clumsy, like every thing else belonging to them.

We were too weak to stand erect, and upon reaching the beach sank in the sand. We made earnest gestures for water, but they paid no attention to our wants till they had stripped us of every article of clothing. Then some water was brought us in calabashes, and some of the flesh of the kangaroo and bandycoot. Refreshed by a moderate meal, and by frequent draughts of water in small quantities, we laid down to sleep under the native blanket, a wide strip of bark, doubled. Certainly never before was sleep so delightful to me, or so refreshing.

CHAPTER VI

At and about Port Macquarrie, and to the north of that settlement, the aborigines of New Holland are probably more savage and filthy in their habits, and less acquainted with any thing like art, than on any other part of the continent. In the southern and western parts, the natives have something like houses; but in nearly every other part of the country, bark shelter, the most slight and rude that can be imagined, answers every purpose, and under this they only sleep. Living in-doors is something that never was embraced in their notions of comfort. A large fire is built at one end, to keep away Poloyan, the devil, whose power is recognised by all the tribes, but not always under the same name, as their dialects differ. Eight or nine months spent among them in reaching Port Macquarrie from the place where the Cape Packet was wrecked, on the northern coast of the continent, gave me opportunity to observe their habits. It is not intended to assert that the distance required that time, but want of acquaintance with the country, and the will and hindrance of the natives, much impeded my progress, or rather led to wasting of labor in profitless wanderings.

One general peculiarity of their superstition, which I do not recollect ever to have seen noted by geographers, is this. If during his sleep a native chance to dream, he jumps up upon waking, and gives the alarm to his comrades. If it be still night, the encampment is immediately shifted to a distance from the haunted spot; no inducement would tempt them to sleep there again, until after the expiration of a long period of time, if indeed they ever would wittingly thus tempt Poloyan. Koyan, God, or the Good Spirit, is, as far as I could learn, seldom invoked, as, like many other savages, they think it more necessary to propitiate the evil than to worship the good. A thunder storm throws them prostrate upon the earth, and such a time appears to be the only occasion upon which they worship. Then their shoutings and howlings are alike terrific and ludicrous.

They are divided into tribes so small that the divisions would almost seem families. In some few of these, hereditary chiefs hold sway; in others, might makes right, and the strongest assert a rule per force. The connecting link between apes and men, they have generally less resemblance to the African negro than the New Zealanders, and, particularly when old, resemble the monkey more than any other human beings do. In stature, they are generally above the middle size, and their bodies bear an apish proportion to their legs, those limbs being shorter than the European's, while the arms appear longer. In complexion they vary from copper color to black; the latter being generally the least ferocious race. No tribes have hair quite so much curled as the African's, and in a majority of tribes it is straight.

Marriage is an institution hardly recognised, and often dissolved at will, or by the desertion of the husband, or the elopement of the wife. There is little in their mode of wooing which would attach a bride to her husband; the method being for the man to select his woman, (always from another tribe,) waylay her, stun her with a blow from his club, and bear her to his temporary bark hut. Oftentimes he goes at night with a band of friends, and a sanguinary knock-down between the friends of both parties is the commencement of the marriage ceremony. If the bridegroom is successful, he bears away his *gin*, as the wife is called in the native language. If beaten back, he defers the happiness to a future opportunity. The natives are horridly licentious, particularly near English settlements, where their vile propensities are aggravated by the potent evil agency of alcohol. Their wives are articles of trade. Upon the birth of twins, one is killed; and white or mulatto children of black mothers are butchered as soon as born, the husband acting the executioner, and the mother consenting.

The wild tribes away from the English are fond of disfiguring their faces with red earth, and of thrusting quills through the cartilage of the nose, particularly when going to war. Their weapons are a rude spear, and the *waddie* or club. They have no bows, and the policy of the English government has prevented the introduction of fire-arms among them to any great extent. Predatory in their habits, they attack isolated residences of stockkeepers, and even small settlements. The government have been compelled to a war of extermination with several tribes, who had become, by forbearance, not only thievish, but sanguinary, when Englishmen fell into their hands. Powerful tribes compel their conquered neighbors to give up tooth after tooth as tribute; and it is the custom of some to cut off the little finger on the right hand of each of the vanquished tribe, men, women and children. Others subject only the women to this mutilation. Most of the native black fish-women who ply their vocation in the harbor of Port Jackson are thus disfigured.

In the interior they exult in the naked majesty of nature; and

91

instances of blacks promenading the streets of Sydney *in puris naturalibus,* were not quite so rare as eclipses. Some would misappropriate garments given them, as for instance, by buttoning the waistband of a pair of trowsers round the neck, and strutting like a Spaniard under a short cloak, or a bashaw of two tails. At the annual fairs at Paramatta, and upon other occasions, the government distribute Paramatta frocks and blankets to each native man and woman, and a hatchet to each man of the crowd of blacks. The chiefs and "bush constables" are also presented with brass plates, and the latter with muskets. Not more than one, however, is ever given to one native. If these and food were the only articles served out to the natives on these occasions, it were well; but empty sugar bags are also thrown to them, which are put into tubs on the spot, and water poured upon them. To this, some of the worst sort of emigrants add rinsings of liquor-casks and slops from the public houses, and,

"To make the mixture slab and good,"

tobacco and other maddening substances are thrown in. Instigated by this detestable compound, rows, fighting, and beastly licentiousness wind up a day originally instituted, among other objects, for the benefit of the natives. Things, however, have probably changed since my visit to Sydney.

Cannibalism is a trait found more or less among the tribes on all parts of the continent, but principally on the northern part.* I have seen parts of human bodies in the bags which the women carry on their backs; and am convinced, from direct oral accounts in which I put credit, that even abandoned white runaways, after a residence with the natives, learn to eat human flesh. Indolence and hunger assist an unnatural taste in preserving this revolting custom; for, salubrious as is the climate and fertile the soil of New Holland, less nutritious plants and fruits are indigenous there than on any of the smaller islands of the Pacific; and cultivation of the earth is scarcely known among the aborigines. Their precarious food is principally the flesh of the opossum, bandycoot, kangaroo, and kangaroo-rat, with such few edible roots and herbs as grow spontaneously. Fish, till

---

* *Cunningham, the author of a work on New South Wales, says the blacks about Sydney speak of the northern tribes as 'white fellers what eat black fellers'.*

the introduction of proper implements by the English, they had not ingenuity enough to catch in any large quantity. Kangaroos they knock down with the club or spear, and to take the opossum, climb trees, with more agility than their natural indolence would seem to allow. They get up the smooth trunks of trees by notching steps for the toe with a hatchet or sharp stone. One species of snake, vermin, any thing, no matter how repulsive, capable of being devoured with impunity, is eaten by them.

The tribes have no fixed residence, but wander each within a certain tract or district, shifting their quarters as impelled by hunger. This mode of living, with their vilely licentious habits, men and women living together in almost indiscriminate concubinage, and children destroyed according to the freaks of their parents, keeps the native black population small. The reader has seen from the description, how precarious their food, and how filthy their personal appearance; the very cattle imported and bred by English settlers will run away from a black native with every symptom of disgust. Yet, under all these circumstances, runaway convicts will live with them. On my over-land jaunt from the north coast to Port Macquarrie, I encountered with one tribe two runaway convict women, and with another a convict man. They had become so utterly degraded, as to be scarce above the savages in their habits; wore next to no clothing, and fell into their indolent and filthy mode of existence. Each was a runaway from a penal settlement, if I recollect, and each professed to prefer life in the woods to the discipline of the penal settlements. Never in my life before had I seen such a complete degradation from civilization to the lowest scale of human existence.

The tribes near the English settlements have become almost entirely dependent upon their English neighbors for subsistence. Low cunning, thieving propensities, and inveterate habits of begging, with the utmost impudence and pertinacity, are their characteristics. They appear to have recognised their title "black fellows," and in return dub the English "white fellows," seemingly perfectly content with the distinction, and considering white the worse hue, decidedly. The connection of adult blacks with the convict settlements imparts to them all the vices of the convicts. Settlers employ them in harvesting for a small compensation, and they have proved willing, occasionally, to work, provided they be starved into it, and the liquor and food be withheld till nearly night, or delivered in such small quantities as barely to sustain the laborer and provoke his appetite. They are wags in a small way, many of them very diverting even in their disgusting filth. Generations must pass before they are brought to any considerable approach to civilization. Missionary enterprises to the interior experience has proved of no avail, attended with great peril, and effecting no good. The only influence upon the future character of the natives must be effected through the charity schools where young blacks are educated. It is, however, frequently the case that nature leads even educated black youth back to the habits of their parents. The experiment of mixing colonial children with the blacks in the charity schools was expected to operate to the prevention of this returning "to wallowing in the mire" on the part of the blacks, by destroying some of their nationality. How far it has been successful, I am unable to state. The probability is, however, that the civilization of the natives of New Holland will, as in other new countries, be synonymous with their extinction.

The position of New Holland is antipodal to our latitude. Consequently our winter is their summer, and our summer their winter. The season is never too severe for vegetation, and English settlers get two grain and two potato crops in each year. The soil under cultivation is hard and clayey, but capable of much improvement by furrowing and compost, an important article, gypsum, or plaster of Paris, being abundant. Salt is applicable also to earth of such a nature. Winter is marked by very heavy and dense dews; and the fall of rain is nearly equal to ours. The atmosphere is, however, less humid, and this arid peculiarity renders the heat more supportable, even with the thermometer at 100°, than with us at 70°. A vessel of water does not gather upon its outside the deposit of moisture from the atmosphere so frequently observable with us. Almost every thing will grow by cultivation; the fruits of tropical and of temperate climates yield their increase in the same gardens, the care of the husbandman being directed to favor the nature of each plant or tree, diversifying his culture to its wants. The pumpkin is a great staple for farm food, and especially coveted by the blacks. Dairies are very lucrative property, and for draught, bullocks supersede oxen and horses, except with the very wealthy. Twelve to twenty pounds per year is the price of free labor on a farm. Wool is a staple product of the colony, and the settler can have it manufactured at the government factory, paying the cost of the manufacture in the produce of his farm.

The most uncomfortable wind at Sydney is the northern and western, producing oftentimes a disease of the eyes called "the blight," and carrying the thermometer up to 110°. The southern and western is cool, and the east, in summer, refreshing. The general character of the climate is healthy, dysentery being the most fatal disease which can fairly be ascribed to the country and climate. Among the convict servants, the seeds of disease borne out with them, and the excessive use of alcohol when their situation permits opportunity to procure it, and other vile habits, produce diseases, less fatal in New Holland than in any other climate.

The native forest trees of New Holland are nearly all evergreens, and are named from their peculiarities. Thus there are the iron wood and the stringy-bark. The acacia is a native, exuding its gum in great purity and perfection. Manna, a gentle medicine, may be gathered in the forests on any morning before the sun is hot. There are two or three varieties of nuts, one of which, the burwan, is highly esteemed by the natives, but must be washed to insipidity to avoid its poisonous qualities. The native pear is hard and woody in its exterior, and will not pay for the trouble of breaking. A principal native root is the wild potato; yams, bananas, bread fruit, are exotics. Grapes can be cultivated, with care, and some wine has been made by theoretical agriculturists. A characteristic of the vegetation is brilliance of color without fragrance. At times, indeed, the forests look singular enough, many of the trees casting their bark, and rearing long black trunks, surmounted with tufts of green at the top. Grass is rank, long and sere on the plains, like American prairies.

Of the animals, one of the most wonderful in New Holland is the duck-bill or ornithorynchus. There are only two species of duck-billed quadrupeds known, and the description of the New Holland variety is as follows. With a duck's bill, it has the web feet of that fowl joined to the legs of a quadruped. It is a water bird or beast, and has a broad tail, resembling the beaver's, for a rudder. Inside of each foot is a single hollow claw, through which a violent poison is infused into the wound it makes. When attacked, it strikes its feet together, clinging to the assailing object like a crab. It has long, thick, coarse hair, and is supposed to be an oviparous animal.

The native dog, or rather the species found in the country by the settlers, is supposed to be an importation at some distant day, as nearly all the other quadrupeds on the island are of the class marsupialia, or nurse-pouched. This animal moans, but never barks; snaps a piece out of the animal it attacks, but never hangs on and worries. In a flock of sheep it will take one bite from each it can catch, and the wound is virulently poison. It emits a strong, offensive odor, will drive the domesticated dog, has shaggy hair, a bushy tail, large head, and nose tapering. The native cat has a long body and tail, cat's claws, and instead of the domestic cat's round face, a nose pointed like a pig's. Of kangaroos and opossums there are many varieties. The wombat is an animal as large as a mastiff, which burrows for its food, and is of the same species as the kangaroo and opossum, having a nurse pouch. The coola is an animal between the sloth and the bear. Of bats there are several varieties, one of which is called the flying fox, and is so large than one of Capt. Cook's sailors ran away from it in affright, protesting that the devil had appeared to him in the shape of a flying ten-gallon keg!

The birds are eagles, hawks, emus, cranes, curlews, wild turkeys, snipes, quails, and an infinity of others. The emu is said to be peculiar to New Holland, walks like the ostrich, and is nearly as large. A blow of its leg is powerful enough to knock a man down. Of pigeons there are two very beautiful varieties, the bronze winged, and the green. The New Holland swans are black; parrots and cockatoos of an infinity of varieties are found in the forests. As a general character of all countries where brilliance of plumage is a feature of the feathered creation, there are few or no songsters; nature denying voice where she is lavish of beauty. The *musk duck* is one of the freaks of nature peculiar to New Holland. It cannot fly, lives usually in the water, has hard, stiff quills like the penguin, and walks on land like that bird.

The guana is the largest species of lizard, usually from two to four feet long. It is said that this animal will kill sheep. Of snakes, the only one not poisonous is supposed to be the diamond snake, the most common length of which is four, although one species has been found twelve feet in length. This snake the natives eat. Our limits would not permit us to go into a description of the insects; nor must this brief notice of the natural history of New Holland be supposed to contain all that is worthy of preservation. Before the subject is dismissed, however, it appears proper to mention that nature appears here to have inverted her usual order in respect to fish, as well as fowl and flesh. Perch are caught in the sea, and cod in the rivers.

After remaining at Port Macquarrie about six weeks, I was shipped to Sydney as a runaway convict. My story had the less weight, because instances are not unfrequent of convicts stumbling upon penal or other settlements in their wanderings, and many could tell as good a story as mine, in every thing but the slight circumstance of truth. It was the proper course so to dispose of me; if a runaway, I should have received a trial at Sydney, and returned to Port Macquarrie with a legitimate right to the peculiar privileges of that settlement. Freemen unconnected with the government are neither anxious to remain at exclusively penal settlements, nor is their presence tolerated at such places. Happy to find a conveyance back, I embarked.

With a brief sketch of Sydney, its appearance and character, and a few general notes upon the government of the colony, my notice of New Holland closes. Anchored in the bay near the mouth of the fresh water cove which divides the town, the appearance of the settlement is a blending of the picturesque and the useful. On the right or north side of the harbor is Bennilong's Point, on which stands Fort Macquarrie. To the south, or left hand, is Dawes' Point, on which stands Fort Dawes. Several islands in the bay, rocky and covered with shrubs, and the gentlemen's seats on either shore, form a pleasing view, in which the wild aspect of nature as she has been from the beginning of time, is relieved by the artificial adjuncts to the scenery of green blinds, verandas, white walls, cultivated gardens and systematic parks, in which the skipping kangaroo destroys the resemblance you were about to trace between this and the mother country; mother, alas! of too many *legitimate* inhabitants of Australia.

To the right of the cove runs George street, the principal Sydney thoroughfare, winding away from the mouth of the cove till it ends on the shore of the bay. The commissariat stores, government wharf, dock-yard, are the first objects noted in the foreground. Then in George street come private warehouses. The principal buildings above are St. James' Church, the Gothic Presbyterian Chapel, and the Military Barracks, with parade ground in front. On the left the prominent objects are the Horse Barracks, Gothic Catholic Chapel, Colonial Hospital, and Hyde Park. Across the head of the cove, at its rise, stretches the governor's house and grounds, called "The Government Domain." Much taste appears in the arrangement of this territory; the trees are planted with as much attention to nature as art is capable of producing, and amid beautiful and useful exotics many native trees, which date an earlier growth than the first arrival of the English, stand sentinels deputed by the solitude which once reigned here, to watch the movements of innovation upon her former precincts. The houses, built of light freestone or plastered brick, rise on either side of the creek, presenting a panoramic appearance, many with verandas and white fences inclosing gardens. The prospect from the bay gives rather a greater idea of compactness than is realized upon landing. The space covered by the settlement is probably a mile in breadth, and a mile and a half in length.

That part of Sydney called "The Rocks" derived its name from the nature of the spot upon which it is built, a ledge of limestone. It is the oldest and least respectable part of the settlement. It is directly behind the government dock-yard and other buildings, and the jail frowns in front, as if by a wonderful coincidence those most fit to be its tenants had clustered around it. In Sydney are four or five respectable taverns, and pothouses an infinity. Of these latter "The Rocks" has a share more appropriate to its moral character than its limits; the cause and effect of its bad order and reputation. In no part of the world which I have visited have I seen more of what may be best conveyed by that significant compound "rum-soaking."

In George street, the grand thoroughfare, the visiter is amused with the motley group of divers nations, kindreds, and tongues that he encounters. New Holland is less exclusively the residence of convicts than the reader may have imagined. Settlers and visiters from all portions of the globe—Spaniards, Frenchmen, Englishmen, Americans, Chinese, Malays, Kanakas or South Sea Islanders, the latter arriving in whale ships, add variety to a scene which, without them, would be varied enough. The convicts marked "P. B." subject to a control which, though strong, is not apparent to the observer; the assigned servants without this distinguishing mark; the "currency," "cornstalks," or Anglo-Australians, upon whom the above two first generic terms have been bestowed, one to distinguish them from the *legitimate* or *sterling* population, the other in allusion to their rapid growth, slender forms, and yellow countenances; soldiers; officers; free English emigrants; and last, the native blacks, walk their short legs and long bodies along the streets, armed with their *waddie* or club, and in all costumes from Adam's to the cast-off teguments of His Britannic Majesty's soldiers: these, one would fancy, need no additions to constitute a variety. The free population of New Holland is divided into three parties: the English free emigrants, siding with the government; the Anglo-Australian, leaning either way, as connection with the free and the third or freed party preponderates; and the third or freed-men, made up of pardoned convicts, or those whose sentences have expired. The latter is numerically the larger party, and rigidly enforce a distinction between themselves and those who have been convicted before colonial courts. In a previous chapter the number of newspapers has been stated at three. In that statement another younger establishment, the Australian, was overlooked. The other two are the Sydney Gazette, government, and the Monitor, opposition.

In 1826 there were in Sydney, established, or in contemplation, two steam, three water, and four wind mills, for grinding wheat and Indian corn; two distilleries; leather and some other manufactories; eight or ten auctioneers; about twenty shipping agents; several vessels engaged in the whaling and sealing business, and some one or two others. Freighting to and from Sydney was principally, if not entirely, done in English vessels. In George street are two banks, and stores of all descriptions, the "variety stores," as they are called in this country, outnumbering the rest. Parrots would seem at the first glance through the street to be the staple product of the colony, so many are exposed for sale in cages; but the exports from the colony in the thirteen months preceding June 1826 have been stated at £300,000; the imports during the same period, at £200,000.

The coal mines at Newcastle and other places are worked by double convicts, as also are the freestone quarries. The coal is of two or three qualities, one as bituminous as the cannel coal, the others less so. The freestone is very soft when first quarried, but hardens upon exposure, and forms the principal building material. In the shape of grindstones it forms sometimes an article of export.

H

The governor-general of New South Wales has two lieutenants, one of whom is acting governor of Van Diemen's Land. The sittings of the executive council are secret, but as New Holland is calculated mainly for a criminal settlement, the chief justice has a veto power over their edicts. Three judges constitute a bench at the sessions for trial of high crimes; misdemeanors and infractions of the colonial regulations for convicts come within the jurisdiction of one magistrate, or a bench of two. Freed convicts can now sit on juries, which were at first composed solely of the army officers and free emigrants.

Archdeacon Scott was at the head of the Episcopal Church establishment in 1826. There were in Sydney two parish churches, in Paramatta one, and in Liverpool one. In all settlements where the population will warrant it, churches are built; where the settlement is not large enough, wooden chapels, as at Bathurst. Where there is neither church nor chapel, prayers are read in the house of the magistrate. Beside the Episcopal churches, and the Presbyterian and Catholic in Sydney, the Methodists had a chapel. The public schools are under the supervision of the clergy. In the education of youth efficient measures were in progress, both by government and private munificence.

Sydney is divided into six police districts, but all the surveillance of the police is not sufficient to keep experienced rogues, enjoying partial liberty as servants and in other ways, from practising their vocation. A Botany Bay burglar does not stop to think of locks and doors, but picks you a clean hole through the brick or freestone wall, so silently that the sleeper is not disturbed. Through this aperture, as the Egyptian embalmers extracted the bowels of their subjects, will these adroit thieves clean a room of its lighter moveables. Beside the transported population, there are growing generations of Anglo-Australians, but, to do them justice, they keep wonderfully clear of the infection of guilt, though there must be its quantum of crime to every people. The girls are in special interesting; early mature, early old, and borrowing from their new and antipodal birthplace a simplicity and artlessness the reverse of the studied manners of older countries.

To sustain the remark made a few pages back, that a much less proportion of the inhabitants of New Holland are convicts than is usually imagined, the following facts are taken from the official report published by the colonial government in 1835, about ten years from the time at which I left the colony. The whole population at the time of making the report was 70,000; of whom 24,276 only were convicts. Of these, 20,207 were assigned servants, 982 were in the road-gangs, 1191 in the chain-gangs, 646 in jail, and 1250 in penal settlements. The maintenance of each prisoner is estimated at ten pounds, except the assigned servants, who are of course supported by their masters.

CHAPTER VII

Mr. O'Connell ships in barque John Bull.—Embarkation of missionaries for Strong's Island.—Vessel strikes a reef.—Deserted by crew.—Mr. O'Connell, five others of the crew, and the wife and daughter of the missionary, escape in one boat.—Lose sight of their comrades.—Sufferings from cold and heat.—Death of the females.—Make land after three days.—Find landing.— Caution of the islanders.—Their attack.—Non-resistance of Mr. O'Connell and his comrades.—Their names.—Conducted to canoe-house.—Hospitable conduct of islanders.—Fear of cannibalism.—Jig by Mr. O'Connell.—Delight of his audience.— Baked dogs.—Jagow.—Arrival of chiefs.—Distribution of the strangers among them.—Jane Porter.—Cut up and sewed into blankets.—Washed away by rain.—Looking-glass a great curiosity.—Smashed to catch the spirits in its back.

In or about the year 1826, I shipped in the barque John Bull, whaler, Capt. Barkus. The common incidents of a whaling voyage, which I have already declined recounting in another place, it is unnecessary to repeat here. After we had been from

Sydney about four months, we put in at the Bay of Islands, New Zealand. Bishop Marsden, at that time on a visit to New Zealand, from his residence at Paramatta, put on board of us a missionary who was appointed to Strong's Island,[3] one of the Caroline Archipelago, with his wife and daughter. We were to cruise among the islands towards Japan, with the intention to reach the shores of Japan at a particular season, when whales were supposed to frequent the Sea of Japan. At eight months out we had taken about eight hundred barrels of oil, and were **endeavoring to make** Strong's Island to leave our passengers. At nightfall we had made no land, but knew from observation and the ship's log that we were within a day's sail of our destination. We were bowling along under easy sail, the wind on our quarter, when, at about eight o'clock in the evening, the vessel struck on a concealed coral reef, which is not laid down on the charts. Capt. Barkus was, as usual, drunk on the hen-coop when **the vessel struck.** In the presence of the master, the mates can assume with success no authority which it is his peculiar province to exercise; consequently, with a drunken, stupid sot for a master, every one followed the promptings of his own experience or inclination. The boats were lowered, but notwithstanding the necessary precipitation with which we prepared to leave the vessel, the boat in which I escaped was furnished with provisions and arms, and we were able, also, to take away some ammunition and little portable articles. In the boat with myself were five seamen, and the wife and daughter of the missionary. He was in the boat with the captain. In the four boats the whole crew escaped from the vessel. For five or six hours we kept together, but when the morning dawned there was only one of the other boats discernible, and that but faintly, a long distance astern, as we crested a wave! Even in a latitude which must have been within fifteen degrees of the equator, a night passed without sleep or food, in an open boat, washed by the continual breakings of the sea over it, chilled our whole frames; we were faint, cold, weak, jaded and dispirited. But the sufferings of the ladies engrossed more of our care than our own situation. We had a sail in the boat, and kept her away before it, both because of the comparative comfort of such a course, and our indifference as to what point we stood for. As I sat steering, I folded

[3] Kusaie, the easternmost of the Caroline Islands.

the shivering, sobbing daughter to my body with my left arm, while two of my shipmates assisted in protecting her by placing themselves on each side. The mother was similarly cared for by the other seamen. We tendered them parts of our clothing, but could not persuade or induce them to accept any thing of the kind. Oh, such a horrid night! The women had much more to endure than ourselves, for, beside the natural weakness of their frames, and the delicacy which is woman's suffering in misfortune as her ornament in prosperity, they suffered acute pain from the excoriation they had received in descending to the boat by the davit tackles; the salt water rendering poignant the smarting pain of their wounds. But in all their affliction they bore holy testimony to the efficacy of that religion whose messengers they were; their fortitude might have put even some of their male associates in misfortune to the blush. If ever true practice as well as profession of religion existed, it was exemplified in this family. On shipboard, before our misfortune, the discreet and feeling manner in which they strove to impress upon rude sailors the truths of religion, had convinced all of their *sincerity*, at least. In the boat we had more affecting proof. They prayed frequently and fervently, and there were none to scoff.

Broiling heat succeeded the chills of night; the wind abated, flattened, at noon we were becalmed; dying with heat and fatigue upon a sea whose dead swell was so tranquil that its glassy, slimy smoothness was not ruffled. Toward night we had a breeze again, through the night the wet chills, and the same heat and calm upon the next day. After two days and three nights' exposure, the daughter died about ten o'clock on the third day. For some hours before she had been apparently unconscious of her situation; she had talked in her wanderings of her father, of her home, and of the island to which she was destined on an errand of mercy: the happy end of her pilgrimage was attained without the toil to which she had in her youth devoted herself to reach it. The mother was by suffering so far bereft of sensibility, that the death of her child hardly moved her. She scarcely appeared to understand us when we informed her of it; or, if she did, the announcement was received with a sort of delirious joy. With as much attention to the forms of civilized society as our situation would permit, we committed the body to the ocean. We at first intended to wrap the corpse in our sail; but the prudence of a portion of the crew, who objected to exposing the living to save a form for the dead, prevailed. The mother, in her weak state, hardly uttered a comment, and in a few hours followed her daughter. Her body was also consigned to the deep.

Upon the next morning after these melancholy duties to the two martyrs to the holy religion they professed, we made the land. We had been in the boat three days and four nights, but, rejoiced as we were to make the land, no immediate prospect of profiting by it appeared, for it was circled with a coral reef, in which it was past noon before we discovered an opening. Effecting a passage we entered a smooth basin of water, and saw hundreds of canoes launching and putting off to us. They would approach within a short distance, then suddenly retreat, and at length commenced showering stones, arrows,[4] and other missiles upon us. We threw ourselves in the bottom of the boat; and when they had satisfied themselves that we could or would offer no resistance, they were emboldened to make a rush upon the boat, which they towed to the beach. After we were landed they stripped us of our clothing, and took every thing out of the boat, whale irons, tubs, muskets, etc. The boat was then hauled upon the beach, and our company, six in number, were led to the canoe-house. In the hope that this publication may be the means of conveying intelligence to their friends, I shall here insert the names of my comrades, and their birthplaces, so far as I remember them. George Keenan, an Irishman, belonging to Dublin; John Johnson, an Englishman; Edward Bradford, of Bristol; John Thompson, of Liverpool; and John Williams, of London. Of the native places of the two last-named persons I am not positive.

We were seated in the centre of the canoe-house, upon mats; and yams, bread fruit, plantains, bananas, fish, bits of cold game of some sort, the class of which we could not at first decide, were brought to us. The building was filled in every chink by natives, seated, the men with crossed legs, like Turks, and the women on their heels. A constant buzz of conversation ran through the assembly, each talking to his next neighbor and gesticulating vehemently. The interjection or sound indicative of pleasure or

---

[4] Modern Ponapeans say that the bow and arrow were never a weapon but only a child's toy. Perhaps the spear is meant here. The major weapons were the spear, club, and sling. Small knives were also employed.

surprise among these Indians is a cluck,[5] and of this sound there was abundance, but we were at that time at a loss how to interpret it. Parties of two or three would come down to where we sat, walking with their bodies bent almost double. They took hold of our persons very familiarly, women and men, and gave frequent clucks of admiration at the blue veins which were marked through our skins, on parts of the body which had not been usually exposed to be bronzed by the sun. My comrades feared the Indians were cannibals, and that this examination was to discover whether we were in good roasting case: a horrible supposition, which was strengthened by the building of two or three wood fires, covered with small stones.[6] Their fear was so excessive that they gave themselves up as lost; but as I had been somewhat acquainted with the manners of the inhabitants of other islands, I reasoned, from the apparent good humor of these people, that they intended us no harm.

In a sort of desperate feeling of recklessness, I determined to try the experiment of dancing upon our savage audience. I proposed it to my comrades, and they endeavoured to reason me out of what they esteemed criminal, thoughtless conduct in the view of a horrid death. The prospect was none of the most agreeable, certainly; but I was determined on my experiment despite their remonstrances. I accordingly sprung to my feet and took an attitude; a cluck of pleasure ran through the savages, and one of them, readily understanding my intention, spread a mat for me. I struck into Garry Owen, and figured away in that famous jig to the best of my ability and agility; and my new acquaintances were amazingly delighted thereat. There was no loud acclamation, but anxious peering and peeping over each other's shoulders, the universal cluck sounding all over the house. Before my dance was finished the cause for which the

[5] This is identical to the click-sound which among ourselves expresses disapproval, or commiseration. In 1947 it could be heard when a boy admired the long beam cast by a new flashlight, or when a man witnessed the operation of an ice-making machine.

[6] This is the stone oven, made by heating a pile of stones in a shallow depression, then raking out the wood ash, placing the food to be cooked on a layer of the glowing stones, heaping more hot stones over the food, and covering finally with leaves, to hold in the steam. It differs from the Polynesian earth oven in that the latter is usually made in a pit and covered over with earth.

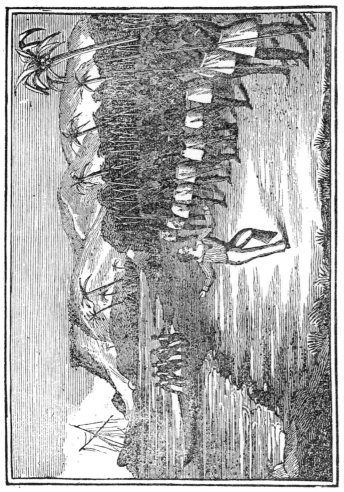

Fig. 7 O'Connell saves his life by dancing for the Ponapeans. This illustration appears in the pamphlets which were sold at circuses to accompany O'Connell's performances. In the original book the John Bull, shown wrecked on Ponape's shore in the background, is said to have been lost a distance of four days by boat from Ponape, and the dance is done not on the beach but in a canoe house. O'Connell's five shipmates are shown in the background at the left.

fires were built became apparent, to the no small relief of my comrades. It was ascertained that the roasting preparations were made, not for us, but for some quadrupeds, which we afterwards found were dogs.[7] Other preparations, such as the pounding of jagow [*sakau*],[8] (cava in the Sandwich Island language,) roasting of game, etc. were making for a feast. In three or four hours all was ready. After my dance was concluded we were separated from each other, each of us making the nucleus of a group of natives, who could not sufficiently admire and examine him. Food was sent us, and jagow. Of the latter I could not drink; it was unpleasant in taste, and a very strong narcotic in effect.

We were now all completely reassured; the conduct of the natives to us was all that uncultivated kindness and hospitality could prompt. At night we slept in the canoe-house, having each half a dozen bed, or perhaps I should say mat fellows. Upon the first day we were each supplied with the mat[9] which is a part of the native costume. For three or four days it was with us a continual feast, islanders crowding from all directions to see the white strangers. Some people claiming to be civilized might take a lesson from the humanity of these people to shipwrecked mariners.

Upon the fourth day after our landing there was an arrival of a fleet of canoes, the head and other chiefs. We were again inspected by the new comers, and it was my fortune to be selected, with my shipmate George Keenan, by the principal chief. The other four of my comrades were also appropriated; and our property and the articles we brought on shore in the boat were also divided. I was astonished at the perfect peace in which, among savages, all these arrangements took place. On the morrow, my new friend, or master, or owner,—I do not know exactly how he considered himself,—left the island upon which we landed, taking with him Keenan and myself. Eight or nine

[7] See fig. 10. Dogs were the only domestic animals.

[8] Ponape and Kusaie are the only Micronesian islands where kava drinking was practised, and only Ponape today clings to it. The root is prepared by pounding, as O'Connell says, the Polynesian custom of mastication being absent.

[9] What is meant is a kilt consisting of coconut leaves suspended from a waist cord and hanging to the knees. This is the men's costume.

hours carried us to his island,[10] where new feasting and *lionizing* awaited us.

A grand feast celebrated the return of the chief to his house, at which I repeated the Irish jig which had taken so well upon my first landing. I have no doubt that in my heels was found the attraction which led the chief to select me from among my comrades. Upon the next day after his return he restored to George and me our "ditty bags," the only property I had preserved from the wreck. In that bag were two odd volumes of Jane Porter's Scottish Chiefs, and a little shaving-glass. These articles were great objects of curiosity, and I may as well relate their history and ultimate fate here as elsewhere.

God bless Miss Jane Porter! I have so good an opinion of the lady that I doubt not it will add to the pleasure which the composition of her Scottish Chiefs afforded her, to know that two odd volumes of the work were pleasant companions in our exile on the Carolines. Intimately acquainted, as we soon necessarily became, with the Scottish Chiefs, I must do the armor-cased warriors the justice to say, that far from tiring, they improved upon acquaintance, and being the only persons to whom we had access who asserted any claim to civilization, we spent hours in their company. I had nearly the whole by heart; every word and every period was recognised upon each reading as an old acquaintance; every leaf was as familiar as the milestones to a coachman. The natives noticed our devotion to the books and shared in it; they supposed printing was the English method of

---

[10] Here and repeatedly later O'Connell speaks of islands, and gives the impression that Ponape consists of a cluster of small islands. Actually there is one large island of 124 square miles, and about 40 small islands, in the lagoon and on the surrounding reef, all of them together making up 5 square miles in area. Since the place at which O'Connell and his shipmates landed is evidently the tribal area of Net, on the north side of Ponape, he may be referring here to the two islets in the lagoon belonging to Net called Parem and Lenger. It is also possible that he thought of Net Peninsula as an island. Whatever is the case it would have taken at the very most, and with contrary winds, no more than two hours to travel between any of these places. The shore line of Ponape consists in large part of mangrove swamp, intersected by many narrow passages and cut through by streams, used by people in canoes in travelling from one place on the main island to another; perhaps these passageways gave O'Connell the impression that they cut off bodies of land from one another.

tattooing, and Miss Jane Porter was in as much demand among them as she ever could have been among the patrons of a village circulating library. I was careful not to permit the volumes to go out of my sight, but allowed the natives to examine and admire it in my presence. A little Cupid with a scroll upon which was inscribed "Finis" was one particular object of the women's admiration; "jeree but a but maco ja-le-le [*seri pwetepwet me kaselel*]!" a nice little white child. In one of the volumes was a frontispiece—a portrait of some female body or other, which likewise came in for its share of attention. At length, upon an unlucky day, after the books had been with me nearly two years, I was careless enough to leave them exposed while I went upon some excursion. When I returned, the leaves were torn out and sewed into blankets, under which half a dozen women were strutting in all the pride of peacocks. In addition to the beauty which the article thus manufactured possessed as a "lagow [*likou*]," (blanket), it had another charm in the tattooing. The wearers imagined themselves connected with the English chiefs while thus wearing the white man's tattoo. Regrets were useless; so I made none, but amused myself with the complacent carriage of my yellow *chere amies* under their new lagows. Their gratification was, however, soon turned to vexation, and then my turn to be pleased came. Situated so near the equator, rains are frequent and violent upon the Carolines. The Jane Porter bedecked belles were surprised in a shower, and their new garments washed off their backs. They were very much chagrined at this, and protested that the white man's tattoo was good for nothing, it would not stand. That the islanders' tattoo will stand, my body is witness.

The shaving-glass did not survive so long. While it lasted I kept it sacred to the eyes of the island aristocracy, never permitting plebeian gazers access to it. To have permitted all who wished to look into it would have converted me into a mere exhibitor of facial panoramas. I carried it with me on all my rounds of visits to the chiefs, and the exclamations of those who were favored with a peep at the magic glass were amusing enough. As many as could look in at once would peep over each other's shoulders, twisting their features into the most grotesque expressions, and *clucking* with delight. They imagined the reflection of their visages was caused by animan [*enih-men*] (spirits) behind the glass; consequently some awe was mingled with their delight. It is, however, a curious fact for the student of mental philosophy, that their respect for those genii did not prevent their destroying the frame of the glass one day in my absence, and scraping off the quicksilver, to detect the animan in their hiding-place, and meet them all at once!

CHAPTER VIII

Mr. O'Connell and Keenan put on board a canoe.—Reach an uninhabited hut.—Unsatisfactory guesses.—Arrival of persons indicating no equivocal purpose.—First impressions of tattooing tools.—Process.—Keenan's outcry.—Ungrammatical swearing.— Application of oil and charcoal.—Dinner.—More tattooing by way of dessert.—Borrowed comments upon mats and rose blankets.—Gratifying reflections upon their previous durability.—Return of operators on the morning following.—Entreaties, unavailing on the part of Mr. O'Connell, but more successful in George's case.—Extraction of hair.—Month in healing.—Flute and violin.—A digression upon poets and poetry.—Return to head-quarters.—Farther impressions.—Music and dancing.— Feasting.—Discovery at the end of second day.—Mr. O'Connell's father-in-law.—His wife, and her charms.—Her jointure.—Her capacity as a teacher.—Her father's practical jokes.—Excursions. —Music and dancing.

We had been about three days at our new residence, when some of the natives began showing us their tattooed arms and

Fig. 8 A tattooing implement used on Ponape. Drawing by Edward G. Schumacher of the Smithsonian Institution.

legs, and making signs, not entirely intelligible to us at first, though their meaning became afterward too painfully marked. On the fourth or fifth day, George Keenan and myself were put on board of a canoe with six natives. They paddled a short distance along the shore of the island, and then turned into a creek, wide at the mouth, but soon narrowing till there was not room for two canoes abreast. It was completely arched over with dependent branches of trees; and altogether the scene was romantic, and would have been pleasing, if we had not been so utterly in the dark as to the purpose of the journey. At length we reached a hut on the banks of the creek, landed, and entered it, directed by our conductors, who remained outside. No person was there to receive us, and for half an hour George and I busied ourselves in guesses and speculation as to the end to which all this was tending. There was nothing in the building to give us a clue to the purpose for which it was erected; it was evidently not a dwellinghouse, and was too defenceless and fragile for a prison. At length our suspense was relieved—ended, I should say—by the arrival of five or six women, bearing implements, the purpose of which we were soon taught. George was made to sit in one corner of the room, and I was seated in another, half the women with me, and the residue with my comrade. One of my women produced a calabash of black liquid; another took my left hand, squeezing it in hers so as to draw the flesh tight across the back. Then a little sliver of bamboo was dipped in the liquid and applied to my hand, upon which it left a straight black mark. The third beauty then produced a small flat piece of wood with thorns pierced through one end. This she dipped in the black liquid, then rested the points of the thorns upon the mark on my hand, and with a sudden blow from a stick drove the thorns into my flesh. One needs must when the devil drives; so I summoned all my fortitude, set my teeth, and bore it like a martyr. Between every blow my beauty dipped her thorns in the ink.[11]

I was too much engaged in my own agreeable employment to watch my comrade, but George soon let me hear from him. He swore and raved without any attention to rule; the way he did it was profane, but not syntactical or rhetorical. He wished all sorts of bloody murder and plagues to light upon his tormentors, prayed that the islands might be earthquake sunken, hoped forty boats' crews from a squadron of armed ships would land and catch the blasted savages tormenting the king's subjects. All this availed nothing but to amuse the women; and even I could not forbear a smile at his exclamations. The operators suspended their work to mimic him; mocked his spasmodic twitches of the arm and horrid gestures. He was a standing butt for it long afterwards, and when the natives wished to revile him, they would act the tattooing scene, ending with the exclamation, "Narlic-a-Nutt mucha purk [*Nahliken Net masa pwehk*],"— Narlic-a-Nutt (his name) is a coward; "Jim Aroche ma coo mot [. . . *me kommwoad*],"—Jim Chief brave!

After my executioner had battered my hand awhile, she wiped it with a sponge. I hoped she had finished; but no! She held my hand up, squinted at the lines, as a carpenter would true a board. Then she commenced again, jagging the thorns into places where she thought the mark was imperfect. The correction of the work was infinitely worse than the first infliction. In about an hour and a half the hand was finished, and the women left us, taking away their tools. Before they left us, however, they smeared the tattooed part with cocoa-nut oil, and then patted pulverized coal upon it. This was repeated often, till there was a thick crust of coal and oil, completely concealing the flesh.

---

[11] The description of tattooing given here and in the following pages is in close accord with that related by modern Ponapeans who have endured the same operation (although young people are no longer being tattooed). The designs would ordinarily have been applied by the female tattooing specialists by or during early adolescence. The dye is made from candlenut soot. The tattooing implement is a kind of rake, consisting of a short piece of hibiscus wood to the end of which is lashed, at right angles, a row of wild orange thorns or sometimes a flat comb of bird-bone with one edge filed to a row of points. See Fig. 8.

The healing properties of charcoal are familiar to chemists. The reader has noted, perhaps, that it will delay the putrefaction of butcher's meat; and, indeed, some over economical housewifes know how to restore tainted meat by an application of it. The women gone, something was sent us to eat, and we flattered ourselves that our punishment for the day was over. However, the afternoon brought a fresh bevy of these tender ladies, who continued operations upon the left arm. At night we were pointed to some mats and informed that we must sleep there. As Logic says in the play, ours were any thing but rose blankets; and we had the farther gratification of reflecting that they were fixtures of this tattooing hospital, and had probably encased the limbs of at least two generations of Indians. I refused at first to accept the embraces of *such* clothing; but, not yet quite used to going nearly naked, I was fain to seek some protection among the mats from the bamboo floor.

On the next morning the gout-puffed hand of the canon of Gil Blas would not have been a circumstance in size to mine; though the color of my flesh, maturated, and grimed with charcoal, hardly looked so aristocratic as a delicately swelled gouty limb. Another squad of these savage printers followed our breakfast. George was outrageous in his protestations, and howled and gesticulated earnestly against a repetition; and I did not spare entreaty. The prayer of his petition was granted, but my reluctance availed nothing. For a reason of which I then knew nothing, they made gestures that I *must* stand it—there was no escape. George was let off, but not without unequivocal expressions of disgust at his cowardice and effeminacy. He was indeed incapable of enduring it; his blood was bad; but physical disability, among all savages, is quite as much a disgrace as a misfortune.

After finishing the left, operations were commenced upon my right arm. George, a blockhead! not only jeered at me for enduring it, instead of begging out of it like himself, but assisted to hold my flesh for the women. It is unnecessary to go into details; eight days were occupied in the process upon different parts of my body. My legs, back, and abdomen, were marked also, and to enable them to operate I was compelled to lay extended upon a mat. The hair upon my body was twitched out with sea-shells—a process which was performed as expeditiously upon my person as the same ground can be cleared of pin-feathers on geese by a dexterous cook. I often thought I should die of these apparently petty, but really acutely painful inflictions. George was compelled to remain with me, not only during the eight days the tattooing was going on, but for the month afterward that I was obliged to remain at this hut for my flesh to heal. During this time the application of the oil and charcoal was continually repeated, till I resembled in skin, if not in shape, the rhinoceros.

A long, dreary month that! We were not absolutely confined to the hut, but peregrinations, to a man in my sore situation, would have been sorry amusement; nor were we allowed to stroll far. To relieve time of some of its weariness, George made a rude fife of a piece of cane, and with his knife he manufactured a very tolerable fiddle from light wood, stringing with the fibres of the plantain tree and whale sinews from his "ditty bag." Had we been poets, we might, taking the dreams of those gentry for truth, have vastly enjoyed this rural retreat, romantic as it was, with a beautiful rill running by our door, mountainous and variegated scenery about us, and, in addition to our music, flocks of parrots[12] squawking. But we soon tired of the scene, and of the faces of our keepers; we saw nothing of the women after the tattooing was finished. Every thing became dull and monotonous —the same dull routine of sunning and shade by day, the same notes from the same birds, and the same nightly howling of dogs at a distance. Never did men in quarantine sigh more earnestly for deliverance. At length it came.

We were heartily rejoiced when the canoe was manned to carry us back to the war canoe house. I came from the tattoo hospital a bird of much more diversified plumage than when I entered, being tattooed on my left hand, on both arms, legs, thighs, back, and abdomen.[13] George had escaped with a few stripes on the left arm, and those unfinished. Upon our return a feast awaited us, and, to give it eclat and variety, George astonished

12 The Ponape lory, *Trichoglossus rubiginosus.*

13 Perhaps this is a variant style of tattooing. Traditionally both sexes tattooed the hands, arms, legs, and thighs, and women in addition the abdomen, *mons veneris,* and buttocks, but neither sex the back. If O'Connell or H.H.W. is being prudish and using 'back' as a euphemism for 'buttocks' he has essentially described on himself the feminine tattooing pattern, which, if it was indeed done on men must soon after O'Connell's time have become obsolete.

the natives with tunes upon his rude instruments,[14] to which I danced.

I had supposed that my tattooing was over, but I had not been ashore three hours, before, by the chief's direction, one of his daughters prepared to mark me still more. She tattooed a ring upon my right breast, another upon my left shoulder, and two about my right arm. This was but the prick of a needle to the extensive printing business which had been prosecuted upon my body at the tattoo-house, and I made no complaint. The feasting continued during the day; many dogs barked their last; jagow in abundance was mauled to express its juice; and my comrade for his fife, and myself for my heels, were in excellent odor with the natives.

The singing and dancing was protracted into the night of the first day. Upon the second, after bathing, their daily morning custom, the natives recommenced the rejoicing; feasting, jagow, and frolic were the order of the day. Canoes with chiefs and petty chiefs were continually arriving from the other islands, and George and I were paraded and examined at each fresh arrival. As when we first landed, the blue veins, showing through our comparatively white skin, were particular objects of admiration. I enjoyed this parading much better than my comrade, fell into the spirit of it, and danced like mad upon every visit from strangers, George supplying the music, and the spectators clucking, or breaking out into an unsuppressed laugh of delight. George's music saved him much contumely, which he would otherwise have received for his cowardice in the tattoo-house.

So wore the second day. It was not until night that I began to suspect to what it all tended. At night I learned that the young lady who imprinted the last-mentioned marks upon my arm and breast was my wife! that last tattooing being part of the ceremony of marriage.[15] Upon the third morning my bride led me away to the bath, and the day was spent in feasting and dancing, as upon the two days preceding; only that the third, being the climax, was more of a day of rejoicing than the two

[14] Both the fife and the fiddle were foreign to Ponape, although a nose-blown flute existed.

[15] The descriptions of the rings on the arm, breast, and shoulder and their supposed connection to a marriage ceremony, when repeated to modern Ponapeans, are mystifying to them.

117

preceding. There was, however, no quarrelling or disturbance, no uproar or disorder. The liquor expressed from jagow (cava) is a tremendously powerful narcotic, and drinking it in large quantities produces deep and stupid sleep.

George also was provided with a wife; but his unwillingness to submit to the process of tattooing wedded him to a woman of no rank. She, however, proved a good woman to him.

My father-in-law was Ahoundel-a-Nutt [*Oundol en Net*, 'watchman of the mountain of Net'], chief of the island of Nutt [Net], and the most powerful chief on the group of islands inclosed by the reef, set down on the charts as one island, Ascension, but called by the natives Bonabee [*Pohnpei*, 'Ponape', lit. 'on the stone structure'].[16] He did not have the grace to give me a separate establishment however, for, during the whole time I remained upon the island, I resided under the same roof with him. He gave me his own name, Ahoundel, but I was oftener called Jem-aroche. George Keenan's island name was Narlic [*Nahlik*, 'Lord of the exterior'].

I never had more reason to complain of my wife than the majority of people in civilized countries have. I can say more than the don in "The Wonder;" had my wife died, I should not only have been far from rejoicing at it, but should have regretted it exceedingly. She was only about fourteen years of age, affectionate, neat, faithful, and, barring too frequent indulgence in the flesh of baked dogs, which would give her breath something of a canine odor, she was a very agreeable consort. During my residence upon the island she presented me with two pretty little demi-savages, a little girl, and a boy, who stands a chance, in his turn, to succeed his grandfather in the government of the island.[17]

---

[16] Oundol ('Ahoundel'), the title of O'Connell's father-in-law, is and was apparently at that time also only the twelfth title in the first line of chiefly titles in most of the Ponapean tribes. The title series in Net was different from those of the other tribes in O'Connell's time, the highest title being Lepen Net, and the title Oundol being far down the political ladder. There is no island of Net; the area known by that name lies mostly on the mainland, and the tribe which occupies it is a small and weak one compared to the others on Ponape.

[17] The missionary Albert Sturges, writing in the 1850s, says that O'Connell's wife was still alive then and describes her as a fearful

Although my father-in-law never permitted me a house distinct from his, but kept me as one of his own household, with a host of other connections—a knight of his majesty's bedchamber—for there was no division wall in the hut, and I slept on a mat next him; my wife's dower in canoes, Nigurts [*Naikat*, 'my people here'], (slaves,) and other Caroline personal property, with the improvement of real, was far from inconsiderable. She assumed a task new to her, and one of course which she could have had no idea of before—that of an instructress in the language. I was a tolerably apt scholar, but my teacher had a very critical ear, and the least deviation from the island pronunciation created vast merriment both for her and others present.[18] It was a long time before I was sufficiently acquainted with the language to know what property I held in my wife's right; and when I had learned I cared little to be exactly acquainted. Covetousness is almost unknown among the Carolines.

My wife accompanied me in my walks and in my canoe excursions; always at my side, and looking up to me as affectionately as ever a novel-schooled miss could, and with twice the sincerity. Her father, who was a practical joker, contrived, in the excursions in which he accompanied us during the lengthened honeymoon, to pop upon places where he knew that, although my name and fame had preceded me, the residents had never seen me. He would direct me to enter a house suddenly, with a howl, and strike an attitude. It would invariably send all the occupants, usually women, flying out at every place of egress. The sight of Ahoundel on the outside, enjoying a hearty laugh, would remove fear, and this rude method of introduction supplied both parties, the visiters and the visited, with rare amusement. Imagine the effect which would be produced on a party of American or European ladies by the sudden apparition of an Albino under such circumstances, and you will have some idea of the fright of the islanders.

---

monument of depraved lust. (Records of the American Board of Commissioners for Foreign Missions, Vol. III, No. 268, p. 3, Houghton Library, Harvard University.)

[18] O'Connell may have viewed himself as 'a tolerably apt scholar' but his knowledge of Ponapean was elementary. This matter is discussed in the Introduction.

To excursions without him Ahoundel was very averse. He would, in answer to my inquiries about the other islands, tell me they were inhabited by cannibals, and assure me, that if I ventured away from him I should certainly be eaten. George and I, if we took excursions, did so in a canoe borrowed of fishermen, because we could not launch our own unperceived. Afraid of being eaten, our trips were at first confined altogether to Nutt, the island upon which we resided; circumnavigating it, and paddling up the creeks. When we were near a settlement, George would take his fife and make its shrill notes echo in the still valleys and mountains. "Narlic! Narlic! Narlic! Narlic!" we should soon hear the natives shouting, as they came running down to the creek side, "Narlic, cudjong [*keseng*]! cudjong!" Cudjong was the name which the natives had bestowed upon George's fife. The shore would soon be lined with breathless listeners, and while I kept the canoe just in motion enough to avoid the banks, George would play some of his sweetest tunes. We were always invited to land, and usually did so. As soon as I left the boat came my turn; I was besieged to dance, and as I always refused to land except when intending to astonish the natives with a reel which might have passed for clever, even

—"*at the fair of nate Clogheen,*"

I usually complied with their request.

CHAPTER IX

Castes.—Moonjobs.—Jerejohs.—Nigurts.—Respect to chiefs.— Succession to authority.—Number of islands.—Names of chiefs. —Condition of Jerejohs.—Of Nigurts.—Houses—description and mode of building.—Gaudy exterior.—"House warming."— Canoe-houses.—Estates.—Relations between landholders and their dependents.—Power of petty chiefs.—Revenue of head chiefs.—Tools.—Twine and cordage.—Mats and sashes.— Weaving.

There are on the Caroline group the same two distinct races of people that are common to almost all the islands of Oceanica,— the olive race, judged by geographers to be descendants of Malays who emigrated at a date which it is impossible to fix, and the ocean negroes, probably the original inhabitants. The whiter race upon the islands of Bonabee are divided into two classes,—the Moonjobs [*mwohnsapw*], composed of chiefs and their blood connections, and the Jerejohs [*seriiso*], or free whites. The negroes form one caste, and are known under the name

NIGURTS. A similarity between this word and the Philippine Nigritos is obvious.[19]

Jerejohs and Moonjobs intermarry with each other, but seldom or never with the Nigurts. When intermarriages take place between the Jcrejohs and Moonjobs, the issue takes the rank of the mother. The children of chiefs by Jerejoh mothers may become petty chiefs, but can never reach the rank of supreme chiefs. The respect paid to chiefs is extreme, no person of less rank approaching them in an erect posture. In a house, where a chief is present, all persons keep in a sitting position, or, if they walk about, it is done with the body inclined forward almost at right angles with the legs. Should a person unapprized of the presence of the chief enter the house, the exclamation "Agai! moondie! Aroche nanname [*ekei! mwohndi! . . . nan-ihmw!*]!"—"Ah! sit down, chief (is in) the house!" rises from many voices at once.

The Moonjobs are the distant and immediate connections, or family of the chief, and are in number to the whole population as one to twenty. The term *moonjob* is also applied to the skies; and the chiefs claim some affinity or connection with the sun and moon.[20] The succession to the supreme authority is very orderly, and no confusion ever takes place. It does *not* descend directly from father to son, but when the head chief dies the next chief in rank—probably his brother—takes his place. The new incumbent's vacated place is filled by the next below him in rank, and his again by the next; thus causing a promotion from grade to grade through the whole, leaving a vacant place at the foot of the scale, into which the deceased chief's eldest son steps, if his mother is a Moonjob; if not, the eldest son by a

---

[19] This description of racial castes is completely unfounded. Modern Ponapeans say that high-ranking people, because they did little outdoor work in former times, were less exposed to the sun than commoners, hence were lighter in skin colour. Andrew Cheyne, describing conditions on Ponape in the early 1840s, gives virtually the same explanation of differences in pigmentation. As for any cognation between the words 'nigurts' and 'Nigritos', this is of course sheerest amateur philology. See p. 124 n. 25 for an explanation of 'nigurt'.

[20] The word moonjob (*mwohnsapw*) means literally 'first of the land', referring to those entitled to receive first fruits. It does not mean sky, nor do chiefs, at least today, claim any connection with the sun or moon.

Moonjob mother; and if the chief leaves no Moonjob sons, the vacancy is filled from the family of the new incumbent. It often happens that deaths of chiefs between the highest and lowest grades create vacancies, which are filled by the head chief's sons before the death of their father; and sometimes the head chief's family is not sufficient to fill vacancies; in which case the next chief's family is drawn upon. Each chief has an estate, the size and fertility of which determines his rank. The group inside the reef consists of about twenty inhabited islands, varying in size from twenty miles to half a mile in circuit.[21] The largest island is called Nutt,[22] and the head of this primitive oligarchy always has to his name the addition Nutt, connected by a sort of particle, thus, Ahoundel-a-Nutt. Nothing else is necessary to designate his rank, though the general term Aroche lap-a-lap [lapalap]—very great chief, is sometimes applied to him. The following is a list of some of the principal islands,[23] and the names of their chiefs in 1833; the word after the particle being the name of the island. The native name for the whole group is Bonabee.

> Ahoundel-a-Nutt, [*Oundol en Net*]
> Wajai-a-Matalaleme, [*Wasai en Madolenihmw*]
> Namatha-a-Chaba, [*Nahnmadau en . . .*]
> Roun-a-Kitti, [*. . . en Kiti*]
> Na-anaho-a-Palaga, [*Nahnawa en Palikir*]
> Wajai-a-Chocoich, [*Wasai en Sokehs*]
> Ahoundel-a-Param, [*Oundol en Parem*]
> Nanamoraki-a-Hoo, [*Nahnmwarki en Uh*]
> Lecunjoni-a-Jounaboo, [?]
> Tuccaree-a-Hand, [*. . . en Ant*]
> Ajongajangkee-a-Corrapin. [?]

[21] See p. 109 n. 10. The main island is actually about 40 miles in circumference.

[22] No island is called Nutt (Net). That word is used in two senses: 1) Net Peninsula; and 2) the entire tribe of Net, which includes the Net Peninsula, other parts of the mainland, and some small islands, principally Lenger and Parem.

[23] Of the identifiable place names given in this list, only Sokehs and Parem are islands within the surrounding reef of Ponape. Sokehs Island is part of the tribe of Sokehs, the rest of which is on the mainland and bears the same name. Parem belongs to Net. Ant is a completely separate atoll, 8 miles distant and belonging to the tribe of Kiti. All five tribal names are given by O'Connell in this list: Kiti, Net, Madolenihmw, Uh, and Sokehs. Palikir is part of the Sokehs tribe, on the mainland. Of the

The head chief sometimes takes the title Bonabee, but more usually that of Nutt. On each of the islands are petty chiefs, taking their titles from the districts which they own. We find it difficult to determine where the title *chief* ceases, as every landholder takes the title of his property; and all under Moonjobs and very prominent Jerejohs are known by the general title "Aroche[24] ticatic [. . . *tikitik*],"—very small chiefs. Perhaps aroche might as well be translated freeman as chief; but then there would be no word in the language signifying chief.

The JEREJOHS, the next class, are all landholders, but never rise above the rank of petty chiefs. They are less noble and independent in their carriage, a bearing evidently the effect of habitual submission.

The NIGURTS are, in effect, slaves. They are of the race of Oceanic negroes, not jet black, but much darker than the higher classes. The hair is not short and curly, but long and straight. The skin is rough, and very unpleasant to the touch. They perform not only the labor of fishing, but nearly all the labor done on the islands. They own no land, and are attached to the estates of the Moonjobs and Jerejohs, who assert a vague claim of property over them. They are the executioners—the butchers—of the only species of cattle killed,—dogs,—and the cooks.[25]

---

identifiable titles, which precede the place names, only the Nahnmwarki of Uh is correctly given as the highest title of that tribe. Wasai is the second highest title in both Madolenihmw and Sokehs, though in the case of Sokehs there was a period of time, which probably included the time of O'Connell, when the highest title, Nahnmwarki, was not issued. This was because of certain misfortunes which befell the holder of that title. Nahnawa is the fifth ranking title in each tribe. Oundol (O'Connell's father-in-law's title) is twelfth or lower, and Nahnmadau is even lower.

[24] See p. 151 n. 64 regarding this word.

[25] O'Connell has only partially understood the chiefly system, as set forth in the preceding paragraphs. His use of the word 'chief' confuses matters. There are two lines of titled persons (or chiefs) in each of the five tribes. These are what O'Connell calls Moonjob and Jerejoh. A more generic term which includes the higher titles in both lines is *soupeidi*, a term not given by O'Connell. The higher titles of one line belong to the men of one particular clan, those in the other line to another clan. Members of all other clans (there are about twenty) are commoners (*aramas mwahl*, literally 'common people'). These commoners apparently are what O'Connell calls slaves, 'nigurts', which is probably to

The houses upon the Bonabee group are simple in construction, but by no means rude, answering every purpose of shelter and convenience. The erection of a house is not considered a servile task; it is an honorable employment, in which the future occupant is assisted by his friends and their dependents. The first step is to build a regular and neat stone wall for a foundation, averaging four feet in height, but regulated to the inequalities of the ground, so as to present a level at its top. The inside is then filled with smaller stones, and squared timbers of about a foot in thickness are placed upon the foundation wall. Into these timbers are inserted squared uprights, about five feet apart, and upon these are placed the horizontal timbers upon which the eaves rest. In a word, a very creditable frame is erected. The sides of the dwellinghouses, between the roof and the foundation, are generally only four or five feet in height, but the roof has a very steep pitch, and is supported at its centre by tall posts, and thatched with cocoanut leaves, overhanging the walls about a foot at the eaves.

The upright posts of the walls are netted with twine, and the space between the posts is filled up with small cane or bamboo, fastened together with twine, which is used in such abundance as to conceal the wood. The twine is of variegated colors, red,

---

be read as *naikat*. Horatio Hale writes it thus too, and it would mean only 'my people here', referring to relatives, dependants, etc.

The two titled clans are different in the different tribes, so that people who are chiefly in one tribe might be commoners in another. Clan exogamy prevails, and the two titled clans in each tribe formerly intermarried exclusively. Since descent is matrilineal, a man's sons would be in their mother's clan and would have titles in the line opposite to his.

The men of each of the two titled lines, being mostly of the same clan, receive their titles and are promoted roughly in accordance with the rules of clan seniority. The two lines are essentially equal, contrary to what O'Connell indicates, the highest title in the first line being Nahnmwarki in each tribe, often translated as 'King', and that of the second line, Nahnken, often called 'Prime Minister'. It is the Nahnmwarki whom O'Connell seems to mean when he refers to 'head chief'. Because of the rules of intermarriage between the two lines just explained, the Nahnmwarki and Nahnken can be and often are father and son or, conversely, son and father.

There is a similar political structure involving ranked titles on the sub-tribe (section) level. These lesser titles are given out to commoners, along with parcels of land formerly, as O'Connell indicates.

black, blue, and is so woven as to form figures upon the outside walls; which, with the assistance of tassels and other decorations, make the house present a very gaudy appearance. The floor is laid of bamboo upon the stone platform, and is also covered with twine. In the centre of the floor a hole four or five feet square is left for the fire, the smoke from which finds its way out through crevices in the roof and in the wall. The entrances are about three feet in height, serving alike the purpose of doors and windows.[26]

The dwellinghouses vary in size and in shape, according to the taste and rank of the proprietor. The sites usually selected are those sheltered by trees, and near streamlets. The erection of a house is an occasion of feasting—a sort of pic-nic party, to which those who assist in building bring not only articles for the feast, but materials for building. The time occupied in building is usually about ten days. Newly married couples seldom build, but remain with the parents of one of the parties, or are quartered upon some chief; "house-keeping" forming no essential part of a bride's privilege.

After the house is completed the priests hold a sort of ceremony of consecration in it, which occupies about three or four hours. The friends of the intended occupants, the chiefs of his district, and other chiefs if they be present, are seated in the house, according to their rank, but no women are allowed to enter. Jagow, dog meat, yam, bread-fruit, etc., are served to the guests, while the priests keep up a sort of song, incantation, or invocation. One sings a sort of recitative song, same and monotonous, and when he has howled himself out of breath the tune is taken up and continued by another.[27]

---

[26] This description of the native dwelling house (*ihmw*) is important, for the structure has long since vanished. The modern house bears little resemblance to it. Nowadays the thatching (increasingly replaced by corrugated metal) is of ivory-nut palm leaf, and Ponapeans assert that this was true also in ancient times, in contrast to O'Connell's description of coconut-leaf thatch; they are probably correct, for the very word for thatch (*oahs*), current also according to Cheyne in the early 1840s, is also the word for the ivory-nut palm. The so-called bamboo in O'Connell's description is actually a kind of cane, *Saccharum spontaneum*, called *ahlek* by the Ponapeans. Blue-colored twine seems doubtful; native dyes do not include that colour.

[27] House dedications, very much modified, are still occasionally held, but any religious elements in them are Christianised.

Dwellinghouses seldom exceed forty feet by twenty, and Nigurts are sometimes contented with ten by six, and less. But the war canoe houses, which serve also the purpose of council rooms and halls for feasting and other ceremonies, are often a hundred feet in length, and forty to fifty wide. They are built like dwellinghouses, except that they are always on level ground, near the beach or upon it, and the floor is not all covered with bamboo. Along the sides is a raised bamboo passage-way, as high from the ground in the centre as the top of the foundation wall, and at one end of the house is a raised platform, which is occupied by the chiefs and Moonjobs upon feast occasions. During two or three months, in the hottest season of the year, the chief with his family and suite occupy this part of the canoe-house as a residence. Upon the ground in the centre of the house the canoes are finished, and upon feast occasions the fires are built for cooking dogs. At the sides of the house the canoes, when finished, and not in use, are suspended. The canoe-house has at one end a large entrance.[28]

Estates all descend from the parent to the eldest son. His is the paternal mansion, his the canoe-house, and his the Nigurts. A large landholder has quite a village about him. The most prominent object in the settlement is the dwellinghouse of the proprietor, always standing in the best situation, and always larger and more tastefully ornamented than the rest. About him are houses, less in dimensions, but also neat, the abodes of younger brothers, connections, and dependents, whom he permits to build upon his territory, and allows the use of a portion of his land and bread-fruit trees; but he never relinquishes his ownership in the soil. Real estate is never passed from hand to hand except by inheritance, and thus is perpetuated the distinction of castes.[29]

[28] These structures (nahs), known variously in English as community houses, meeting houses, canoe houses, and feast houses, serve all the functions inferred from those names. In contrast to the dwelling houses they persist today and except for the substitution of building materials are essentially as O'Connell describes them. There is a central ground-level area; there are three walls, the front being left open; the 'passage-ways' are the two raised platforms along the sides, and at the back is the still higher platform where persons of high rank sit.

[29] Inheritance was basically matrilineal until the German land reform of 1912. Land belonged ultimately to the highest chief in each tribe, the Nahnmwarki, and was held in fief by lower-ranking chiefs who in turn

These dependents pay a sort of voluntary rent in presents of fruit, yams, and jagow, if they have it. At a greater distance are the huts of the Nigurts—the slaves of the proprietor of the soil, who till the land for the white tenants and their landlord; fish, cook, pound jagow, and, in fine, do all the servile work. There are some descriptions of employment, as I have already noted, which are honorable; such as the manufacture of twine, the building of houses, and decorating of canoes, by the men; and the weaving of wywies [weiwei], and manufacture of mats, by the women.

Canoes may belong to people who hold no land, being a description of personal property. Over every thing else the proprietor has control, and exerts over his tenants and slaves a patriarchal power. He can punish minor offences, but being in his turn subject to the head chief of the island, he reports flagrant crimes at head-quarters, where he also pays a tribute, not a stated one, but regulated in quantity by his means and will.

The principal chief upon an island has a similar clan of his immediate connections and slaves about him, and a large landed estate. Every thing is similar to the establishment of a petty chief, except that his dwellinghouse is larger, his canoes more in number, larger and better decorated, and the canoe-house calculated for numerous assemblages. Beside the direct products of his own land, he is in the continual receipt of tribute from the petty chiefs upon his island, and, if he be chief of Nutt and head of the group, of presents from the chiefs of the inferior islands.

The principal mechanical tool is of course the hatchet. It is made of a hard white stone,[30] found on the beach, broken to something the shape of a hatchet, and rubbed to a very good edge on rough rocks. A native will be sometimes two or three months preparing his hatchet, working at intervals upon it, before he fastens it to the handle. The piece of wood selected for a handle is a small branch of a tree, in which there is an

---

parcelled it out to still lesser people. On the death of a land-holder the land reverted to the Nahnmwarki, who usually confirmed the normal matrilineal inheritor in possession, but he could and sometimes did interfere with the normal succession. With land was inextricably bound the system of titles, a title being associated with each parcel. Only the title-system persists.

[30] The material is not stone but the hinge of the giant clam, *Tridacna gigas*. Adzes, not hatchets, were the principal tools.

elbow. One part of this elbow is cut off; the other left long forms the handle. The back of the stone rests against the angle, and round the stone and wood are passed strong bands of bark, hemp, or twine. The hatchet is so fitted upon the handle that its blows are like those of a cooper's adz, but it will at once be perceived that with such an instrument no deep blows can be struck. For smaller work sea shells are used, and coral forms their rasps. They have also dogfish skin for polishing. With these simple tools they are very dexterous, and turn out work which would reflect credit on some European and American craftsmen, who bungle, with every advantage upon their side.

Vines supply much of their cordage for common purposes, made to their hands. They manufacture very neat twine from hemp, the silk or fibres of the plantain tree, and the shells of cocoa nuts. The hemp and cocoa-nut bark is soaked, beaten, and dried before twisting. It must be cleared with the fingers, and is twisted between the knee and the palm of the hand. The fibres of the plantain and banana tree are very fine and soft, and are used only in the manufacture of sashes. They are drawn from the pith of the tree, and after washing, are woven into a texture which much resembles silk.[31]

Men make the twine, and use it, in the finishing of houses and canoes. Women plat the mats for sails, for clothing, and for the beds. The sails are very neatly woven of split rushes; the mat worn about the body is made of the tuft of leaves which crowns the cocoa-nut tree; they are bleached, and then strung together by the women. The mats upon which they sleep are made of rushes. The mat worn by the women is made of the bark of the cocoa-nut tree.[32]

---

[31] Twine is made principally from the inner bark of the hibiscus tree and from coconut husks—hardly from the coconut shell or bark, which produce no fibres. It was still made by the ancient technique of rolling on the thigh by hand in 1947, largely for fishing lines and nets and for lashing together the parts of the outrigger canoe. The so-called hemp and plantain twine (actually several varieties of *Musa textilis*) was not really a twine, the fibres being very loosely twisted together and used for the manufacture of the loom-woven sashes to which O'Connell refers. These sashes are no longer made but are common in museums.

[32] The so-called rushes for sails and sleeping mats are actually pandanus leaves. The men's 'mat' is a kilt of young coconut leaves suspended from a waist cord. It was still worn in 1947, having experienced a revival

For preparing sashes, or wywies, the women have a rude process of weaving. To a sailor it will be description enough to say it is something like weaving spunyarn mats; but for the ladies, a more particular account is necessary. The web, or threads which run longitudinally of the belt, are fastened to a post at one end, and at the other about the weaver's body, who thus keeps it straight. A stick is then passed over and under alternate threads across the web, and, turned upon its edge, opens them to permit the shuttle to be passed. With the same stick the weaver drives the thread to its place. In this way are manufactured narrow belts to wear beneath the mat, and gaudy sashes for ornament.[33]

---

because of the shortage of cloth in the post-war years. The woman's 'mat' was a wrap-around, waist to knees, made not from the coconut tree as O'Connell says but of either banyan or breadfruit bark; it was manufactured in the same way as Polynesian *tapa*.

[33] O'Connell describes here the horizontal belt-loom, widespread in the Carolines but no longer used on Ponape. The warp was wound in a continuous spiral around both beams, measured lengths of different colours being knotted on at predetermined intervals to produce vari-coloured panels on the face of the cloth—a surprisingly sophisticated technique which occurred only on Ponape and Kusaie. The weaver kept the warp taut by means of the back-strap. Omitted from O'Connell's description are the heddle, shed-roll, pattern sticks, and the warp-winding bench. The intricately woven and often beaded articles were primarily the loin-cloth, worn as O'Connell says under the kilt, and the sash, worn by men around the waist. (Incidentally, in Hambruch's translation the word 'sash' is given as 'Vorhänge', and in another place Hambruch refers to these articles as jalousies, then adds that they no longer existed in his time, 1910. Of course they never existed at all.)

CHAPTER X

The first care in making a canoe is to select a straight, clear tree. Then five or six persons attack the base at once with their axes, and fell it. If intended for two small canoes the trunk is divided, or if for one long one, trimmed only. The branches are lopped off, and the trunk hollowed out, rudely at first, the principal object being to lessen the weight. Vines are fastened to the

K

trunk, and taking hold of these, the laborers haul it to the nearest creek or shore, and it is towed to the canoe-house.

The first rough work of felling and transporting is done by the Nigurts. At the canoe-house the work falls into more skilful hands; petty chiefs, Moonjobs, and Jerejohs being the canoe builders. The outside is first made to assume something of the form and comeliness of a canoe, then the inside is carefully hollowed out. Four or five hands generally spend about a week upon a canoe; and after the shape is given, and the rough wood taken off, it is carefully and elegantly polished. This latter is done with coral; as many as can get about the canoe working at once, and lightening labor with a song. After the polishing is completed, a coat of red paint is rubbed inside and out with a piece of cocoa-nut bark, and the boat is placed in the sun to dry. Then a coat of cocoa-nut oil is put on over the paint, giving it quite a high varnish and polish. After the oil is completely dry, the thwarts and outrigger are fitted. The thwarts (seats) are all neatly worked with twine. The outrigger is made of two pieces of wood, extending over the side of the canoe about three feet, and three feet apart; these things regulated of course by the size of the boat. At the outer end of these pieces is fastened a long pole, parallel with the boat, and extending its whole length. Between the ends of the outriggers and the pole are stanchions, adapted in length to the depth of the canoe, in order that the outriggers may be as near horizontal as possible. Upon the two pieces is laid a platform, covered with mats, and protected from the sun by an awning, under which the chiefs sit or lie down. The platform does not cross the canoe; consequently the passengers are as little in the way of those who propel the boat as if they were on shore. On common occasions and excursions Nigurts manage the boat, but when they go to war no people of different castes are allowed in the same boat. The platform is capable of bearing from one to half a dozen persons, according to the size of the canoe, and the mariners, if I may so designate them, are in number from two to eight. Canoes are made in length from five to thirty feet. The canoes of the Nigurt fishermen are less finished, and the platform is barely large enough to carry a basket; being confined more to its original intention—the support of the outrigger. All the joints of this frame are ingeniously secured with twine.

A canoe is the islander's pride. They are very highly finished, pearl shell being worked in about the gunwhale, and the heads, as each end of the boat is the head by turns, are ornamented with a neatly carved billet of wood. The state canoes are always kept in the house, which opens toward the water; the boats of the Nigurts, and a few hacks, being the only ones constantly afloat. The wood of which all canoes are made is a strong white tree, bearing no fruit, and called in the native tongue kyup [kiop]. The sails are triangular, such as are called in the sailor's vernacular, shoulder-of-mutton sails, and are platted by the women of split rushes. A yard and a boom at the foot secures two sides of the sail, and the third side has no leach rope, the strength of the material rendering it unnecessary. In putting about, it is only necessary to shift the craft end for end, and make that her bow which was before the stern, as the outrigger must of course always be kept on the windward side.[34]

The paddles are made of the same wood as the canoes, stained red, and polished in the same way. Paddles made for use are plain, and kept in the canoe-house; but every man has one or more fancy paddles which he sports in processions and dances. These are carved and ornamented, and are never dipped in the water, but are kept in the owners' houses during their lives, and buried with them.[35] The platform of a chief's canoe is generally painted white, with lime made by burning coral rock. Mixed with cocoa-nut oil this makes a very good paint, extremely white and tenacious of its hold. The same mixture is an excellent cement for cracks in the bottom of a canoe.

Uneven as is the bottom of the basin inside the reef, frequently changing from very deep water to shallows of a few inches, the canoes, notwithstanding the labor bestowed upon them, are short-

[34] This is an excellent description of the Ponapean canoe and its manufacture, which is still followed. The 'pole' is the outrigger float. The red paint, now often replaced by commercial paint, was made from a red earth. The varnish was not coconut oil but oil from the nut of the *ais* tree (*Parinarium glaberrimum*). Pearl shell worked into the gunwale is unknown today and the ornamental end-pieces have disappeared. 'Kyup' (*kiop*) is not a tree but a spider lily; the most frequently used trees for the canoe hull are breadfruit, *Campnosperma*, *Elaeocarpus*, *Myristica*, and *Terminalia*, but other woods are used for other parts of the canoe. The sail was plaited from pandanus leaves; nowadays it is of cloth but retains the same lateen shape. Putting about is still done as O'Connell describes.

[35] These dance paddles are still used but are mostly made as curios for sale.

lived, seldom lasting more than a couple of years, the coral bottom grinding them through. The largest, used only on state occasions, last, indeed, longer, and decay of dry rot. Even then they are preserved, as are the regalia of royalty among civilized nations; but the canoes are infinitely more safe, because the reverence of the islanders for them is universal, and there is no cupidity to tempt to their conversion to cash, were it possible. There were canoes hanging in the house at Nutt, the origins of which were almost lost in tradition, and the age of which it was impossible to fix.[36] The smaller and more useful, when worn too much for the chief's pride, are passed to the Nigurts, who divest them of their ornamental frippery, as a gentleman's span of horses may be degraded to a barkmill.

The need for building returns periodically about once in two years. Three such jubilees—for jubilees they are—occurred while I resided upon Nutt. The permission of the chief first obtained, all the petty chiefs upon the island went to work, each at the canoe-house in his own district. When the building was finished, all the new canoes were brought to the head chief's quarters. The natives paddled them about, performing skilful evolutions to test the behavior of their new craft, Ahoundel, the head chief, alone standing erect. After an hour or so spent in this way, the canoes formed a line to the number of hundreds, and each chief, on his own platform, danced and flourished his fancy paddle, the whole assembly singing and keeping perfect time. Such are among the few occasions upon which any but women and priests sing. The day was wound up with a feast, and the usual draughts of jagow. The whole scene—the decorations of the canoes, the chiefs in their gala dresses, and the women on shore with their heads dressed with flowers—formed a pageant which I thought seldom, if ever, surpassed among civilized nations.[37] Then the universal hilarity and good order, the absence of all jealousy and quarrel-

[36] The large state canoes are no longer made nor are canoes preserved in this manner today.

[37] The canoe ceremonies, now long in abeyance, seem actually to have been held annually, not every two years. In each tribe every section, about January, became completely absorbed in the building of a new canoe of the large, elaborately decorated state type. The local section chief directed the work. People worked on the hull, outriggers, and end-pieces, and others prepared the vari-coloured twine for the decorative lashings. Still others formed bands of singers and dancers and practised

ling, for precedence, rendered impossible by the established order of castes and standing, is a feature in their rejoicings which the pomp of civilization never possesses. No individual distress or inconvenience follows them; there is nothing in the customs of the Indian to make it necessary that he should

> ———— *Defraud his daily cheer*
> *To boast one splendid banquet once a year.*

The belt of coral reef about the Bonabee group incloses a comparatively still basin of water. The canoe navigation of this is the most quiet and beautiful motion conceivable; much of the time the canoe is propelled by putting the end of the paddle against the coral floor, which is distinctly visible through the clear water. Fish are sometimes speared with great dexterity by the natives, the stillness and transparency of the water permitting the perfection of skill in thrusting the spear. This is the amusement of amateurs, the fish caught for food being taken in nets by the Nigurts. There are within the reef many places where the water suddenly deepens to many fathoms—interregna in the coral bottom, of various circumference. As well acquainted with the floors of their fishing places as with the floors of their houses, the Nigurts divide themselves into two parties, one party stealing noiselessly to the edges of this deep water, and there holding their nets. A method of walking in the water, peculiar to the natives, is worth description. The leg is lifted up straight and quick, bringing the foot almost to the surface of the water; then, the toe pointed as gracefully as that of a danseuse, the foot is planted again some two or three

---

for weeks, under teachers, and prepared the dance paddles, costumes, and other paraphernalia for the performances. In April the canoes were launched, with religious ceremonies. Any canoe not ready on the appointed day had to be abandoned where it lay, or destroyed, and the delinquent section chief was punished.

Despite the idyllic description given by O'Connell, there was a strong element of competition in the canoe races and canoe dances held between the people adhering to the two highest chiefs in each tribe, the Nahnmwarki and the Nahnken, to whom all the canoes were given, some to keep and some to re-distribute. The canoe ceremonies seem to have been in large part a form of prestige competition between the highest chiefs, the lower chiefs gaining merit, and favour in title promotions, in proportion to their success at the canoe building, racing, and dance performances, just as they still do in the modern feasts and other forms of competition.

feet in front of its first position. This method of progression offers next to no resistance to the water; consequently very rapid progress is made, without any splashing and splatter. The net holders stationed, the others, if possible, surround them in a circle, if not, as near as may be, and with their spears and legs create as much hubbub as lies in their power. The frightened fish make for the deep water, and are intercepted by the nets.[38] Fishing with lines is seldom attempted; as the natives are very unsuccessful with their rude tortoise-shell hooks.[39] I made some very tolerable hooks from the ramrods of the muskets preserved from the wreck; but it was necessary when a bite was felt to keep the line taught, as, there being no barb, the fish would otherwise escape.

So servile is the respect paid to chiefs, that a party of fishermen immediately suspend their work upon the appearance of a chief's canoe, scramble into their boats, cross their arms, and incline their heads in obeisance till the chief has passed them, then follow, and offer him a selection from their fish, if they have taken any. A neglect of this observance would subject them to severe punishment, probably death.[40]

Fish are plentiful, and a main source of subsistence; but I am neither Billingsgate woman nor naturalist enough to specify the varieties. The skin of the dogfish and shark supply the natives with a means of polishing wood and cocoa-nut shell utensils, and the shell-fish furnish utensils for cutting. The shark is seldom captured, and when captured it is in shoal water with spears. Upon every island some species of fish is *majorhowi* [*me sarawi*], or tabooed; and it is not unfrequently the case that different families upon the same island have each a species of fish which they may not eat.[41] The reason for this will appear in the account of their religion. As a proof that sophistry in reasoning upon religious points does not require a knowledge of the technicals of the science of logic, it is not esteemed wicked for a man to furnish another with food the consumption of which he esteems

[38] O'Connell describes here only one form of fishing. Many others are known.

[39] But trolling with a line was done anciently, using the bonito hook, a two-piece device made of clam-shell.

[40] These are but a few of the many forms of deference which must be shown to social superiors.

[41] This is a reference to clan totems—most, but not all of which are fishes.

profanity. When the spoil of a fishing excursion is landed, it is divided by species; he who cannot lawfully eat a particular fish turning it over to one who has no such scruples. Thus, as the indefinite restriction of Mahomet, who, in stating that

> "*There is a part in every swine*
> *No friend or follower of mine*
> *May eat,*"

neglected to specify the particular portion, has left his followers to go the "entire animal," all the finny salt-water tribe are devoured by the Bonabeeans. Even parts of the shark are eaten upon one island.

There is one species of fish universally held sacred by the islanders, a species of eel, inhabiting the fresh water. Keenan and myself had resided upon Nutt, and eaten at many feasts, beside the regular domestic fare, but in all this eating no eels had furnished their share. To our inquiries why this fish enjoyed such a peculiar and universal exemption, the only answer had been "Majorhowi!" This we knew was a partial defence for all fish, and not being aware that the respect for eels was more strenuously insisted upon than that shown their cousins the dwellers in salt water, we determined upon indulging ourselves in a feast upon them; taking the precaution, however, not to invite any of our copper friends to be of the party.

We selected for the occasion a fine night, and with elbowed sticks poked the fish out of the water at a sudden bend in a brook. Unlike the eels which were used to being skinned, these were not so much as used to being caught, and having enjoyed an immunity from the snares of the fisher from time immemorial, our trouble was in avoiding to take too many, rather than in catching enough for our purpose. Building a fire and broiling them in an unoccupied house, we had a sit down alone, and demolished them with an appetite which was not abated by the circumstances under which we feasted—the wise man having recorded his opinion that "stolen waters are sweet." Our feast finished, we wiped our mouths, as beseems those who have committed a secret crime, and returned to our island friends with all the conscious rectitude of rogues undiscovered.

Murder will out. We had neglected the precaution of concealing the bones, and, with an aptitude for detecting sin like that which characterizes some civilized people, who are supposed to

137

be innocent even of the knowledge of iniquity, some of the natives recognised in the bones the fragments of the forbidden fish. Our first intimation of the discovery was taken from seeing the natives repairing to the house, and, not at first understanding the reason of it, we fell in upon the tide. When we reached the hut, we found men, women, and children kneeling or completely prostrate, beating their breasts, and rocking to and fro, or rolling on the floor. Of the noise they made, we had been, of course, apprised by our ears before we reached the house, and had concluded that some accident or sudden death was the reason of the outcry. Nothing was there however—no broken bones but the bones of the eels; the pyramid of which, as George and I had left it, might indeed have caused cries of surprise that two persons could have left such testimonials of appetite; but as the aspect of affairs looked like an expression of something more than surprise, we esteemed it prudent to keep our own counsel. For two or three days was the lamentation continued; it flew from place to place and from hut to hut; on every side was weeping and lamentation. George and I thought we saw some looks indicative of suspicion, and when the bones were fairly buried by the chief's orders, and the hubbub ceased, we felt relieved from a load of fear which had been sufficient to give us a distaste for eels; which operated better for their safety, as far as we were concerned, than all the acts passed by the legislature of Massachusetts have done for the shad and alewives in Taunton River.[42]

---

[42] The logbook of the *Gypsy*, a Sydney vessel (microfilm in Dept of Pacific History, Australian National University), at Ponape in March 1841, states that the river eels 'are worshipped by the natives, and in such veneration are they held, that should they be caught and cooked on board ship and the natives get knowledge of it, every soul would directly abandon her with the greatest abhorrence'. The taboo against consuming the fresh water eel persists today, but at least some Ponapeans say it is because of the horrid, frightening appearance of the fish.

CHAPTER XI

Marriage.—Approbation of a chief necessary to unequal matches. —Marriage celebrated in canoe-houses.—Arrangement of the guests.—Preparations for feast.—Pounding jagow with peculiar ceremonies.—Expressing the juice.—Order of drinking.—Women averting faces.—Mode of building fires to cook dogs.—Mode of dressing and cooking them.—Serving up.—Carving.—Day ends with dance.—Paddles and music.—Breaking up.—Ceremonies of next day.—Priest's mummery.—Polygamy.—Connubial bonds.— Tattooing one cause of wives' fidelity.—Its meaning.—Different in different castes.—Conjugal spat between Mr. O'Connell and his wife Laowni.—Cause of it.—Manifestation of grief and rage on her part.—A disagreeable visit.—A relenting wife.—A vindictive husband.

If a man affects a woman, the rank of the parties being equal, he has only to obtain the consent of herself and her parents. Women are never compelled to accept as husbands persons whom they dislike. When a match is proposed between a Moonjob and a Jerejoh, the approbation of the chief is necessary, before the match can be ratified.[43] I have often known instances where this consent was refused, and the match broken off. I never knew a marriage between a Nigurt and a person of either of the two upper classes; and I never knew an instance of the occurrence of incestuous intercourse between the white castes and the black.[44]

It is one feature of the patriarchal government and habits of the islands, that marriages are celebrated in the canoe-house of the district in which the husband resides, and under the patronage and superintendence of the petty chief. The ceremony commences with drinking jagow, while the dogs are roasting and the other preparations making by the Nigurts. The petty chief is seated in the centre of the platform against the wall, and on his right hand are seated the bride and her female friends, their heads dressed with flowers. On the left are seated the bridegroom and his friends, dressed in the holiday decorations.[45] No paint is used upon the body on any occasion. The Nigurts never come upon this dais, except to pound jagow, or present jagow and food to the chief, but remain upon the floor in the centre of the canoe-house, where all the preparations for the feast are made,

[43] It is not political but consanguineous relationships that are here involved. It is still the practice, in modified degree, for parents to ask permission of the senior man of their child's sub-clan for that child to marry. Because the Nahnmwarki of a tribe (which is what O'Connell means by 'chief' here) would ordinarily be the senior man of his sub-clan, he would be the one approached for such permission by the parents of 'moonjob' (mwohnsapw) children, since such 'moonjobs' would be in his sub-clan. But permission is asked of him in his role of sub-clan head, not that of ruler of the tribe. Moreover, seniority of descent does not invariably coincide with political seniority. Relative age, military exploits, and expediency could result in a man receiving a title higher than that of a man senior to him by blood. Thus in 1947 the sixth chief of the first line of Net (the Nahnpei) got permission for his daughter to marry not from the Nahnken, who is in her sub-clan and the highest chief of the second line, but from the Lepen Net, who holds a lower title but is the Nahnken's consanguineous senior.

[44] Whatever O'Connell means by the word 'incestuous' here, while it is true that men of both chiefly lines (what he calls Moonjobs and Jerejohs) took their senior wives from the opposite line, it is also true that they did often take 'black' women, that is to say, commoners, as secondary wives.

[45] The reference to right and left hand is to the two side platforms of the canoe house. The couple did not sit on the main platform.

except the jagow pounding.[46] Meanwhile the guests keep up a buzz of conversation, for these islanders are far from being remarkable for taciturnity. All remain seated, the women on their heels, and the men crosslegged.

The jagow* root is pounded with peculiar ceremony. If either of the contracting parties be of the direct connections of the head chief of the island, the marriage is solemnized in the principal canoe-house. The jagow, whether from his own ground, or from the bridegroom's, or presented by the guests, is brought and laid at the chief's feet. Sometimes also sugar-cane is brought in by the women as they arrive, and placed at the chief's feet, all who approach him walking bent nearly double.[47] The chief then proceeds to cut the root of the jagow from the plant, in which he is assisted by the friends or favorites who are seated nearest him. Nigurts are then called, who take the root and carry it to a large flat stone upon the platform, but as distant from the company as the size of the dais will permit. From six to twelve[48] Nigurts then commence pounding it, the root and the stone having been first washed. Each has a small round stone in his hand, and all strike together. If a head chief be present the blows are given thus, in perfect time: one, two, three,—then a pause,—one,—another pause,—one, two, three. If a petty chief is the highest in rank present, the blows are one, two,—a pause,—one,—another pause,—one, two.[49] Thus carefully are the distinctions of rank

---

* Piper methysticum *is the botanical name.*

[46] Kava pounding on the main platform is very seldom seen nowadays. O'Connell describes here the 'early kava', which is prepared before the ovens are cleared away from the central, ground-level area of the canoe house, after which two rows of kava stones are set up to replace the ovens and the main kava preparation begins.

[47] The kava is brought by male bearers, often in singing and conch-blowing procession. If sugar cane is brought it is carried by women as well as men. Both are presented root foremost. The posture described is conventional in approaching persons of high rank, whose heads must always be higher than those of their inferiors.

[48] The number of pounders is usually, at least today, only four or five at each stone.

[49] O'Connell has given only a simplified version of the ceremony. There are other pounding rhythms also, which vary according to kind of feast, tribe, and who is present. The large, flat stones on which the

preserved by all possible means. After the root is pounded fine, water is thrown upon the mass, and it is stirred together with the hands. A quantity of it is then wrapped in a bunch of plant fibres, about a foot in length, resembling hemp,[50] and the juice of the root, or rather the water poured upon it and thus impregnated, is wrung out into a calabash. This is carried up to the chief by a Nigurt, who passes up the aisle between the men and women, and presents it to the chief, kneeling, holding it in both hands. He drinks, and passes it to the next in rank.[51] Every calabash is first presented to the chief, whether he drinks or not.[52] I must do them the justice to say they are generally very temperate; and although jagow forms a liquor very potent as a narcotic, it is seldom drank in quantities to stupify. When it is, a dead and stupid sleep of three or four hours is the consequence. It makes them loquacious when temperately drank, but seldom quarrelsome. The women never drink it in public, and while the men are drinking often avert or conceal their faces. It is *majorhowi* to all except Moonjob women, and as even their entire abstinence is considered a virtue, those who do take it do it very privately.

While the root is pounding, the chief distributes joints of the

---

pounding is done are propped up off the ground on coconut husks so that they resonate like bells when they are struck. A large feast, with many stones in use, all being pounded in the same rhythm, is an impressive affair.

[50] Actually *Hibiscus tiliaceus* bast.

[51] The bearer presents the cup, which is not a calabash but half a coconut shell, with only one hand. The hand holding the cup is supported by the crooked elbow of the other arm. This is done in a seated position, both legs bent to one side, the crooked elbow towards the receiver of the cup, the bearer's face lowered and turned away. But, depending on the type of occasion, more often the bearer hands the cup to an attendant, who then gives it to the chief in the conventional posture just described. Passing of the cup from one chief to another is not done. The cup is handed back to the bearer, refilled, then given to the next drinker. The motions of the hands in the use of the wringer, the footsteps taken by the bearer, his posture, the manner in which the cup is received—all are conventionalised and vary in detail according to the kind of feast being celebrated.

[52] It is considered good form to refuse the proffered cup occasionally and to direct that it be given to another.

142

plant among his favorites. It is eagerly coveted, and it is a mark of great favor to receive it, as the joints, set in the earth, take root. They are, however, ten or twelve months in coming to maturity; and as the culture is barely enough to supply the demand, it is a plant esteemed of great value.

While the jagow is being prepared and drunk, the preparations for the more solid parts of the feast are going on in the area. Fires are built of wood, covered with small round stones, like a pyramid. As the wood turns to coal, the stones fall in, and are heated to a red heat, forming a glowing platform. As soon as it has ceased smoking, the dogs,[53] previously killed, and their entrails extracted, outside the house, are brought in and the hair singed off. They are then scraped and laid upon a floor of the hot stones, and other stones are piled over them, the Nigurts handling them very adroitly with sticks. Over the whole are spread green leaves to prevent the escape of any steam, and in half or three quarters of an hour Pedro comes out of this impromptu oven, delicately cooked.

Baskets of cocoa-nut branches, made expressly for the occasion, and never used afterward, are then brought, into which the dogs are put; and the Nigurts carry one at a time to the chief, with baskets of yams and bread-fruit as condiments. The chief, with a bamboo knife, officiates as carver, distributing bits of the flesh to those present, and modestly reserving the quarter, the best part, to himself.[54] Dogs are seldom cooked in larger quantities than to serve as a bare relish to the yams and bread-fruit; and are usually provided at the expense of the bridegroom. The rest of the material for the feast comes in presents from the guests, every convivial meeting on the islands being a sort of pic-nic. The chief takes his tribute out of every dog, and carries what he cannot eat away with him. The Nigurts may occasionally get a dog's head thrown to them, but their usual share of such a delicacy is only permission to suck their thumbs. There is, however, always an

[53] Nowadays more often pigs than dogs. Dogs are pre-European; pigs were introduced very soon after O'Connell's time.

[54] If O'Connell is here describing 'Ahoundel', his father-in-law, officiating at a feast, that chief did indeed hold a low position, as we have already suggested. At most feasts there is an official food divider, who supervises the butchering and distributes the portions according to various conventions.

abundance of fish cooked. All the eatables pass through the chief's hands in their distribution.[55]

The feast finished, and washed down with jagow, the day winds up with a dance. The males and females stand opposite each other on the raised walk which goes round the house inside, the women upon one side and the men upon the other. The chiefs present remain upon the dais, the bride is in the centre of the line of women, and the bridegroom opposite with the men. In dancing they do not skip, run about, or change places; a foot square is abundant space for each person. They stamp with each foot alternately, bringing the right or left side forward as the foot is moved, and flourishing the arms. All have fancy paddles in their hands, men and women, and as they turn either side of the body to the centre of the building they strike the paddles together in perfect time, shifting them from hand to hand to keep them inside. All sing together, and to aid in the time a person is seated in front of the chiefs, on the dais, with a stick in his hand, with which he hammers time on the bottom of an old canoe.[56]

This dance is the breaking up for the day. What of the fragments of the feast are not carried away by the guests, fall to the Nigurts, who have been spectators from the floor in the centre of the building. The bride goes home to the house of her lord, or the house of the friend upon whom he is quartered. Presents from chiefs and friends, mats, wywies, tappas, etc. follow them, sometimes immediately, and sometimes after the interval of a month.

Upon the next day the newly married couple repair to the great canoe-house of the head chief of the island; not to the canoe-house where the feast was held the day before. There is another gathering of friends and acquaintances, and all seat themselves as for a feast, women and men apart, on the dais. A priest enters the house, and goes to a part of the dais as distant as possible from the company. He then makes a circle of a mat, about four or five feet in circumference, by setting it upon its

55 O'Connell has in this chapter given a general and rather sketchy description of the feasting pattern. It applies to all feasts, not just the wedding feast, although there is much variation in detail.

56 This dance is the *kahlek*, written 'gurlic' by O'Connell in the vocabulary, and is the same as the dance he previously described as done aboard canoes. The 'raised walk' refers to the two side platforms of the canoe house. It is surprising to read that women participated in this dance, for it is strictly a masculine dance today. There is another man's dance done without paddles and there are two women's dances.

edge, and walks inside of it.[57] His whole person is thus concealed from those present. The head chief walks up to his side, and a sort of recitative conversation is kept up between them for about a quarter of an hour. It is done in a voice so low, that the words are not distinguishable to the company, a low monotonous sound only reaching them, while they sit in the most subdued silence, their countenances wearing an aspect of deep gravity. I never was able to understand the subject of this mummery by listening to the words, or by inquiry, as all appeared to be in the dark, except so far that they knew it was a part of the marriage ceremony. A draught of jagow concludes it.[58]

The foregoing is a description of the marriage of a Jerejoh. Nigurts are yoked together among themselves with very little ceremony. At the marriage of Moonjobs, the feasting sometimes begins a couple of days before the wedding, and continues a day or two after. The feasting and preparations vary, of course, according to the wealth or standing of the parties.

I have said polygamy is common. A man may have as many wives as he can support, but the largest number I ever knew one man to have was eleven.[59] Concubinage and promiscuous intercourse is common among the Nigurts and lower Jerejohs, but very rare among the Moonjobs. The Moonjobs are morally superior to those beneath—superior in intellect and character, as in standing. Adultery committed by persons of standing is punished by burning, preceded by an infliction of torture upon both

---

[57] This is not the plaited floor mat but the sewn sleeping mat. This is a long, narrow mat made of two layers of pandanus leaf strips. The strips are laid side to side, the edges of each folded so as to interlock with its two neighbours. Other leaves are used as stuffing between the two layers, which are then sewn together.

[58] This description of the priest and his behaviour applies to all occasions when a priest officiated, not just to weddings. The 'mummery' that puzzled O'Connell was a dialogue in the form of question and answer, the priest, concealed behind the mat, being possessed on such occasions by a spirit, who spoke prophecies through his lips. The questions and answers had mostly to do with the fate of planned enterprises. Classes of diviners other than priests also existed and followed similar procedures. Living Ponapeans who recall witnessing these occasions describe an eerie whistling as the spirit took possession and a shaking and muscular rigidity on the part of its human vessel.

[59] The highest chief of Sokehs, ruling in 1870, is said to have had some thirty women in his harem.

parties too horrid and disgusting to describe. Among the lower castes it is unnoticed. During my stay upon the island I never knew an instance of its commission, by persons of note or standing enough to call for punishment.[60]

Polygamy, as already stated, is allowed, and yet there is no necessity for restraint upon the women, or the exertion of harsh authority over them. A resort to blows is seldom, if ever had, and the same odium that would attend such conduct here, visits it there. Of their children the islanders are remarkably fond. The little beings run naked for the five or six first years of their lives, and are the pets and playthings not only of their parents, but of all. Tattooing is commenced on children at about four years of age, the first marks being upon the back of the left hand. These first marks are made at the residence of the parents; at six or eight years of age the child visits the tattooing hospital, and again at different periods, until at about the age of eleven the tattooing is completed. The reader will recollect that in my case it was necessary to apply all these usually periodical inflictions at once. The art of tattooing Moonjobs and Jerejohs is a profession, confided to a few women—female professors of heraldry, for tattooing is the preservation of a species of heraldic symbols. The marks upon my body have often been read to me, being expressive of the names of deceased chiefs and Moonjobs. At the end of the catalogue the reader almost invariably adds,—"midjila! midjila! midjila [?]!"—"dead! dead! dead!"

The introduction of tattooing in this connection is not, as it may at first sight appear, a change of subject. While different methods of tattooing distinguish the two upper castes from each other, and from the Nigurts, who are only permitted to make a

[60] The information in this paragraph is directly contrary to descriptions of conditions in former times related by aged living Ponapeans. According to them a man of very high title could demand the favours of any woman he desired, and none could deny him, whether she was married or not. The Nahnmwarki, the highest chief of all, could even take a woman of his own clan, even a parallel cousin (who in the kinship terminology counts as a sister), whereas incest meant death to others. The adulterous wife of a high chief was usually put to death, along with her lover, but a woman of higher rank than her husband had sexual privileges similar to those of the high chiefs. A man of low status who was cuckolded usually had to be content with beating his wife, and punishment of her seducer, which he usually attempted if his clan was strong enough compared to that of the seducer, was in his hands only.

few awkward marks upon the front of the legs, tattooing also serves to bind husband and wife. On a Moonjob man's right arm two rings signify the names of the nearest deceased ancestors of his wife, if she be a Moonjob; and on the wife similar marks preserve the ancestry of the husband. In the case of a man who can afford a half dozen women, the ceremony is not so particularly attended to; but the women make it a point of family pride to cover their shoulders with the family tree of their husband.[61] The reader will perceive that this is a contract incapable of erasure, and could a woman be tempted to desert her husband, she would still wear the recollection of what she had been; the honors and name of his house, no longer a gratification to her vanity, but a memento of her fallen state. The generally kind treatment of her spouse—her fondness for her children—her religion, education, the traditionary lore, of which her body carries an edition, and to the glory of which as wife she is heir in her husband's right, are reasons sufficient why a Bonabeean woman should remain faithful and attached, although her return is but perhaps a decimal part of her husband's affections. Accustomed to polygamy, and unaware that in any country the wife has undisputed and entire possession of her liege lord, the Carolinean woman sees nothing shocking in the system of a plurality of wives. It were nonsense to assert that there is no jealousy and quarrelling—as it would be asserting a position contradicted by reason, and the nature of things. Even in Christian countries we often see that one wife is enough to quarrel with; and although early education had taught me better than to wish for more than one wife, it is not to be imagined that Laowni [probably *Liauni*] (such was her poetical name) and myself had none of the disputes which appear incidental to conjugal life. Upon one occasion, when I was sick, a journey was projected, as was the usual course with invalids. I, however, refused to be cured in such a way, preferring ease and quiet.[62] All the preparations having

---

[61] Nothing is known today of any connection between tattooing and marriage, except that it was regarded as a prerequisite to marriage to have had the full pattern applied to the body. (O'Connell omits from his description another prerequisite to marriage, namely the excision of one testicle on the part of males and the artificial elongation of the *labia minora* by women.) Nor is there any remembrance of use of the designs as heraldic symbols or of reading them as names of the dead.

[62] Taking sick people to new environments was practised to recent times.

been made for the journey, it was taken without me. I thought my wife might have had the grace to remain at home with her sick spouse, but she chose to accompany her father. Upon her return I had pretty well recovered, and I welcomed her by taking my wedding gift—a few blue beads—from her basket, and breaking them between two stones, before her eyes. As soon as I had done the mischief, Laowni ran from the house to a stone in the edge of the water, where she sat down and commenced crying like an infant. I followed, and endeavored to pacify her, but it was of no use. The only answer she made was to kick like a spoiled child. The tide flowed in, till she was in water to her elbows; then I was enabled to coax her away, but still she ceased not bellowing for her beads. If I had bitten off her finger, it would certainly have grieved her less.

At night I went to sleep and left her weeping. She had refused to eat, though fish and the most delicate bits of canine venison had been offered her. Happening, however, to awake at midnight, I detected her solacing her grief, not, like Mrs. Oakley, on boiled chickens, but like a delicate savage, on a dog's drumstick. I said nothing, thinking the return of her appetite was a good omen; but when I waked again in the morning clouds and darkness still sat upon the countenance of Laowni.

The day long she wore the same sulks, giving me an occasional look of any thing but affection, but not vouchsafing a word. At night I took George with me, and instead of sleeping in the canoe-house, which was then Ahoundel's quarters, went to his house proper. There we built a small fire for its light, and just as we had propounded to each other the sage conclusion that his Majesty of Nutt and family were not in the best humor, we were surprised with a visit from that dignitary himself, accompanied by a native who was particularly indebted to me for detecting him in stealing my knife, and two others, all armed with spears. Without saying a word they sat down at a little distance, biting their nether lips, as is always their custom when vexed or in a passion. I spoke to them, and inquired the reason of the visit, but received not a word in answer. George shivered beside me like a leaf, although I assured him he need fear nothing, as the visit was undoubtedly intended solely for me. At length our agreeable state of suspense was relieved by the appearance of Laowni, who beckoned them outside, and we saw nothing more of them. It was two or three days afterward before the reconciliation between myself and wife was completed, as I took it upon me, upon the most approved civilized plan, to become sulky when she relented. This lesson, however, taught me better than to trifle again seriously with the property or comfort of a wife, whose father might inflict summary punishment upon me without being amenable for it to any power. Such I afterward ascertained was the intention of the visit. Ahoundel left the canoe-house with a determination to put me to death, and it was the intercession of Laowni, who followed the party, that saved me. Upon the whole, the adventure had a good effect. Ahoundel respected the courage with which I faced him, though God knows it was as much in outward seeming as genuine; and respected the firmness which led me to maintain my ground, even after the threat of death.

CHAPTER XII

Priests.—Their rank—power—vocation.—Use of tattooing.—
Edyomet *a synonyme with* Aroche.—Jure divino.—*Island wor-*
ship.—Theory of mind.—Apotheosis of chiefs.—Native notions of
English printing. —Animan, *or spirits.—Metempsychosis.—Treat-*
ment of sick.—Incantation.—Fatal embracing.—Time and mode
of interment.—Perambulations of the ghost of the defunct.—
Yearly procession round the grave-yard.—Inheritance.—Strength
of custom.—Proportion of the castes to each other.—Journeying
for sickness.—Cure of elephantiasis.—Cleanliness.—Feeling pulse.
—Mr. O'Connell's calls to visit the sick.—Influence of his opinion
on the patients.

The priests upon the Bonabee group are Jerejohs, and rank as
petty chiefs.[63] Their profession is hereditary, and their support is
drawn from presents, for, though generally landholders, their
possessions are small. They are much respected, and are the con-

[63] The now extinct priests seem to have had a title series of their own,
like the two series described on p. 124 n. 25. Apparently only the higher
priests were 'Jerejohs' (*Seriiso*). The principal priest, the Nahlaimw, suc-

fidants and advisers of the chiefs. Tradition and the usages of
their religion have given them much power, and they also exert
a powerful influence through their interest with the chiefs. Called
upon on all occasions,—feasting, house-warming; canoe-launch-
ing, sickness, death,—present at all ceremonies and assemblages,
and in fine directing not only the public but the domestic business
and economy of the islanders, as they are main depositaries of the
traditions, it is their care to enforce the observance of all the
minute distinctions between castes and ranks. Tattooing, spoken
of in another connection as embalming the memory of the dead,
is an art essential, in its symbolical language, to the preservation
of the traditionary usages of the natives. Even the ornaments
worked in twine upon the walls of the houses assist in this main
object—the perpetuity of their tradition and religion. Every thing
combining to render the priests powerful as they make themselves
necessary, their name, *Edyomet* [?], is almost synonymous with
Aroche [?], chief; the terms are, indeed, often confounded. In
inquiring for the chief, or king of England, the natives used
Edyomet and *Aroche* indiscriminately.[64] Their ideas of govern-

---

ceeded to the secular office of Nahnken when the incumbent Nahnken died.
This title of Nahnken, sometimes called 'Prime Minister', is the highest
title in the second series of chiefs. The second highest priest was the
Nahnapas. These two priestly titles, which nowadays are secular ones,
were in the 1880s fitted into the second series of chiefly titles, in the second
and fourth positions in that line. Supposedly it was the Nahnmwarki of
Madolenihmw, 'King' Paul, who did this after the priestly functions had
lapsed. The other four tribes then copied Madolenihmw. Some lesser
priestly titles have also continued as secular ones.

[64] These two words do not occur in modern Ponapean, nor are they
recognised by present-day speakers of the language. O'Connell is
apparently the only person who ever recorded 'Edyomet' for priest. The
usual word is *samworau*, and there was a lower level of priests called
leiap. For 'Aroche', however, there is independent supporting authority.
Kittlitz in 1828 noted that Ponapeans, like Kusaiens, called their chiefs
iros, although the Ponapean form sounded more like *uros* to him (F. H.
von Kittlitz, *Denkwürdigkeiten einer Reise nach dem russischen Amerika,
nach Mikronesien und durch Kamtschatka*, Gotha, 2 vols., 1858, Vol. 2,
pp. 69 *et seq*). Horatio Hale, who interviewed O'Connell in 1837,
corrects 'aroche' to read *arōtç*. Hale later recorded information in
Honolulu from a man named Punchard, who had lived for a year on
Ponape; from him he got *li'rōtsh* as the word for noblewoman (Horatio
Hale, *Ethnology and Philology*, Vol. 6 of United States Exploring
Expedition during the Years 1838-1842, under the Command of Charles

ment connect the priest and the chief, as it will be found in tracing all earthly power to its primitive source that the original rulers claimed a direct mission from, or connection with, heaven. The reader will remember that in speaking of the Moonjob chiefs, it was stated that they claimed affinity with the skies; the term which defines their caste being also a term for the heavens. Great as is the power of the priests by their connection with the chiefs, it is but doing them justice to state that they attempt no increase or arbitrary exercise of it, and in their adherence to traditionary form, which it is their interest to press upon the people, is their strength. They are established—their dogmas and their power were never disputed, and it is therefore only necessary to assert their belief, and to permit the silent and almost imperceptible operation of their strength through the nominal, ostensible chiefs.

The whole theology of the island, the most singular imaginable for such a people, appears to be a worship of MIND, intelligence, or life. They appear to have an idea of its action, independently of the body,—to imagine it a separate and superior existence—a guiding genius over the conduct of the body. They have no temples, no idols, no altars, no offerings, no sacrifices; but worship a world of spirits, the disembodied souls, if I may so speak, or, more properly, the exalted minds of their dead chiefs. A chief's apotheosis takes place almost before his death; nay, invocation of his spirit commences before breath has left the body. The spirits of the deceased are supposed to hover in and about the scenes which, alive, they frequented. Aside from the general and universal worship of the ancestors of the chiefs and Moonjobs, each family has the worship of its own ancestry—its household gods or *lares*. When I told them of the Supreme Being they admitted his existence, although they never address prayers to him; but recognising such a power as the *Aroche lapalap*, great chief of their world of spirits, they persisted in prac-

---

Wilkes, U.S.N., Philadelphia, 1846, p. 83). These are obvious cognates with the Kusaien word, spelled in a variety of ways, and with the Marshall Islands forms usually spelled *iroij* and *liroij*, and we may accept 'aroche' as genuine, though obsolete today. (Hambruch and Eilers apparently regard the word as cognate to Polynesian *ariki*, but this is etymologically impossible.)

tically acknowledging only the power of the *animan*,* as they style their deified progenitors.[65] Of these, as the reader has already seen, the names are preserved by the practice of tattooing, no name of a living person being imprinted on the flesh. I have a vague impression that the surviving friends sometimes tattoo themselves upon the death of a connection, but am positive that it is not an invariable custom. The next marriage of a descendant, however, or the next regular tattooing of a youth, after a chief's decease, is sure to preserve his name. I never learned to read their marks, but imagine they must be something like the system of the Chinese, from this circumstance: before Miss Jane Porter was washed away in a rain-storm, many of the natives had learned the alphabet; that is to say, they "knew the letters by sight," but, counting large letters and small, figures, points of reference, points of punctuation, and every other printer's character, they gave us many more than twenty-four letters. When they saw these repeated, they signified that it was superfluous; they had no clear idea of the combinations, but said there was too much of the same thing, evidently imagining that each letter conveyed in each place one and the same idea.

To the *animan*, vested with absolute power for good or ill, are attributed all the good and all the evil which befal them. Every thing for which it is impossible otherwise to account is attributed to them, and all inquiry into things uncertain or perplexing is barred at the outset by the assignment of the sufficient cause, the agency of the *animan*.[66] Good comes from them in reward for good, and evil for evil. When I told them that worship belonged only to the One God, they asked me "how I knew; if I had been in heaven." Singular as it may appear, they have such an opinion of the whites, gathered from the specimens of their superiority which they had seen, and from the distance which they supposed their white visitors traversed to see them, that they thought the possibility of the whites having visited

---

* *Upon the Ladrone islands, where a similar worship prevails, the term is stated to be* anita *by geographers.*

[65] This paragraph is a fair description of the native religion. But not all gods are ancestral beings. Some, known as *enih-wos*, are said to have existed always.

[66] But there is also a strong belief in witchcraft as a source of ill.

heaven was probable enough to tempt the question. My answer, no, of course, would put us on an equality again as to what we had seen, and when I referred to "the Book" in proof of my assertion, they sneered at once at the admission of such scanty evidence—such repetition of the same letters, such abundant poverty as the doubling and trebling the same marks to infinity, for the sole purpose, as they thought, of display!

Engrafted into their worship of mind is a rude system of metempsychosis. The species of eels, celebrated in chapter ten of this work, furnish the favorite residences of the superior *animan*, and are universally venerated. It must not be supposed that they worship the fish, although a superficial observer might so imagine; and the preservation of the distinction between the worship of the animan and their visible representatives is creditable proof of their sagacity, and of the industry of their priests in their vocation.

As among all savages, the priests are also doctors; and almost all their remedies are spells and incantations. They have, to be sure, as a universal specific, a mixture of cocoa-nut oil and curry. The dose is measured and mixed in the palm of the doctor's hand; and is administered externally as well as internally, the whole body of the patient being smeared with it.[67] This uniform prescription for all diseases serves better for savages, whose ailments are all of a similar type, proceeding from similar causes, than the specifics of the British Hygeian College of Health can possibly serve for the thousand diseases which flesh is heir to under the abuses of civilization. The natives generally attain a good old age; and even if a patient does occasionally slip his wind under the simple quackery of the priest, we must forbear to censure *his* practice, till the civilized world shall cease to build up the fortunes of empirics, by buying one nostrum for all diseases.

The Edyomet sits beside the mat of his patient, with his legs crossed like a Turk or a tailor, rubbing his hands slowly upon

[67] Though the priests are extinct, there are still many healers (*sounwini* and *kedinwini*, male and female practitioners) who know a great number of specifics for different diseases, mostly concocted from plants. The mixture of coconut oil and 'curry' (turmeric powder) described by O'Connell, widely used in the Caroline Islands, is not really a specific but is regarded simply as being healthful and strengthening when applied to the body.

each other, and upon his legs, alternately, after the manner of a "Pease-porridge-hot" solo, with variations. This motion is accompanied with a solemn chanting, the burden of which is a guttural "e-e-e-ah!" "o-o-o-ah!" commenced slow, and snapped off short, as the hands reach the knees, or are taken apart. The subject of their chant is, of course, a particular supplication to the tutelar genius of the sufferer, and to the whole family of genii incidentally.

The sick-room is always crowded with the friends of the patient, and air is carefully excluded. He is pronounced dead as soon as he ceases to notice those about him, but before respiration ceases. As soon as it is supposed that the seal of death is set, a pyramid of bodies is formed upon the dying person, by those present, who throw themselves upon the body, each anxious to embrace, or, at the least, touch some part of it. There is usually a furious struggle, those in the rear catching the first who throw themselves upon the mat by the heels and pulling them back. The poor sufferer, beneath this living hecatomb to his memory, must die of suffocation. During all the time a deafening howl is raised by the whole company, something after the manner of the Irish, only that Hibernians have the grace to wait till a man's breath is out of his body before they commence to "wake him."

After this first rude embracing has ceased, the patient is usually entirely dead; but cases have occurred, I am compelled to believe, when sufferers, still living, have been buried. Before burial, the defunct is made to leave "p. p. c. cards" at the houses of all his connections and friends in the village, being carried from hut to hut on the shoulders. At each house the procession tarries about ten minutes, and the same outcry is made as in the dying room. It is the invariable custom to bury the body before the next sunset; unless death occurs within a **very short time of night, in** which case the interment is postponed to the next day.

With no other protection for the body than a roll of mats, it is buried about three feet below the surface of the earth. All the persons present, except those who place the body in the earth, remain in a sitting posture, and weep and howl till the body is covered, when they leave the spot. The season of *active* mourning lasts about twelve days. On some of the islands in the group

155

there are stated places for burial;[68] on others, the dead body is buried near the hut which it occupied while living. If a male, a paddle from his canoe is buried with him; if a female, her spindle or distaff.[69] Over the grave a small hut is built, in which the nearest surviving relative sleeps for five or six nights; after which it is taken down: a beautiful proof of affection in its holiest simplicity! The mourners, male and female, except chiefs and their families, cut off their hair, but do not maim or disfigure their bodies.[70]

Another part of the ceremony is a piece of mummery got up by the priests—no less than a personation of the character of the ghost of the deceased, by one of their number.[71] Be the dead male or female, old or young, his ghost was invariably of the masculine gender, and of years enough not to be frightened should he meet a brother ghost in the night. This personage parades the village for five or six nights after the burial, with a spear in his hand. There is no pretence that the walking gentleman is *indeed* the spirit of the departed; it is a sort of testimony of respect to the memory of the deceased.

There is upon the island of Nutt a grave-yard.[72] It stands upon the shore, so near the water that at high tides it is flowed; it is inclosed by a strong stone-wall, and filled with cocoa-nut trees, the fruit of which is seldom if ever disturbed. It is a custom to plant over each grave a cocoa-nut tree, and, beside the paddles buried with the deceased, to lay one or more near his grave. Once a year, at low tide, these were taken out, each by a descendant of the former owner, and all the inhabitants of the island walked in procession round the inclosure. The procession bore no funeral aspect; the persons forming it were decorated with flowers, and in their gala dresses, and flowers were placed

[68] A number of stone structures containing human remains survive today. They are mostly large rectangular chambers, constructed of basalt prisms, but some are small and dome-shaped.

[69] And other personal belongings.

[70] Part of the mourning behaviour also included the feigning of madness, running about wildly, besmearing oneself with filth, and the loosening of normal inhibitions generally. Virtually none of the practices described by O'Connell survive.

[71] Nothing is known of this custom nowadays.

[72] This does not exist today. The burial practices described in this paragraph are unfamiliar to modern Ponapeans.

upon the graves. This ceremony, like all others, is under the superintendence of the Edyomets, and in the procession they walked next the Moonjobs. Thus does every part of the conduct and observances of the islanders tend to a reverence for ancestry; and the strength of the government is so based on hereditary rank, and perfect order and observance of precedent, that nothing less than an entire change in their religious belief and in their customs can produce a revolution. The custom of burial in yards is only practised upon Nutt and two other islands in the group; upon all others, and even upon Nutt in isolated instances, the patriarchal custom of laying a man down in his own "field" being preferred. The usual time of mourning is about a month, and during that period there is every day a stated hour for weeping—that upon which the friend died.

The order of succession to the property and rank of the defunct has already been spoken of. With his estate the heir inherits the incumbrance of the maintenance of the former proprietor's wives, children and dependents. No court of probate, no legal quarrels ensue. Where each man is, in a sense, a lawyer, and perfectly acquainted with the condition of the deceased, and the simple rules by which his effects are to be arranged, there is no possible manner in which a person can disguise fraud in attempting to take possession of what is not his by inheritance. It is seldom if ever attempted; being a crime not only against the individual wronged, but against the whole island population; having a tendency to subvert and undermine the institutions over which Moonjobs, Edyomets and Jerejohs watch with jealousy.[73] The proportion of the white or upper classes is as eight in twenty of the population; the other twelve being Nigurts, or slaves. Of the aristocracy one in eight are Moonjobs, and of the Jerejohs one sixth are priests. With the advantage of power, tradition, and superstition on their side, the priests and Moonjobs easily control the Jerejohs, who derive whatever power they possess from the same order of things that places another class still above them. The knowledge that union is necessary to control the

[73] Nevertheless, at least in later times, a state of lawlessness might follow the death of a Nahnmwarki. The missionary reports of the 1850s describe general destruction of coconut trees, yams, and dogs at the place where a high chief had just died, and to some degree elsewhere too. His lands and other property would be taken and divided up among the other chiefs, usually in an orderly way along matrilineal principles, but

slaves, and of the fact that the priests represent their order in the government, makes the Jerejohs assist in maintaining a system, the least infraction of which would set an example to the Nigurts, ruinous to their masters.

To return to the treatment of the sick. It is a common and very judicious mode of commencing the course of island practice, to remove the sufferer from place to place by the canoe, in easy stages, and try upon him the effect of change of air and scenery, while he can yet bear the journeying. This course is, in very many cases, a preventive of fixed disease, and is infinitely better than to wait until a complaint becomes seated, and then travel, when the only object possible to be gained is its amelioration. I am unable to describe the different characters of all the island diseases, or even to enumerate them by their native names. The variety is, however, small. The fevers generally are similar, and of the diseases peculiar to civilized countries they have none, of course. Elephantiasis, or something very like it, is sometimes seen upon the islands, and the remedy the natives universally apply is worse than the disease. It is their practice to pass a stick burned to a coal, and all alive with fire, over the affected limb, keeping it near enough to scorch, but not actually touching the flesh. Eruptions of the skin of the face, and soreness of the mouth, frequent during some seasons, I attributed to their practice of eating bread-fruit, which, deposited in the earth for keeping, had become impregnated with some mineral or other poisonous quality.[74] Their food is simple, and their scrupulously cleanly habits

---

sometimes a rush was made by all to seize whatever movables they could. This was true sometimes after a commoner died too; his balls of twine, his mats, sometimes even his house would be appropriated and the widow turned out. Perhaps these descriptions apply only to the abnormal conditions which prevailed after the smallpox epidemic of 1854, when the population was reduced by half and the power of the chiefs was much weakened. But even in O'Connell's time the dead chief would be buried immediately and in secret and the ordinary people would not learn what had happened until they were summoned to the feast in the canoe house and saw the new incumbent in the place of honour on the main platform; the purpose of the secrecy being to avoid the general anarchy and the excesses of behaviour which might otherwise have followed.

[74] This is preserved pit-breadfruit, eaten when ripe breadfruit is not in season, and prepared in this way in many places in the Pacific. The breadfruit becomes somewhat fermented but as the pit is lined with leaves it is doubtful whether minerals from the soil could affect it.

and frequent ablutions are sufficient almost to insure an immunity from disease. Twice or thrice a day, men, women and children of the upper castes bathe themselves. For cleanliness they bathe in fresh water, each caste having its own bathing place, into which it is a crime for one of a lower order to step. When swimming they do not move in the water like us, but take the dog's short paddling for a model.

After I had some time resided with them, I happened accidentally to feel a sick man's pulse. This was noted by the observant natives, and I was called upon to explain what it meant, and why I did it. I gave them the best illustration in my power, beating time to show them how fast the pulse should beat, and telling them that any thing faster or any thing slower was "no good." The beating of the pulse at the wrists was a remarkable discovery to them; all the old women, and indeed all the young, made a dive at the wrists of every one when first suspected of ill health. Once on the scent, they followed it, and detected the throbbing of the temples; so if there was not room enough at the wrists for all examiners, a portion would settle on his head. It was really amusing to see how like civilized people they could ride a hobby to death. Inquiries ceased. As phrenologists are said to read a man's whole character without other data to proceed upon than the external developments upon his head, so the native professors of the new art of pulse-feeling wished only to find rest for the finger on the patient's body. He or she would find rest only when the tormentors were asleep; the sleep of the patient being of too little consequence to interrupt the medical examinations of the thousand friends.

An islander sick is an object ghastly enough. With the smearing I have described, his original sallow face is resplendent in ghastliness. The accompanying objects, the gloomy visages of the attendants, and their howling and moaning, give such scenes a character gloomy as the most inveterate old-lady lover of sorrow, rendered doubly sorrowful by exaggeration and anticipation, could desire. If possible, I was always called to pronounce whether a patient would live or die; and by caution in pronouncing judgment, and care in forming it, my word, as I gained experience, was considered with the islanders life or death to the patient. By a favorable opinion, confidently pronounced, I question not I saved many lives, as the natives would redouble their efforts when hope was encouraged, and the patient's imagination, thus relieved, would assist the recovery.

CHAPTER XIII

We have already remarked that the natives have a very accurate ear for music. The priests have their religious howlings, but other men seldom sing, except to relieve labor, or while dancing. In hollowing out a canoe, the workmen strike together, singing the while; and in polishing there is the same attention to concert in motion. The oarsmen, or rather paddlemen, in canoes move together to songs. There are however no war songs, other than such as a civilized nation may have, commemorative of the feats of countrymen in arms.

The women are very fond of singing, and do not, like the men, confine their vocal exercises to labor and dances. A favorite arrangement is to seat a hundred or more in the canoe-house, with strips of dry, strong bark from knee to knee, on which, at certain points in the song, they strike their hands together, the men remaining silent auditors.[75] The subjects of these songs were, their ancestors or the *animan*; the stars and constellations, of which the natives are attentive watchers, and for which they have names; their bread-fruit, dogs, fish; and sometimes they would chant for hours a bare catalogue of the names of their chiefs and their possessions. One song I recollect celebrated the barking of a dog on board of some vessel which had visited them. So simple a circumstance was an event, as the reader is already aware of their affection for the canine race. The figure-head of a vessel which had drifted ashore, and was preserved by the natives in the canoe-house at Nutt, was the subject of another song. It was a bust of a female figure, and along with it they had stored the arm of a figure broken, probably, from the stern ornaments of some vessel. Another was the commemoration of a man riding a dog, which, upon my inquiry, proved to be Neptune, or some other ancient worthy, figuring with his establishment on a vessel's stern.

Singing is, like tattooing, an important method of perpetuating the history and fame of the island, ancient aristocracy, religion, and traditions. In general character tending to the perpetuity of their institutions, there are still songs in which the lighter matter of love is introduced; but these are for convivial meetings of a few—private jagow bouts. The musical instruments in use are only two, and rude in make—a drum, and a description of pipe, or fife. The drum is made by stretching a fish-skin over a hollowed log, and the fife has three finger holes, and is blown by the nostrils, instead of the mouth of the player.[76] For war trum-

[75] In modern times this women's dance consists of a row of women, seated side by side, with a long plank or planks laid across their laps, on which they strike in unison two small sticks, one held in each hand, to accompany their singing.

[76] The drum, now extinct, was made in hour-glass shape, and the head was of shark or ray skin. An identical drum was found also in the Marshalls, Kusaie, and some of the atolls of the eastern Carolines.

pets they use shells, or conches. My comrade Keenan's instruments were, beside these, as a German flute to a penny whistle, and the admiration of the natives at his "execution" was unbounded.

Night dances in the canoe-house were without other light than that of the moon or the stars, entering at the large door. Standing up in rows, as has already been described, their dancing was mere stamping in time to the singing, and the precision with which they struck together their paddles was truly astonishing. Moonlight nights were always improved, if not for dancing, for singing. The natives are passionate admirers of the study of the heavens, and will even sit alone and watch some particular star.

These are indeed a happy people. War, as in all primitive nations, is with them an occasional occupation and a glory, but it is by no means a propensity; occurring less often than among nations who have the technicalities of written treaties to quarrel about. The government, while it is exact and unchangeable in its requirements, being secure and based on the habits of the people, offers them no unwelcome innovations, and finds few bad subjects. Prompt in the visiting of punishments upon all offenders, however powerful, the idea of resistance to it seldom is conceived; but when conceived, the whole strength of the people goes with the chiefs to suppress it. The government is an oligarchy, where the power is so divided and subdivided that some chief can take cognizance of every man's conduct; and minor faults are punished by the petty chiefs as soon as committed. A dig in the flesh with a shell, a blow with a stone from a sling, or a knockdown with a club, the offender daring not to resist, tells the whole story of trial, conviction, and punishment. No petty chief can inflict death; and all the worse crimes, except adultery, are punished by crushing the head with stones, burning the body of the executed malefactor and strewing his ashes to the winds, or by throwing his carcass to the dogs.[77]

In character, after about five years' residence with them, I pronounce them hospitable, sagacious, and benevolent. Vindictiveness of character is no more a universal trait of their character than of any other nation living between or about the same

[77] In later times one or two cases of burning alive occurred, but the customary method of execution was by clubbing or spearing.

degrees of latitude. They are tidy in appearance and in thought, affable and pleasant in manners, delicate in conversation before women and children, and critical in their knowledge, so far as it goes, particularly in their pronunciation of the language. They are accused, in common with other South Sea Islanders, of being thievish. As far as these people are concerned, I can answer for them, that they have not even an idea of barter. The land is parcelled out in "entails," and is nominally the property of its holders, but no person would go hungry by another's food, and, except trinkets and little valuable articles of "personal property," no one would think of withholding his possessions from the needy. They, like all other people, value articles by the estimation in which the owner holds them; and deeming that such things as they most covet are held, on account of their abundance, in least esteem among the English or Americans, they take them, as a miser would appropriate a pin, a button, or a nail, in the street. I have asked them the question why they stole from vessels, and have found it difficult to convince them that such conduct was more than a trifling error—a mere taking of a "liberty." They reasoned that their visiters have every thing in useless abundance, and every thing better than themselves, and could not miss what was taken; judging it no more difficult for ships to replace articles lost, than for themselves to obtain any island commodity. The restitution to myself and comrades of our little property, even to our knives—jewels in their sight—is proof of their honesty where they are sensible of the need and justice of such a virtue. I do not say that there are not exceptions, that they are without exception this excellent, conscientious people, as I had myself a difficulty with one Namadow [*Nahn-madau*, 'Lord of the Ocean'], a Jerejoh fellow, who stole my knife. Ranking as a chief, I took restitution into my own hands, striking him when I saw the knife in his possession. Though he dare not resent the blow, he held the stolen property, till Ahoun-del compelled him to restore it.

In person the Moonjobs and Jerejohs are about what we call the "middle size," and erect in their persons and carriage, except when ceremony requires abasement. In features they resemble the Mongolian race, having high cheek bones and broad faces. The hair of males and females is black, long, and flowing, and softer than is usual to Indians. Upon the head both sexes wear a conical hat, with no rim.[78] The men wear a mat made of bleached cocoa-nut leaves, strung together. Beneath it is a sash of soft fibres wound about the waist and loins, and over it a sash of gaudy red, the quality and arrangement of it denoting rank. The women's dress is a much closer mat, manufactured with care and skill from the cocoa-nut bark. Sometimes a "lagow" or mat is worn, like the "poncho" of the Chilians, on the shoulders, with a hole in the centre through which the head is thrust.[79] Passionately fond of flowers, the women wear them in their hair and in their ears, perforating the latter for that purpose.[80] The only pigment ever applied to the flesh is the oil of the cocoa-nut, with a little of some powder resembling curry;[81] and their very frequent ablutions prevent any thing offensive in this. Like all Indians they are fond of beads, and manufacture them from white stones,[82] found on the beach, spending a day upon one. They chew nothing like the "betel" of the Malays, but keep the teeth white and clean. None of these remarks apply to the Nigurts, who are as filthy as degraded; their dress is coarser, and their skin rough and unpleasant to the touch.

With these people, after George and I had become habituated to their customs, and learned to appreciate their character, we resigned ourselves to circumstances, and were content, in the absence of almost all hope of escape, to be happy. In about a year from our arrival, Ahoundel grew a little less cautious about our wandering; a forced remission of care, as we had become too well acquainted with the people to believe them all cannibals. Still he insisted upon our being frequently in his company. The difficulty with Laowni, detailed in a preceding chapter, my father-in-law's conduct in which he was, I suspect, instigated by Namadow, left my situation not quite so pleasant as before. Ahoundel seemed inclined to repair his harshness with over

[78] This conical hat, made of strips of pandanus leaves sewn together, is widespread through the Caroline Islands. It is usually worn for fishing.

[79] See p. 129 n. 32, p. 130 n. 33, for descriptions of all these items of clothing. *Likou*, a term which was later applied to any kind of cloth, here refers to the bark cloth from which blankets (see p. 110), the woman's 'mat', headbands, and this poncho-like article were made.

[80] Love of flowers persists. Both sexes wear them.

[81] Turmeric.

[82] Actually seashells.

affection, and it was with much difficulty George and I obtained permission to leave Nutt even for twenty-four hours.

Outside the reef which bounds Bonabee are two islands, one called by the natives Hand [*Ant*], about twenty miles distant, the other Pokeen [*Pakin*], about sixty miles distant. The latter, called on the charts Wellington Island,[83] is inhabited; Hand is **not. The inhabitants of Wellington Island** resemble those of Bonabee, except that they are addicted to cannibalism,[84] a practice which is unknown on Bonabee, except, perhaps, so far as tasting an enemy's heart goes. Hand is visited for its cocoa-nuts, which are very abundant. Keenan and myself visited it once, and found it bounded by a reef, through which there is but one passage. Beche le mer was deposited in large quantities upon the sand at low tide. We were detained by a storm longer than we bargained for, being weather-bound ten days.

Upon Wellington Island we remained nearly six months. The language was essentially the same as at Bonabee, the customs similar; the three castes of people also existed there. It is oftener visited by vessels than Bonabee, as the bits of iron hoop, an officer's coat, and other articles in the possession of the natives proved. Beche le mer and tortoise shell were plentiful; the latter in possession of the islanders, and the former neglected from an ignorance of the method and means to cure it.

The natives of Wellington Island are in the habit of frequently visiting Bonabee, bringing presents of mats, fruit and other articles; and it was upon the return of a party from Wellington that we visited their island. The inhabitants of Bonabee hardly reciprocate these visits, as their canoes are less adapted for the open sea than those of Wellington Island, and they are also less skilful mariners. I did not believe, till my visit, that the natives of Wellington Island were cannibals; then I had ocular demonstration. It seemed with them an ungovernable passion, the victims being not only captives, but presents to the chiefs from parents, who appeared to esteem the acceptance of their

[83] This is a confusion with the atoll of Mokil; see the Introduction. Ant, still uninhabited and still visited for coconuts, is part of the tribe of Kiti. Pakin, inhabited today by a colony of Mortlock Islanders, is part of Sokehs.

[84] This is a surprising remark. The people of Pakin at that time were identical to Ponapeans in every respect. Perhaps O'Connell witnessed some extraordinary and highly irregular event.

children, for a purpose so horrid, an honor. Wellington Island, laid down on the chart as one, is, in fact, three islands, bounded by a reef. One of them is inhabited, and the other two are un-inhabited spots, claimed by different chiefs, as if to afford pre-text for war, and the gratification of their horrible passion for human flesh.

Shortly after our return from Pokeen, or Wellington Island, our four comrades, Johnson, Brayford, Thompson and Williams, paid us a visit, as had been their occasional custom. At these meetings we sparred, danced, sung, and conversed in English, relating to each other our various experience and discoveries in the language of the people, and their character. The reader may well imagine we enjoyed these opportunities to revive old asso-ciations, and speculate upon the chances of our escape from Bonabee.

Upon this occasion my comrades proposed to George and me that we should leave Nutt, and spend a twelvemonth with them, dividing the time with the different chiefs with whom they were quartered, and devoting the first month to an excursion from island to island. This proposal was eagerly embraced by us. I had frequently expressed to Ahoundel a wish to the same effect, giving as a reason my weariness of the monotony of an abode upon one island, but he uniformly refused his consent. My visit to Wellington Island was protracted, by the strength of the north-east trades, much beyond his pleasure, and although I was an involuntary absentee, and of course not liable to blame, that long absence had so proved the need of my presence to him, that it made him averse to my going from his sight: a fatherly solicitude that was horribly annoying. Knowing therefore the certain answer to an application for leave of absence, I deter-mined to take liberty without. What I fancied a good oppor-tunity soon offered. Ahoundel and his whole household, and connections, launched the canoes for an excursion or visit. I was excused from the party on account of the presence of my friends, who declined accompanying Ahoundel. When they were fairly off, we stepped into the canoe, but had hardly got under weigh, when a rascally Nigurt, who had evidently been watching us, shoved his canoe off, and paddled before us like lightning, shov-ing, or rather poling his canoe over the shallows, and working like a windmill in a gale with his single paddle in the deep water. When he reached a creek or inlet, into which we knew

Ahoundel had turned, he shot up the opening, and we began to see his intention, and the meaning of the hoohooing he had kept up as he preceded us. In a few moments we saw the canoes of Ahoundel in pursuit. We used paddles and sail, and cracked on, esteeming it more a frolic than any thing else. As we had the start, and the canoes of the islands differ but little in speed, it was nearly two hours before they had neared us enough to be within hailing distance. They then commenced fair promises if we would stop, offering us fish, and bread-fruit, and yams, and using all the logic of persuasion of which they were capable. Still we cracked on; but Ahoundel's canoe at length shoved alongside of us, upon the weather or outrigger side, and we gave up the race as useless. My friend Namadow was the first to lay hold of the outrigger, and gave us the first intimation of their rough intentions, by endeavoring to capsize us. We hung to windward to trim the boat, and finding his strength ineffectual to upset it, he had the brazen impudence to climb on the platform with the intention to board us. In the heat of the moment I administered a settler with my fist, which knocked him into the water. Then half a dozen of the Indians laid hold of our outrigger at once, and esteeming it useless to struggle against such odds, we all jumped out of the canoe. Others of Ahoundel's fleet had by this time gathered around us, and the Indians commenced beating us with the flat sides of the paddles whenever we showed our heads. Our canoe was smashed to smithereens, and my comrades were allowed to climb into others in the fleet, without much beating; indeed, they were assisted in; but I did not fare so well. Ahoundel made frequent feints with his spear, and so did others, but not one was thrown, nor had any person any such murderous intention; as I afterwards learned their orders were to frighten and beat, but not to hurt: a consoling circumstance, of which I had not then the benefit, but considered myself a case. During all this time my father-in-law was upbraiding me with my ingratitude, reminding me of my rank, connections, wife, and the benefits he had heaped upon me. I protested my purpose was only to make an excursion with the intention to return. The paddle pounding had ceased after the first rude attack, and this conversation was carried on, or rather his scolding, while I was eyeing the spears, and dodging in anticipation of the expected blows. I made several attempts to climb into Ahoundel's canoe,

Fig. 9 O'Connell and Keenan, having left to visit another of their castaway shipmates on Ponape against the wishes of O'Connell's father-in-law, are pursued and taken captive by Namadow, O'Connell's enemy

but my particular friend, who had by this time been fished out of the water, rapped my fingers with his paddle as soon as they clasped the gunwale. The fleet, which had received additions from Nutt, of people who came out from curiosity, seeing the fray, now turned toward Nutt again, and Jem Aroche, Moonjob as he was, was fain to crawl into the canoe of a Nigurt, and return to the house of his father. My shipmates accompanied me, and Ahoundel, satisfied that I should not repeat my attempt to escape, proceeded on his excursion. I should have mentioned, that no women accompanied our pursuers, as the precaution was taken to set them ashore before the boats started in pursuit.

Three or four days passed before Ahoundel and his party returned. During that time I had ample opportunity for reflection, and came to the conclusion, that, considering the stealthy circumstances under which I left Nutt, the chief had reason for his jealousy of me. Nay, I could not help acknowledging to myself that my punishment was not altogether undeserved, as my treatment of my father had, to say the least, been unhandsome.

When the party returned, Laowni immediately sought me upon landing, as she had heard vague rumors of my adventure, and was not sure that I was not killed. She was overjoyed to see me, rubbed her nose against mine, (think of that for a method of kissing, ladies!) threw herself on my neck, and fairly wept tears of joy at my safety. Ahoundel himself made a sort of half apology, and excused himself by recapitulating the suspicious circumstances against me. Laowni was clamorous in her complaints of my treatment, and even appealed to her father by asking him how he would like such usage if he was a stranger in London.

Laowni questioned all the particulars of the attack out of me, and worked herself into such a rage with Namadow, the friend who struck my hand, that she ran up to him, and struck him with her codjic [kesik?], or small wooden knife. It was a severe blow, too, she dealt him, doing her savage notions of friendship more credit than her sex. He had no refuge but flight, being a Jerejoh; and the others, who had been busiest in abusing me at the time of the encounter, noticing the reconciliation with Ahoundel, did not afterward venture into the canoe-house when I was present, till they imagined they had propitiated me with

169

presents. Ahoundel was much better pleased with Laowni's attack upon Namadow than I was. He called her "brave" for it; not exactly to her face, but as any father among us would rather commend than regret the pranks of a spoiled child; for such was Laowni, his only daughter.

CHAPTER XIV

Kissing is the universal token of affection, every nation under
the sun having some variety of the interesting ceremony; and
even the brute creation show some indications that the practice
is not the exclusive attribute of reason. The dog kisses his master's
hand or face, in his own way; and there are lovers of horseflesh
who would challenge one who should assert that there is not a
horse-kiss as well as a horse-laugh. The modern Greek belles

kiss with their eyelids; the Spanish coquette kisses her fan from the balcony; our own damsels, British or Yankee, have an honest meeting of lips with the person saluted. The ancients were in the habit of throwing their kisses to the moon or stars; the Laplanders press their noses firmly together; while many of the South Sea Islanders, and among them the Bonabeeans, are content with a gentle, titillating, thrilling meeting of the nasal protuberances. Thus it was, as stated in the last chapter, that Laowni saluted me after my escape from the tender mercies of Namadow; but the reader is, perhaps, arguing from her rude treatment of that person that her temper could not have been uniformly gentle. Namadow was so severely wounded by her, that his death, occurring within a couple of months, was attributed to the combined effects of his bodily injury and his shame at being punished by a woman.

"What a savage!" the lady reader will exclaim. Gently, gently, madam; have the charity to suspend judgment till you have heard my plea in extenuation. Let us look for parallel examples among civilized nations; in royal families first, if you please, for was not Laowni a princess? Elizabeth of England boxed the ears of the Countess of Nottingham on her death-bed, for causing the death of a favorite. Shall we say that Christian England, in the days of good Queen Bess, was less civilized than pagan Bonabee? The death of Mary Queen of Scots; the death warrants signed by Mary of England; the female influence in the Massacre of St. Bartholomew; the ladies who formed applauding portions of the spectators of chivalric combats of *outrance*; the ladies who, even now, grace the ring of admirers of the Spanish bull-fights; the women who looked on unmoved at the procession preparatory to an *auto-de-fe*, nay, who even witnessed the horrible immolation of the victims of superstition; —shall we, in view of these historical reminiscences,—not a tithe of what might be quoted,—denounce Laowni for an act which spoke the affectionate wife as clearly as the impetuous Indian girl, unrestrained by the influence of civilization? The same promptings of the heart in its warmth would, among us, only have induced a wife to urge her husband to legal protection and redress. Laowni had the law in her own hands, and only performed summarily what a Christian woman near the throne would have done by *influence*.

Our shipmates lengthened their visit some days after their

capture under the apparently suspicious circumstances of running away with George and me. Ahoundel had the justice to present them with a new canoe, the civility to invite them to prolong their visit, and the delicacy to restore their property so soon after the explanation, that their visit could not seem a detention forced by the lack of means to escape. Not the least interesting among our occupations and amusements on the islands was conversation with the natives, and watching the avidity with which they swallowed whatever we told them, and the dexterity with which they applied the information thus gained to the improvement of their arts; always excepting when it interfered with such part of their customs as were based on their religion. It was a practice with us to impress their minds with an idea of the power of the chiefs of England and America. We told them of musketry and of cannons, but never, with the guns in our hands, could convince them that those guns were the death-dealing engines, of which, from tradition, they had some idea. Our powder was all spoiled in the boat, before we landed.

In illustrating geography to my adult scholars, I drew, upon bark, a rough skeleton outline of America, large, a small spot for England, and to show them the comparative size of their own islands, a small dot. This however would not suffice to make them understand, till they inquired how many days' journey it required to go round America and England. To the first I assigned an indefinite time, very, very long—too many days to be counted. My inquirers would cluck, cluck, in astonishment. England (not to let her appear too insignificant) I bounded by a year's travelling, the name England comprising the three kingdoms. They would then revert to their own speck in the ocean, almost incredulous to the statement that other inhabited spots so much exceeded it in size. Small as is their territory, it is very thickly peopled, however. As it never entered into my head that, uncertain as was my escape from the island, my observations would ever appear in print, on this subject, as on many others, I am unable to give accurate information respecting numbers. *Emigration* is resorted to when the population becomes too dense for comfortable subsistence; a practice which is not peculiar to Bonabee over other South Sea Islands. When it becomes certain that such a step is necessary, a number of the natives, with their wives and children, take to their canoes, victualled as liberally as the boats will bear, and trust to chance for a harbor or a

173

landing. No such dismission took place during my residence, but my information was gathered from the statements of the natives, and is corroborated by the fact that canoes have been picked up at sea with natives in them. Upon one of the Bonabee group I saw and conversed with an old man, the last survivor of a party who came to the island, years before, exiles from their original homes. It will be readily supposed that emigrants are always from the lower or poorer classes.

Among other objects of curiosity on the group, we found one no less a miracle with the natives than with ourselves. It was a woman, from some freak of nature's, perfectly white. She was frequently visited by the natives of other islands than that upon which she resided, her fame being spread all over the group. In features she resembled the Mongolian, but her complexion would have been clear beside many European women. Pretty, she was upon that account visited, and, aware of her personal advantages, as proud of them as any regularly trained coquette.

Each of us having an island name, we returned the compliment by dubbing our hosts with titles, which they always remembered, and wore with much pride. My father Ahoundel I called King George, apprizing him of the rank of the potentate for whom I had named him. Wajai, chief of Matalaleme, upon hearing of the new title of his friend, made an implied demand upon my civility for a title also, intimating that, as the name of the great English chief was appropriated, the next in my disposal was that of the chief of America. As the American "chiefs" change periodically, and it was impossible for me, so far from any post-town, to see the newspapers, I christened Wajai, Washington.

Some of the islanders, seeing us at our famed old English sport, boxing, insisted upon an initiation into "the art of manual defence." In this some of them became quite expert, but few were philosophers enough to take a blow with entire good humor. They could never quite learn to love tobacco,[85] a few hands of which article, brought ashore in our bags, served us, with economy, for nearly a year. Fond of imitation, the women and children could imitate some of the most simple sounds of verses of songs which sometimes escaped us; and a few of the most

---

[85] By the 1850s the natives of Ponape, including children, were inveterate smokers.

common phrases of a sailor's vernacular they learned by their frequent repetition, and would repeat without always knowing their meaning. In sarcasm and the bandying of opprobrious epithets—in a plain word, "blackguarding"—they were very expert; generally, however, in good humor, as a quick perception of the ridiculous is a characteristic of their minds, untutored though they are. Seldom resulting in quarrels, these little altercations sometimes ended in the exchange of a blow or two with the small wooden knife or fish-shell. Chiefs, as before stated, deal summary punishment for all disturbances or infractions of order in their presence. I have more than once seen Ahoundel throw a spear or club at a native for merely standing or walking erect in his presence.

During my whole residence on the island I formed a part of the family of Ahoundel. At night we slept in the same apartment; the houses seldom having any division, except, perhaps, a small apartment for the storing of valuables. Mats were our only bed furniture, and these, removed in the morning, left the floor clean. During the night a small fire was kept alive for its light, in the place left for that purpose in the centre of the floor. By this a young girl slept, who occasionally replenished it. I have many times been awakened by the calls of Ahoundel to the girl when she had permitted it to go entirely down. In the large house the heat was not felt, of course, although it subjected us to some inconvenience from mosquitoes. The islands swarm with rats, which sometimes, but very seldom, are appropriated as an article of food; and the natives appear to have no means of systematically ridding themselves of so great a pest, though, as an amusement, they are sometimes dexterously caught with a noose. The little mischievous quadrupeds, emboldened by such a tacit immunity in mischief, run across the house in the day-time, as familiarly as flies; but at night their gambols were to me annoying, and almost frightful. They would nibble at the tough skin on the soles of the feet, and even essay the fingers. No kicking would purchase deliverance longer than while the foot was in motion; but I must do the little torments the justice to say that they dexterously avoided touching the quick.

Having spoken of the sleeping arrangements, the other furniture of the houses may be despatched in a few words. Beside the mats, there are only calabashes and cocoa-nut shells polished for holding liquids, and impromptu baskets made of leaves and rushes, and used only once or twice, for holding food. Then there are the baskets which are the exclusive property of individuals, made neatly and permanently, to contain the little et ceteras belonging to their owners—the shell knives, coral and fish-skin rasps of the men, and the beads, knives, bone-tags or needles, etc. of the women. The walls were hung with the paddles, spears, and clubs of the men, and the women's weaving apparatus. These walls are elaborately finished with twine, as is also the floor, the bamboo sticks in the latter being of equal size. No particle of litter is permitted to remain about the house, the cleanliness of the natives in every particular being wonderful. Through the centre of the building runs a row of upright posts to support the peak of the roof, all also grafted or netted with twine. The heavy cooking being done out of doors, or in the canoe-house,[86] there is too little smoke to stain the walls with more than a mellow brownness; not enough to conceal the variegated colors of the twine.

Day opens with bathing; a neglect of so necessary and healthy a custom being sufficient, if not to deprive the offender of caste, to degrade and subject him to opprobrium. Food is taken lightly and in small quantities, principally at the close of the day. The occupations of the males, beside those already stated, are the manufacture of lime from coral rock, red paint, beads, and other little matters. The weight of the labor, the reader is aware, is done by the Nigurts. Their children in their gambols furnished the natives abundant and interesting amusement, and their instruction, occupation and amusement blended. Night was the season for recreation—the singing of the women; conversation, particularly with us; dancing, or watching those women who are dancers, *par* excellence, almost by profession, being famed for their grace or agility; less however of the latter than the former.

Messages are sent from one chief to another by means of leaves of a particular tree, the points folded in differently to express different messages. I was led to notice this by some of the natives, who, noticing my attention to the Scottish Chiefs, produced a leaf, and folded it, to show me their method of "talking at a distance;" remarking of my book that it was "*lakya toto, mijiwid [lokaia tohto me sued]*,"—"too much talk, not

[86] Usually in a cook-house.

good;" their single leaf being "*lakya tic-a-tic macojalale* [*lokaia tikitik me kaselel*],"—"little talk, very good."

The leaves, thus folded, I never could learn to read, and in this obtuseness was behind the natives. Their messages would seem at first thought to be very limited in signification, but a reference to the volumes which may be spoken by telegraphic signals will correct such an opinion. Inclosed in a plantain leaf and secured by twine, one of these primitive letters accompanies donations of presents and demands for them, declarations of war and promises of submission; in short, all the state despatches. No earth, or arrows, or other palpable symbols accompany the message, the language of the leaf being systematically arranged and understood.[87]

The face of these islands is mountainous and the land rather rocky, the most common description being a bluish rock of a slatose formation.[88] Brimstone[89] is found in abundance; but of the mineralogical wealth or paucity of the islands I have obtained no data upon which to speak. The islands are well watered and fertile, producing spontaneously the bread-fruit, cocoa-nut, plantain, banana, and mangrove. There are beside a variety of nuts, and an inferior species of lime, or lemon. Agriculture is confined to the cultivation of the yam and jagow, the demand for and value of the latter rendering pains in its production necessary.[90] Naturalists all know how important a fruit is the bread-fruit, and its singular adaptation to the wants of the natives of the countries in which it is found. Fruit may be seen upon the same tree in all stages from the bud to dead maturity. It is gathered with a long stick with a forked end, with which it is twisted from the stem. When it ripens faster than it is consumed, it is gathered, parcelled in leaves, and buried in the earth, being first prepared by the removal of the rind and seeds. It will thus keep for many months, and the natives prefer it to fruit just gathered, kneading it with cocoa-nut oil before baking.[91] Wild flowers are abundant

[87] These messages went out of use during the last century, but a similar utilisation of folded leaves persists for augury.

[88] Basalt.

[89] This is mystifying. There are no sulphur deposits on Ponape.

[90] O'Connell omits from this catalogue of useful plants arrowroot, mango, pandanus fruit, sugar cane, turmeric, and three aroids which are cultivated—*Alocasia*, *Colocasia*, and *Cyrtosperma*.

[91] See p. 158 n. 74.

and gaudy in color, but generally possess little fragrance. There is one, however, a little yellow bell, which is an exception, being very odoriferous.[92] The women string them upon vine tendrils, passing the tendril through the bell, and thus make a wreath for the head or pendants for the ears, alike beautiful and fragrant.

Fruit is common stock, though an occasional wisp of twine or bark about a tree marks it *majorhowi*, not to be touched under the penalty of trespassing;[93] but yams, jagow, and dogs are private property, sacred to the use of their proprietors. The dogs furnish the only article of flesh eaten, save an occasional rat, and are much coveted and cared for. Women nurse the pups at their breasts in case of the death of the natural parents of the little canine infants; nay, I believe, in some cases, to prevent the impoverishment of the mother dog before a feast, when her carcass may be in requisition. Dogs are not valued for their docility or attachment to their masters; familiarity is discouraged; so that they may be pronounced generally most unsocial quadrupeds, and their "howl o' nights" is the most decidely unmusical I ever happened to hear. These, with rats and mice, form their only quadrupeds, and one common name, with the qualifying adjectives *lapalap*, large, and *ticatic*, small, serves for both.[94] There are millions of lizards, a sprinkling of centipedes, of which latter the natives live in some dread, but I do not recollect to have seen a snake. The reader is not hence to judge that there are none, but that they are not sufficiently numerous, or venomous enough to inspire terror, and thence observation.[95]

Among the birds, parrots and paroquets in untold varieties are the most common. There are few singing birds, and none very musical, the feathered race here, as in other tropical climes, being more gorgeous in plumage than musical in song. A species of pigeons,[96] larger than our wild pigeons, but otherwise re-

[92] *Fagraea.*

[93] This act of tabooing a tree is strictly speaking *inepwi*, taboo. 'Majorhowi' (*me sarawi*) means sacred rather than forbidden.

[94] O'Connell says the same thing in the vocabulary, labelling dog 'kitty' and rat 'kitty-ticatic', but this is an error. Dogs are *kidi* and rats and mice *kitik*, the qualifying adjectives, large and small, serving to distinguish not dogs from either rodent but rats from mice.

[95] There are no snakes.

[96] *Mwuroi (Ducula oceanica).*

sembling them; and common hens are plentiful. The first are, of course, indigenous; the latter the natives state to have sprung from a pair of fowls presented to one of the chiefs by some people with moustaches, who came to the island in a big canoe with one stick. They would seem to mean a sloop. It is possible that such a craft might have visited them from some of the eastern Portuguese or Spanish settlements, but I have concluded from their answers to my questions, unnecessary to repeat here, that it must have been a Portuguese or Spanish schooner. One stick would give a sloop no bowsprit; so that it is quite as likely to have been a schooner as a sloop from the description, and more likely from other reasons. This visit was stated to have been made about forty years before my arrival.[97] The natives will eat no birds of any description, nor will they kill them.[98] They are *majorhowi* to all classes. The cocks and hens are pets, preserved and fed as things of amusement. What is a little singular, we found the natives up to cock-fighting, though they were not civilized enough to make bets upon the fowls, or to supply them with weapons in addition to those nature has given. George and myself often killed and cooked a fowl, but though we sometimes persuaded the natives to put a bit of the flesh in their mouths, they would spit it out again with the greatest expression of disgust in their countenances.

Beche le mer, a sort of fish which is found upon rocks and the beach at low tide, and is cured upon other South Sea Islands for the Chinese market; and tortoise shell, form the principal articles for which these islands would be worthy of a visit in a commercial view, although I cannot undertake to say that they are the only available products. The only good harbor for vessels is at Matalaleme, and without a pilot that would be difficult and dangerous to reach. How safe it would be *now* for an unarmed vessel to visit them, the reader will see from a subsequent

[97] Rosamel (in Hambruch, 1932, I, p. 117) and Gulick, Luther H. ('Micronesia', *Nautical Magazine and Naval Chronicle*, Vol. 31, p. 175) both, in later years, refer to this introduction of fowls, occurring about this time but by a Chinese junk wrecked at Ponape. Yet the native name of the fowl, *malek*, occurs in the same or cognate forms westwards all the way to South-east Asia, suggesting a more complicated explanation of the introduction.

[98] Hambruch reported these same restrictions in 1910, but by 1947 many Ponapeans kept domestic fowls and occasionally would eat them.

part of my story. That they had been visited before is evident, both from the fowls and their traditions. That those traditions preserved some ungracious memory of the whites is clear from our first reception; that they are capable of kindness after they are sure their visiters are weak or harmless, our treatment from them can testify. During our residence we had succeeded in giving them a favorable opinion of Europeans and Americans; how that opinion was *corroborated* by the first vessel which had ever anchored in their waters within their memory, I shall not here anticipate my relation to state.

CHAPTER XV

After remaining restricted principally to Nutt for about two
years, George and I determined upon an excursion, cost what
it might. After an abortive attempt to get away in a borrowed
Nigurt's canoe, we obtained a larger one, and started. To avoid
suspicion it was borrowed, as launching one of my own would
have been attended with a parade that would have led my
honored father-in-law to suspect even more than was my inten-

tion. I had taken the precaution to note on a plantain leaf the names of the other islands and their chiefs. Five or six hours brought us to Chocoich [Sokehs], and upon nearing the chief's canoe-house George struck upon his fife, flute, or cudjong a lively tune, while I kept the canoe in motion. When we reached the landing, a host of the natives, many of whom had never before seen us, were ready to receive us. With Wajai, the head chief,[99] we remained one night, and were feasted and entertained. A like reception we met at other islands, which we visited in succession, occuping nearly a month in the trip. Possessed of the names of the chiefs, it was my custom, upon ascertaining the name of an island, to inquire for its chief, to whom I first paid my respects. George's flute and my looking-glass were assurances of good reception, as their fame and ours had preceded us.

Notwithstanding the representations of Ahoundel that we were in danger of being eaten if we ventured out of his sight, nothing but the most courteous treatment was received by us. My tattooing, speaking my relationship to Ahoundel-a-Nutt, was better than letters of introduction. We were frequently accompanied from island to island, and Nigurts were put in our canoe, to save us the labor of propelling it. During a month thus most agreeably spent we met all of our shipmates. These meetings were indeed the most pleasant part of the excursion, as the reader will well imagine. My friends were much diverted at the respect paid me on account of my tattooing; so far was it carried that the natives often insisted upon my shipmates sitting down, as a token of respect to Jem Aroche, *alias* Ahoundel-a-Nutt, *alias* James O'Connell.

But the most wonderful adventure made during the excursion, the relation of which will put my credit to a severer test than any other fact detailed, was the discovery of a large uninhabited island, upon which were stupendous ruins, of a character of architecture differing altogether from the present style of the islanders, and of an extent truly astonishing. At the extreme eastern extremity of the cluster is a large flat island, which at high tide seems divided into thirty or forty small ones, by the water, which rises and runs over it. It differs from the other

[99] The Wasai is the second highest chief in the first line of titles in each tribe, but in Sokehs for a period which included O'Connell's stay there was no Nahnmwarki and the Wasai ruled. See p. 123 n. 23.

islands in its surface, which is nearly level. There are no rocks upon it which appear placed there by nature. Upon some parts of it fruit grows, ripens, and decays unmolested, as the natives can by no persuasion be induced to gather or touch it.[1]

My companions at the time of discovering this island were George and one Nigurt, who directed our attention to it, promising us a surprise. And a surprise indeed it proved. At a little distance the ruins appeared like some of the fantastic heapings of nature, but upon a nearer approach George and myself were astonished at the evident traces of the hand of man in their erection. The tide happening to be high, our canoe was paddled into a narrow creek; so narrow that in places a canoe could hardly have passed us, while in others, owing to the inequality of the ground, it swelled to a basin. At the entrance we passed for many yards between two walls, so near each other that, without changing the boat from side to side, we could have touched either of them with a paddle. They were about ten feet high; in some places dilapidated, and in others in very good preservation. Over the tops of the wall, cocoa-nut trees, and occasionally a bread-fruit spread their branches, making a deep and refreshing shade. It was a deep solitude, not a living thing, except a few birds, being discernible. At the first convenient landing, where the walls left the edge of the creek, we landed, but the poor Nigurt, who had seemed struck dumb with fear, could not be induced to leave the boat. The walls inclosed circular areas,[2] into one of which we entered, but found nothing upon the inside but trees and shrubs. Except the wall, there was no perceptible trace of the footsteps of man, no token that he had ever visited the spot. We examined the masonry, and found the walls composed of stones, varying in size from two to ten feet in length,[3] and from one to eight in breadth, carefully propped in the interstices and cracks with smaller fragments. They were built of the blue stone which abounds upon the inhabited islands,

[1] These are the well-known ruins of Nan Madol. They consist of some ninety artificial islets, all square or rectangular, with canals between them. The construction is of coral fill, built up on the shallow reef to above high tide level, with the exposed sides along the canals generally faced with basalt slabs and prisms. On these islands are constructed walls, courtyards, burial chambers, house platforms, etc., again of basalt.

[2] Square or rectangular, in one case L-shaped, but never circular.

[3] Some are much longer.

and is, as before stated, of a slatose formation; and were evidently split, and adapted for the purpose to which they were applied.[4] In many places the walls had so fallen that we climbed over them with ease. Returning to the canoe, we plied our Nigurt with questions; but the only answer we obtained was "Animan!" He could give no account of the origin of these piles, of their use, or of their age. Himself satisfied that they were the work of *animan*, he desired no farther information, and dared make no inspection, as he believed them the residence of spirits.

Before the tide left our canoe aground we returned to Kitti, from which island[5] we had taken the Nigurt. Upon stating to Roan-a-Kitti,[6] the chief, my intention of inspecting the island upon the day following, he told me I ought not, that it was *majorhowi*. My rank, however, superior to his, prevented his assuming authority to forbid it.[7] He then endeavored to frighten me out of it, assuring me that the animan would not permit me to leave the place alive, if I intruded upon their sanctuary. Upon the next morning George and I absolutely struggled away from the natives to our canoe. They set up a howl in concert, "Acoa ban midjila [*O kowe pahn* . . .]! Acoa iningah landjob toto [?]! midjila [*O kowe inengieng . . . tohto*]!"—"You will die! You wish to look too much! You will die!" We pushed from them, and my rank, and their fear of the "majorhowi" spot, prevented pursuit.

Arriving a second time at this deserted Venice of the Pacific, we prepared for a deliberate survey. Having with us no native to annoy us with his superstitious fear and haste to return, we fastened the canoe, and staid upon the island till the next tide. For many successive days we repeated our visits, returning to Kitti at night. No native ever ventured with us after the first day, though one would think familiarity might have lessened

---

[4] None of the stones are split or otherwise worked. Their prism-like shape is naturally produced, by scaling off cliff walls.

[5] Kiti is not an island; it is almost entirely on the mainland.

[6] Given as Roun-a-Kitti on p. 123. But in neither form does such a title exist. Rohnkiti is the name of a section of the tribe of Kiti, and the high chief of Kiti probably lived there at this time.

[7] O'Connell's title, given to him in Net, would have given him no authority in Kiti, even if it were as high in rank as he pretends it to be.

their awe, as, at low tide, one might walk from Kitti to the haunted spot; indeed, it is considered a part of that island.[8]

These explorations were sufficiently interesting to engross all our thoughts. Nothing during my residence on the Carolines was productive of so much deep yet vague speculation. The immense size of a portion of the stones in the walls, rendered it impossible that they could have been placed there without some mechanical contrivance superior to any thing I met among the natives; and no contemptible degree of architectural skill was manifested in their construction, though their dilapidated state afforded no clue to the purpose for which they were piled. Always nearly circular, they inclosed areas from a quarter of a mile to a mile in circumference, sometimes elliptical, and sometimes a perfect circle, or rather a parallelogram, with swelled sides, conforming in shape to the ground.[9] We seldom found any water inside the walls, as they circumscribed the highest portions of the island, making it present at high tide the appearance of a cluster of small walled islands. At its eastern end the spray, which broke over the reef which bounds the islands, washes one of these walls. It must be visible to vessels passing outside the reef, but, to a person unprepared to expect any such thing, would present nothing remarkable in its exterior.

The largest cluster of these ruins merits a particular description.[10] The outside wall incloses a space about a mile in circum-

---

[8] It would be quite impossible, by canoe or on foot, to get from Kiti to the ruins and back again in one day. Further, the ruins are not part of 'that island' but of the immediately adjacent tribe, Madolenihmw, to and from which it is indeed possible to wade at low tide. If O'Connell on this long excursion was proceeding around Ponape in a counter-clockwise direction, as he would have done if he had gone, as he says, first to Sokehs, then he would have passed Kiti before he got to Madolenihmw and the ruins. It may therefore be that he thought he was still in Kiti. But it would also bespeak a very limited knowledge of the geography and the political relationships and would reinforce the view, expressed already, that his stay on Ponape was much shorter than he says it was.

[9] The areas are much exaggerated and the shapes are wrong.

[10] This paragraph describes the most spectacular of the ruins of Nan Madol, the one known as Nan Douwas. Most of the details O'Connell gives are inaccurate or exaggerated. For example, the outside wall, which encloses a rectangular area, has a perimeter of 238 metres, not a mile. There are not five or six walls, only two. The front side of the outer wall

185

ference. This area is not, as in the other cases, empty, but at about twenty feet distance from the outside wall is another, exactly parallel to the first; then at the same distance another, and still another, to the number of five or six. The centre wall incloses a space only about forty feet across, and is perfectly square. The outside wall was, upon one end of the edifice, about twenty-five to thirty feet in height. Upon the other three sides, which had been more exposed to the tide, the walls had become undermined, and had fallen in many places, but the inner walls were all perfect. The standing side of the outer wall had evidently been the front, for square pillars, which had formed a part of some portico, or similar structure, lay across the creek. The entrance, or aperture in the wall, was about four feet in height. Upon entering, no aperture in the next wall presented itself, but after working our way among the brush we discovered an entrance at the corner of the wall, to the right of the first. Passing this, we found an aperture in the next, at the left; and thus, finding doors alternately at the right and left, we penetrated to the inner wall. In walking inside of this, by the accidental falling of a piece of wood, we discovered a vault, into which I descended. My first supposition was that it was a burial place, but all that appeared to sustain such an opinion was one skeleton, which lay at the bottom, its parts scattered to and fro about the ground. This distribution was probably done by the rats. I found no paddle or war-club in the vault. This body was accounted for after my return to Nutt, where I was informed that a chief of Kitti had been buried there. Upon the island of Kitti the natives were unable or unwilling to give me any information. The logs, and the sods which covered them, concealing the top of the vault, must have been placed when the body which I found was deposited there. The fact that the vault was used for a burial place, even in this isolated instance within the memory of the living natives, would seem to speak some vague tradition of the purpose for which the place was built;

---

is completely open at its middle and provides unobstructed passage through a similar entrance in the inner wall and to the central burial vault, corresponding not at all to the labyrinth O'Connell describes. So different are these and other details from the reality that there is serious question whether he did not suffer from some visual defect. This would perhaps also explain his repeated references to mainland places as islands.

but I never could get hold of any more satisfactory tradition than that the ruins were built by animan. In one of the creeks on this island of ruins lay a large square stone, which the Nigurt who accompanied us on the first day assured us an animan had dropped from his shoulders as he was trying to transport it! The person who was buried there was an Edyomet of high repute. There must have been some extraordinary motive to overcome the repugnance of the natives to visiting the place; probably the request of the man himself.[11]

Brown beche le mer, which may be found on all the islands, having never been disturbed as an article of traffic, is particularly abundant on the Island of Ruins. At low tide the water leaves it in immense quantities upon the bottoms of the inlets. This circumstance will lead, undoubtedly, to future visits and exploration for commercial purposes, and then, as science and mercantile enterprise go hand in hand, a more particular account of this interesting spot will be given to the world. Persons familiar with eastern antiquities will visit it, and may be enabled, by the resemblance of the ruins to those of some ancient nation, to fix the probable origin of this people. Unassisted by any such knowledge, and unaided by the natives, who pettishly avoided inquiries as reflecting discredit upon what they considered a sufficient explanation, I was unable to find even data for a theory. The story that "animan built them, and that they are the abode of *animan*," and *majorhowi* to every body else, appears to have descended from generation to generation. It is evident they are the remains of a people superior to the present inhabitants; nay, I may almost say dissimilar.[12] Conjecture was vague and entirely unassisted. The vault, favoring the idea that the labyrinth was intended for a burial place, was the only feature about them that appeared to betray any purpose in piling these huge stones together; and it is not certain that even

---

[11] Reluctance to visit the ruins, from dread of the spirits, persists today. Nevertheless, annual religious ceremonies involving large numbers of people were held on certain of the artificial islands as late as the 1850s.

[12] Either O'Connell did not sufficiently persist in his questioning or there was greater reluctance than in later times to discuss the history of the ruins. Many stories, some undoubtedly quasi-historical, are known about events supposed to have occurred among them and about the people who were the actors. There is little doubt that it was the ancestors of the present-day Ponapeans who were the architects and builders.

that vault was not made expressly for the burial of the Edyomet. His bones alone being found there, makes such a supposition probable. Again, the method of building the stone walls on the inhabited islands differs so entirely from the masonry on the Island of Ruins, that the latter are proved the work of another people. Upon the islands, in the walls now made for foundations, etc., though very neatly built, for untutored Indians, stones of all shapes are used; in the Island of Ruins the stones seem broken, if not hewn, for the very places which they occupy. They stand firm, and bid fair to remain everywhere except in places where their foundations have been sapped by the water. The foundation is laid below the surface, while walls now built are commenced upon the face of the earth. I looked in vain, particularly about the entrances, for marks or hieroglyphics; finding nothing of that description.

George and myself, in committee of two, but without authority to send for persons and papers, at the end of about a fortnight rose and reported that the remains were evidently those of some ancient city or settlement, the date of the existence of which, or the cause of its desertion, we could not even guess; and that the creeks or inlets were formerly land passages, which the water had encroached upon, from the contiguity of the island to the reef. We decided, also, that the reason of the comparative height of the inclosed land is owing to the protection afforded it by the foundation of the walls. Where the walls are broken down the water enters the inclosures. Finally and lastly, we paid their ethereal worships, the animan, the compliment to pronounce them better architects than any of the race now extant upon the islands. Before leaving the ruins, I christened the little group "the O'Connell Cluster," after the agitator.

At length I began to tire of exploring and to long for home; for, strange as it may appear, my consort Laowni, savage though she were, by classification, made my island home quite an attractive spot for me. George, too, began to tire of rambling; so we set the head of our canoe toward Nutt. On our way home we touched at Matalaleme, where Wajai-a-Matalaleme hospitably received us. As a curiosity, upon this island we were shown a pit full of human bones, the product, we were told, of a destructive war, years before. The chiefs of other islands sometimes refer their disputes to the chief of Nutt for decision, and submit to the edicts issued from that island without resistance;[13] but as reference is not always effectual in settling disputes, many old men upon the islands bear what are esteemed honorable scars, the effects of the overboiling of their young blood, and of the quarrels of the chiefs under whom they live.

Upon my return to Nutt I found my wife and father had learned my wanderings, by report from the islands I had visited. Laowni was rejoiced to see me, and Ahoundel pronounced George and me *macoomot*, brave, for venturing as we had among strangers. We soon had a chance to put this recommendation to the test, for we were informed that Wajai-a-Hoo* had declared war against Ahoundel-a-Nutt, on account of my marriage. It appeared that Laowni was promised to him previous to my arrival. The daughter never much affected the match, as Wajai was old, and the husband already of something like a dozen. It may be to her disgust for that union, quite as much as to my own good looks, that I owed my marriage to her. Be that as it may, Ahoundel, after stating the case, asked me if I was willing to fight, and as I saw no honorable mode of escape, and am a native of a country whose boys have no very decided aversion to a bit of a row, I consented; but George showed the white feather, and positively refused.

---

* *Nanamoraki-a-Hoo, mentioned in the catalogue, was Wajai's successor.*

[13] Again O'Connell inflates Net's lowly position, no doubt to enhance his own. Since the semi-legendary times of a culture-hero named Isohkelekel, who was the first Nahnmwarki of 'Matalaleme' (Madolenihmw), his successors in that tribe have held the paramount position among the other tribes, have had a kind of arbitration role in those tribes, and have sometimes assumed authority when the other rulers were unable to solve their problems. Net has never had such a role.

CHAPTER XVI

Preparations for war.—Muster of force.—Description of weapons.—Order of sailing.—Formal character of challenge.—Order of reception by Wajai.—Preliminary shout.—Battle opens with slings.—Arrows—spears—hand to hair!—clubbing—knifing— —death of Wajai.—Temporary respite.—Renewal of engagement.—A landing forced.—Ground disputed.—Women fled.— Males follow example.—Plunder and burning of the Hoo houses. —Return to Nutt.—Wailing for dead.—Chivalric distinction of castes in fight.—Reflections thereon.—Feast.—Cannibalism, almost.—Nanamoraki's policy.—Fortifications.—Sail ho!—Pleasure of Messrs. O'Connell and Keenan, and pain of Ahoundel and family, thereat.—Promises of return by Mr. O'Connell.—Reluctant consent of Ahoundel.—A disappointment!—Canoe launched.—Swamped.—Escape from drowning, by aquatic skill.— Mr. O'Connell reaches the reef.—Taken off by native canoes.

Preparations were immediately set on foot to visit Hoo [*Uh*], and "carry the war into Africa," by answering Wajai's challenge at his door. Natives to the number of about fifteen hundred[14] were mustered, from Nutt and two contiguous small islands, called Hand and Param.[15] The order of sailing was thus: Moonjobs to the right, or in the van, Jerejohs next, the Nigurts bringing up the rear. Each canoe was furnished with smooth stones, which were stowed in the bottom, and each native was furnished with a sling, a spear, a bow and arrows,[16] and war-club. The spears are from five feet to eight in length, and barbed with the back bone of a fish, preserving five or six joints, with the protruding bones, like arrow barbs.[17] The clubs are made of heavy wood and notched, similar to the thousand specimens of the war-clubs of the Pacific preserved in museums; except that they are only about eighteen inches or two feet in length.

The natives were dressed in their best savage articles of adornment, their heads dressed with flowers, but no paint was put upon their flesh, except the everlasting smearing with cocoa-nut oil and curry. The castes were kept entirely distinct in the canoes. The Nigurts, who on ordinary occasions navigate the canoes of their chiefs and masters, were by themselves in their own canoes, and the Jerejohs and the Moonjobs each in their own. As war is an honorable enterprise, the labor of paddling the canoes, if the lack of wind or a wrong direction make it necessary, is done by Moonjobs and landholders, and even chiefs, who on no other occasion touch a paddle, except for momentary exercise.

The day and place had been appointed with all the circum-

[14] This seems altogether too large a number. Estimates of the total population of Ponape, made between 1828 and 1854 (the year of the smallpox epidemic) run between 1,000 and 15,000 (Riesenberg, *Native Polity*, 1968, p. 6). Taking the largest figure, 15,000, Net, which has always been one of the two smallest tribes among the five (the other being Uh) could have had at most a total population of 3,000. It is hardly likely that half of that number would have been adult, fighting men.

[15] There are indeed two small islands immediately adjacent to and belonging to Net. They are Lenger and Parem. O'Connell names the latter, and perhaps he says 'Hand' instead of Lenger from lapse of memory. Elsewhere he has referred to 'Hand' as an uninhabited island 20 miles distant from Ponape, evidently meaning the atoll called Ant (actually 8 miles away), which belongs not to Net but to Kiti. Or perhaps he meant Mwahnd, also nearby but belonging to Uh.

[16] Bows and arrows existed, but they were not used as weapons of war.

[17] The spear point is not a fish bone but a sting-ray spine.

stance of a duel, or rather of an ancient joust at arms, with the exception that there was no stipulation or limitation as to force on either side; each party bringing all the strength he could muster. Treachery sometimes occurs in island warfare, and attacks by surprise are made; seldom, it is true, but often enough to induce those who are aware that they have enemies to be on their guard. This engagement with Wajai was, however, a fair fight, preceded by a challenge and its acceptance, and of course Wajai was prepared to receive us, though with an inferior force.

His canoes were ranged in the water, in front of his settlement, and as soon as we were near enough to distinguish features, our chief, Ahoundel, and Wajai sprung simultaneously to their feet, upon the platforms of their canoes, and flourishing their spears, set up a shout of defiance, the conches blowing an accompaniment. The inferior chiefs upon both sides then rose and joined in the cry, and the engagement commenced with hurling the stones with slings. These stones are seldom less than a pound in weight, and are thrown with tremendous precision, the parties being from thirty to forty yards apart. Several canoes were broken and sunk on both sides, and many men killed. The stones exhausted, arrows and spears followed, the parties nearing each other, till the battle was canoe to canoe, and hand to hand. The natives would seize each other by the hair, and thrust with a small wooden spear or lance, without barbs, and cut the flesh with sharp shells. In the onset Wajai was killed by one of the party in our canoe. A shout of joy on one side, and a murmur of grief on the other, suspended the battle a moment; but it was soon renewed with unabated fierceness. At length we forced a landing, and the vanquished or broken foe, failing to prevent it, also sprung on shore, and disputed every inch of ground, to the very doors of their houses. The land engagement was fought with the jagged spears and the short war-clubs. It may be necessary here to state that direct thrusts are seldom made with these spears; they are generally used for striking, and inflict mangling wounds in the flesh. The clubs which are worn in the belt, like a North American Indian's tomahawk, are the last resort, but are never hurled.

An hour and a half of hard fighting brought us to the estate of Wajai. The women had long before deserted the houses, taking with them such of their effects as they could conveniently transport, and the men, fairly overpowered, fled to the interior. No attempt had been made to take prisoners on either side, and the fugitives were not pursued. The natives of Bonabee never slaughter in cold blood after a foe ceases to resist. Our party plundered the houses of whatever moveables were left, set fire to them, and, returning to the beach, broke up the canoes of the foe, and taking with us the spears, mats, and other plunder, we returned to Nutt. We brought back such of our own dead as we could find, and the body of Wajai and other chiefs, who fell upon the other side.

The first duty upon our return was the interment of the fallen. From the lamentation an uninformed spectator would have supposed that the inhabitants of Nutt had suffered a defeat instead of a victory. The number of killed upon both sides was between three and four hundred; of whom one hundred and fifty were of the victorious party.[18] In the engagement no man of one caste attacked another—Moonjobs against Moonjobs, Jerejohs against Jerejohs, and Nigurts against Nigurts. This chivalrous distinction was kept up in the very hottest of the fray, no man daring to aim a blow at a superior, and none descending to strike an inferior. It was like the encounter of three distinct parties.[19]

Here, again, it is worth while to note the admirable system and policy which controls island usages. Even in time of an engagement is the respect for rank chivalrously kept up. If it were permitted to a Nigurt to strike even a free foe in battle, the bonds of their feudal relation to their masters would be weakened, and, in smaller island feuds, the same principle of war would be distorted to apply even to their proper masters, who by circumstances might be placed as foes in relative position to them. The jealousy with which all the grades of society are watched and kept in place would do credit to the policy of high civilized tories.

---

[18] Again probably an exaggeration. Informants living in 1947 who had participated in wars recall at most twenty deaths in a single engagement, except against the Spanish. The missionaries, writing in the 1850s, after the introduction of guns, describe military encounters as exchanges of volleys at safe distances, until one side exhausted its ammunition, when the other attacked, killing a handful of people, then destroying or carrying away movables. The result of a foray might be one or two women, boys, or old people killed; the largest number mentioned in any of these accounts is six men.

[19] This segregation by rank during fighting is denied by present-day Ponapeans as ever having existed.

For the credit of a people whose character is generally humane, for uncultivated savages, I should rejoice to stop here; but the truth compels me to speak of a custom differing so entirely from their usual character, that I am at a loss to account for it. Upon the next day after our return there was a feast held. The usual preparations of jagow and dog venison were made, and the bodies of Wajai and his chiefs were burned; but previously to the entire consumption of the bodies by fire, the heart of Wajai was taken out, and presented to the chiefs on a large plantain leaf. Whether it was eaten or even tasted I cannot say, as I was not present at the disgusting ceremony. The presumption, however, is, that eating the hearts of the chiefs killed in war is a custom with them.[20] Of this I can speak only so far as I have spoken, having had but one opportunity for ascertaining. No other part of the body than the heart was eaten, and that rather as a ceremony than a gratification.

No territory is gained by war, as the victors never pretend to hold a vanquished district, but relinquish it to the conquered party, only plundering it, and burning the houses. They never destroy the trees or natural products. Wajai was succeeded by Nanamoraki,[21] the next chief in rank upon his island, according to the rule of succession already noticed; and the first act of the new chief was to invite Ahoundel and his suite to the island of Hoo,[22] to cement a reconciliation over jagow. A feast was had, of course, and a perfect understanding formed between the successor of Wajai and the chief, to whose good offices in removing his predecessor the new incumbent owed his possession of the authority.

Fortified in the traditions and immemorial usages, the island chiefs pay little attention to breastworks and walls of defence. There are, however, on Nutt and some other of the larger islands, works breast high for the shelter of parties when defending the

[20] Ceremonial cannibalism as described here was a frequent custom. It was considered to do honour to a brave dead enemy.

[21] This is a peculiar statement. The 'Nanamoraki' (Nahnmwarki) is the highest tribal title, the 'Wajai' (Wasai) ranking second and normally succeeding him, not the other way round.

[22] 'Hoo' is mostly on the mainland of Ponape, but it also includes four islands in the lagoon, and the battle may have been waged at one of these, giving O'Connell to think that 'Hoo' was an island.

canoe-house. Invading parties are always met at their landing. It would be an impossibility to surprise a settlement on the land side; as some *animan*, walking ghost, or star-gazer would detect the enemy, even in the night.

So far I have described prominent events in the order of their occurrence, and without pretending to fix very definitely their dates or the intervals between their occurrence. The arrival of the vessel in which I left the Bonabee group is, however, an event of the date of which I can speak with more certainty, as one of my early inquiries on board was, how time had progressed. On the island I must acknowledge such disrespect toward the scythe-bearing baldpate, that I did not count the turns of his glass. It was in the early part of the month of November, 1833, that I discovered a vessel from Nutt; the first vessel that I am positive of having seen while on the island of Bonabee. My comrades often said they saw vessels, and I frequently imagined that I did, but none approached near enough for us to distinguish their class.[23] It was about sunrise in the morning when I first discovered her, and I called up George immediately. We ran to the top of the nearest hill, and anxiously watched her, as well as the mist and occasional rain would permit, for it was a dull morning. After we had satisfied ourselves that it was a European or American vessel, we ran down to the chief and informed him that there was a vessel in the offing, and that we wished to board her. He was not half so much elated at receiving the information as we were in imparting it. He eyed me some moments. "What!" said he, "a ship? Cho! cho [*Soh! soh!*]!" (No, no.) I repeated my assurance, and led him to the hill. My wife and the whole household followed. George and I bounded about for joy, skipping up the hill, as if our feet could not serve us fast enough. The pace of our companions offered something of a contrast; they were still incredulous, and my wife and father were evidently hoping against the truth of my discovery, as they saw in my joy any thing but a pleasant indication of my feelings respecting remaining upon the island. I pointed out the vessel, and satisfied them that it was not, as they supposed and hoped it might be, a native war-canoe. I repeated my request for a canoe, assuring

[23] At least two Sydney whalers visited Ponape in November 1832, a year before O'Connell's rescue (Riesenberg, *Native Polity*, 1968, p. 4).

Ahoundel that I would make the vessel *"moondie,"* literally, *"sit down,"* or come to an anchor. At the canoe-house, whither Ahoundel, Laowni, my children, and others, followed me, Ahoundel granted his unwilling consent that I should go off to the vessel, following it up with questions, while Laowni anxiously watched the expression of my face for an answer. "Do you love your wife? your children? Do you love them much, very much? Will you certainly return?" To all this I answered yes, yes; and my heart smites me now, as I recollect the gratified expression of my wife's countenance upon receiving the assurance. No civilized person however, theorized and philosophized though he were into contempt for the shackles of civilization, could content himself with innocent, unsophisticated, natural men forever. Blunt, plain man that I am, I could hardly disguise my joy at the hope of an escape, although at times, as I looked at Laowni and her children, and the thought of Ahoundel's kindness intruded itself, I could hardly conceal my grief at parting. To have betrayed either joy or grief would have revealed my purpose of escape; so I was compelled to hide both; and it was only the bustle of getting ready, and the diversion of the attention of the natives to the vessel, that enabled me to do it.

A large canoe was prepared to launch, but the tide was out. We were obliged to wait for it two full hours! Oh the impatience we felt, the snail-like progress of time! Knowing perfectly well, had we been cool, the time of the tide, still we could not avoid running down every ten minutes to look. Meanwhile I prepared a quantity of tortoise shell, yams, bread-fruit, and cocoa-nuts to take off to the captain. We watched the vessel—she tacked and stood off—our hopes fell—she stood back again—we were re-assured—she hove to, and we were happy, till—we recollected we were tide-bound.

At length the tide served us to launch the canoe. Ahoundel and Laowni accompanied me to the boat, the former reminding me of my promise to bring him trinkets, the latter melancholy, and half doubting that she should see me again. There was a fleet of some dozen canoes beside mine. I was accompanied by Keenan, a young chief, and two Nigurts. We went outside the reef, and had neared the vessel so that we could distinguish the men on her decks, when the Nigurt who had the steering oar let the canoe get into the trough of the sea. There was a tremendous sea on, and it was carelessness on my part to let the paddle go from my hand; the consequence of getting the canoe broadside on to the sea was, that we were swamped. As is usual with the natives, we all jumped overboard, two taking the outrigger side and the others striving to bail out the canoe. There was however too much sea running, and all endeavors to bail the boat proved futile, while the tide and the swell were drifting us toward the reef. The young chief, who was quite a lad, made no ado, but cutting away the twine fastenings with his fish-shell knife, stripped the board off the outrigger, laid his breast across it, and paddled away like a dog, for the reef. Seeing no alternative, I disengaged the pole which formed the fore-and-aft part of the outrigger, and, with one of the Nigurts, made also for the reef, with the pole beneath our breasts. As we reached the crests of the waves I could see the vessel, and the other more fortunate canoes every moment getting nearer to her. The very dress of the men on the vessel's deck was distinguishable. And here, in the very sight of the first white men, except our shipmates, that we had seen for years, George and I were apparently devoted to death, before we could exchange a word with them. I should have mentioned, that before leaving the canoe I fastened my mat to the mast and waved it, but the vessel's crew, imagining us natives, paid no attention to the signal. George, with one of the Nigurts, remained with the canoe, contrary to my advice, as he insisted that a native of the islands must know better how to conduct in an emergency like this than I could. In a few moments I heard him hailing, beseeching me for God's sake to wait for him to overtake me. The Nigurt who was my companion objected, and for a moment I listened to the Indian and paid no attention to the cries of my friend. My better feelings, however, prevailed, and I waited for my shipmate, who reached us panting with exertion, and seized the outrigger just as he was nearly exhausted. I had trembled for him, but it was impossible to turn back and face tide and surf. One moment and I caught a glimpse of his head on the top of a wave, the next he was invisible. My joy at the relief from suspense which his arrival gave was second only to his reaching us.

We had by this time reached the surf. Taught by former experience, I watched the rollers, and when I saw one coming let go of the outrigger, faced the sea, and clasped my hands over my head. Down it came upon us, but my hands and arms broke the force of the water, and I was driven down, but emerged again, many feet nearer the reef. My companions, George and the native, followed my direction and example, and we rose nearly together. The outrigger was thrown upon the ledge at second or third roller, and had we clung to it we should have been dashed to pieces among the rocks, by the force with which we should have been driven. The young chief had reached the ledge before us, and between our forced plunges we could see him encouraging us by swinging his mat. After being thus swamped five or six times we reached the rocks, more dead than alive, and crawled where the water had least force. Here, taking the pole of the outrigger, which, as before stated, had preceded us, I attached my mat to it, and made signals of distress. On board the schooner they paid no heed to it, although she stood at one time almost within hail of us. Taking us for natives, and supposing us used to such mishaps, her master thought we could manage for ourselves; had he, however, been inclined to assist us, no boat would have lived in the surf. We were two or three hours on the reef before we were discovered by the natives; then some fishing canoes came to us from the inside, where the sea was comparatively nothing, and the reef approachable, and took us off. One of the party, the Nigurt who remained with the canoe, was drowned, his body being picked up a day or two afterward among the rocks which formed the reef.

The rapidity of thought is never better exemplified than in seasons of imminent danger. Years pass in review in moments; but we had ample time for reflection, and that none of the pleasantest. It was over an hour from the time the canoe was swamped before we reached the reef, and that with the tide and swell in our favor. Perhaps the vessel was as near us as the reef, but in endeavoring to reach it we should have been compelled to contend with wind, tide, and swell, while all assisted in drifting us toward the reef. During the last few moments before we landed we considered our death next to inevitable, and the prospect was embittered by the reflection that it would occur just at the moment when we hoped to regain communion with civilized beings again, after a sojourn of years with uncultivated savages.

CHAPTER XVII

Return to Nutt.—Astonishment of Ahoundel.—Anxiety.—Despair.—Return of hope.—The Spy returns.—Putting off again.—Canoes alongside.—Invitation on board.—Dinner on board.—The Spy anchors at Matalaleme.—Purchase of a canoe.—Stolen back by the natives.—Fruitless pursuit.—Capt. Knight shoots a Nigurt.—Swivel in the fore-top.—Capt. Knight's fright.—Under way again.—Blazing away at the natives.—One day's retrospections.—A change comes over Capt. Knight's deportment.—Ship's cook left at Matalaleme.—Altercations with Capt. Knight.—Arrival at Manilla.—Irons.—Guard boat.—Agreeable position, enlivened with music.—Landing.—Arrival at a building opposite a church.—Their affectionate care of us, and commendable precaution.

Upon reaching Nutt, Ahoundel was astonished with the story of our escape, coupled as it was with the loss of the Nigurt. The young chief described our conduct to him, and his astonishment was increased, that two white men should prove better or more fortunate swimmers than a native fisherman. We were weakened, bruised, and sore, as the reader will readily conceive; but our bodily suffering was forgotten in our mental anxiety, as the last light of day showed us the schooner standing off shore.

Would she return? The night long we passed in anxious doubt, and were out with the dawn to look for the sail; but

"The blue above and the blue below"

was vacant, vacant. Cloud after cloud we watched, till our eyes ached; they only mocked us, preserving awhile an illusive semblance, then vanishing or spreading into broad, honest vapors, incapable of deceiving even a landsman. The sun was well up, the water calm, compared with the swell of the day preceding, the day bright, and every thing propitious where every thing frowned before, save the slight circumstance that the vessel was not in sight. At length I saw her, just a speck. Heavens! how my heart leaped!

A half hour more and the tide was right. The vessel, standing in, was now fairly visible, and, prepared with a fresh load of tortoise shell and provisions, with George and two Nigurts for companions, I set sail again. As we went out by the reef, we were forcibly reminded of our escape of the preceding day, by a fleet of canoes which were paddling as near the reef as they dared, in search of the body of the drowned man.

When we reached the schooner she was hove to, with her boarding nettings up, and her men mustered, with boarding pikes and muskets in hand, or at hand. Two or three other canoes got alongside at the same time that we did, and others were coming off. Upon the day before no natives had been allowed to board the vessel, though a barter traffic for yams and bread-fruit was opened between the canoes and those on board the vessel. We passed under her stern, and I read the name, "Spy, of Salem." She was brig rigged forward, and schooner aft. Passing round to her weather bow, I sung out, "Shipmates, throw us a rope's end, will you?" There was a bustle on deck, a buzz of surprise, but no answer, and in a moment I heard somebody exclaiming, "Captain, the *natives* on this island speak English!" The anxiety to get a peep at us through the boarding netting was now redoubled, forward and aft. One of the men, after much hesitation, threw us a rope, and the captain came to the gangway and asked us on board, requesting us to keep the natives in the canoe, which we did. The captain did us the honor to ship the side-ladder for us, and George and I needed no second invitation to come on deck, but, taking up the tortoise shell with us, directed the natives to pass up the yams. To my first question the captain answered that the name of the island was Ascension, the group being laid down as one island on the chart. He inquired particularly into our story, and proceeded, while he did so, to offer us, with a sailor's hospitality, a rummer of grog. It was the first I had tasted for years, of course, and a bare swallow of it burned my throat, flushed my face, and played the deuce with my head altogether. Poor George was even worse flabbergusted than I was. The joy we felt at a prospect of return to England was sufficient to intoxicate us, aside from the liquor.

In answer to Capt. Knight's inquiries, I assured him of the peaceable character of the islanders, and that there was abundance of tortoise shell and beche le mer for commerce, and yams, bread-fruit, water, and wood for provision upon the islands. In a short time Capt. Knight expressed a willingness that I should permit my Nigurts to come on board, and we dropped the canoe astern. Other natives were not so fortunate; they huddled about the vessel, and, coveting iron, strove to pull out the iron work under the chains with their hands. The schooner filled away again, and we stood off with a fleet of canoes in tow, dashing and plashing through the water, their outriggers foul of each other, and getting continually carried away.

I dined on board, with George, at the cabin table. The condiments of my own furnishing, with the salt provisions, ship bread and butter of the ship's stores, furnished a more savory meal than I had sat down to for many a day. I undertook to pilot the Spy inside the reef to an anchorage, at Capt. Knight's request. At four or five o'clock in the evening she came to an anchor in the harbor of Matalaleme. By the natives who went that night to Nutt I sent Ahoundel a large broad axe and an adz, and to Laowni I sent beads, red kerchiefs, and other trinkets; while George and I remained on board, afraid to trust ourselves on shore again.

In the morning the vessel was again surrounded by canoes, and Capt. Knight purchased of the natives, through me as an interpreter, tortoise shell and other articles, and one canoe, which he purposed to carry away as a curiosity. This was dropped astern and fastened by a rope to the counter. In about two hours from the time of purchasing some of the natives slipped into it, and before we were aware were making off with it, induced probably by some island superstition. Capt. Knight immediately fired upon the thieves, and, lowering a boat, sent some men in pursuit; but it would have been impossible to have overtaken them, even if the water had not been too shallow in places for the keel of the boat. Capt. Knight now began to fear that the natives intended to take his vessel, although George and I assured him to the contrary, and told him that their worst fault was an irresistible propensity to thieve, where they saw articles they so earnestly coveted. We represented to him that harsh treatment might bring about the very event he dreaded, and that, at any rate, the next vessel which came within their reach would suffer for his conduct. Still he was nervous, agitated, and acted like one beside himself, begging me to prevent treachery and keep the natives quiet. Instead of acting like a discreet person, which had he done, he might have lain at Matalaleme weeks, with profit, he blowed out the brains of a native who was climbing in at the cabin windows, and threw out the body. Luckily for Capt. Knight, the murdered man was a Nigurt, so that the dissatisfaction of the natives amounted only to a murmur; had he been a Moonjob, or even a Jerejoh, the capture of the vessel and murder of the crew would have atoned for his death. It did not seem long to intimidate them, but after they had clamorously inquired of me the cause of his death, and I told them it was for thieving, they seemed, in a measure, satisfied that it was just. During the time that the Spy lay at Matalaleme no natives were permitted to come upon her deck, but stood in the chains, and in their canoes. No chiefs of note came off to the vessel at all—a precaution adopted by their friends, I presume, and in accordance with the habits and policy of the people; else so simultaneous a measure could not have been carried out by all the islands. In the short time after the native was shot in the cabin, a small swivel was hoisted into the fore-top, charged with nails, slugs, and musket balls. Every fresh arrival of canoes put Capt. Knight in additional perturbation; he had commenced hostilities, and even I began to have fear for the consequences. Constant persuasion, and even the exercise of authority, was necessary, on my part, to prevent a rush upon the vessel by the natives. At about ten in the morning the Spy got under way, and Capt. Knight ordered his crew to fire upon the natives, and even wished Keenan and myself to take arms against people who had for five years been our friends and protectors. We flatly refused. The musket shots were answered by occasional stones hurled from the canoes, none of which took effect, save one, which struck the mate; but from being spent, or some other cause, it injured him but slightly. During all the time the number of the canoes about us rather increased than diminished, and I was in continual conversation and parley with the natives. They complained of the treatment of the Aroche tic-a-tic (petty chief) of the vessel. I answered that I was not to blame for it, and appealed to them for the fact that I had not taken up arms against them. I was anxious that a good report of my conduct should be carried back to Ahoundel.

As we beat out—for the wind was against us—fleet after fleet of the canoes, nothing daunted by the death of the few natives who had fallen, put off for us, from various parts of the group. The echo of a musket report, in the harbor of Matalaleme, was of itself startling. It rang from rock to rock, and from hill to hill, probably for the first time; that generation of the islanders, at any rate, knew nothing of the use or character of fire-arms. Capt. Knight's perplexity was doubled by his want of that knowledge of the harbor which was necessary to safe conduct of his vessel.

The sight of a fresh fleet putting off toward us made Capt. Knight desperate. He sent a hand with a match into the foretop, clewed up the sail, and sent the charge of the swivel among the thickest of the fleet. I saw several natives drop like dogs over the sides of their canoes. There rose a howl of mingled rage and defiance among the survivors; but the cruel expedient answered the purpose—the natives fell back, and though they followed us far outside the reef, it was at a great distance. In the passage through the reef we narrowly escaped getting on the rocks. Had the vessel been wrecked, the lives of all on board would have answered the death of the natives. The crew of the next American or English vessel which touches at the islands of Ascension will probably be sacrificed in revenge, should they fall, by any inadvertence, into the power of the islanders.

The shot from the fore-top was not repeated. The mast was strained, and the sailor who officiated as gunner came down the backstays by the run, protesting he would not again fire the swivel.

Nothing which occurred during my connection with the islands affected me so unpleasantly as the butchery of my friends by Capt. Knight. Knowing perfectly the language and character of the people, I knew that, until they were roused to revenge by the death of the Nigurt, no thought of farther mischief than theft was entertained by them. This might easily have been guarded against by mild means; at any rate, the course taken did not answer. I proposed to Capt. Knight, as we entered the harbor, that the vessel should lay there a month or six weeks, informing him of the quantities of beche le mer which I proposed to cure for him, taking the requisite tools from the vessel. I did not expect that any thing but peace and good fellowship between the natives and the crew of the vessel would grow out of the visit; but the hasty and cruel conduct of Capt. Knight marred it all. I was grieved at the death of the natives; but I was astonished at the effrontery with which Capt. Knight called upon us to fire upon our friends. We told him we were anxious to get away from the island, but that we should prefer to be set on shore again, rather than purchase our freedom by such an abuse of friendship.

Fairly out of the harbor of Matalaleme, the deportment of Capt. Knight materially changed toward us. He was no longer the supplicant for intercession with the natives, but the master, imposing his authority upon us in every possible manner. In about fourteen days we made Guam, one of the Marian Islands, where Capt. Knight would have left us, but the authorities would not permit it. By the way, I should have mentioned that the ship's cook was set ashore at Matalaleme, with his own consent, and I directed the natives into whose canoe he stepped to carry him to Ahoundel, and treat him well, for my sake. Whether he, and the four comrades whom I left upon the islands, did not fare worse for Capt. Knight's conduct, I had no means of ascertaining; but must do the natives the justice to express the opinion, based upon a knowledge of their character, that they have too much benevolence and perception of right and wrong to abuse known friends for the conduct of strangers, though those strangers were of their color and language. I saw nothing of my four friends during the stay of the Spy, although it was my intention, if Capt. Knight had not compelled himself to take such hasty leave, to have carried them away with us.

After leaving Guam I had some altercation with Capt. Knight, which resulted in no very agreeable consequences to myself. During the whole passage I had been sick, from a cold, exhaustion, fatigue, and derangement of my whole system, from the change of diet. Under my right arm was a large and very painful swelling. One night I had the watch from eight to twelve, the first two hours of which I spent on the top-gallant yard, upon the lookout. When I came down I laid myself on the forecastle by the heel of the bowsprit, exhausted, and in agony from the swelling under my arm. Capt. Knight came forward, and the first intimation I had of his proximity was a kick. "What business have you here asleep, sir?" I pleaded my weakness and ill health, and the suffering I had already endured by the lookout at the mast-head. He collared me, and I returned his grasp with interest; he freed himself from me, went aft, and returned with a brace of pistols in his hand, threatening to shoot me. I told him to do it; that I was tired of life, and would willingly die. He then let me alone for the night, and indeed we had no more words, but he hove to near the first land we made, lowered the boat, and ordered me into it. George insisted upon accompanying me, to which Capt. Knight at first objected, but afterward consented. He then sent the second mate and two men with directions to leave the two Irish villains (he used a worse word) any where—on a rock, or a sand bank, but not to bring them on board again. This was in the straits of Barnardino. Upon reaching the shore we found bullocks grazing, but saw no house, or shelter of any kind, and persuaded the second mate to take us back. He did so, and upon returning to the vessel told the captain that he could not drive us from the boat, but that we insisted upon coming back.

We were taken on board, and the vessel filled away again. I very foolishly, as the event proved, threatened Capt. Knight that I would represent to the authorities at Manilla his treatment of the Indians at Ascension, and his abuse of me. Upon arrival at that port he anticipated me, making all sorts of charges against us, as runaways from punishment at New Holland, pirates who strove to cause the capture of his vessel by the Indians, and mutineers on board. Upon being boarded by the captain of the port at Manilla, just as we thought we had reached the end of our vexations and were in a way to return home, we were agreeably surprised by a present of leg safety-chains, and were placed, ironed, in the bows of the captain of the port's barge.

Captain Knight soon came down over the side, and seated himself under the awning in the stern sheets, with the captain of the port, the quarantine and custom-house officers; and as we sat, we could perceive we were the objects of the conversation. We bore this *talking at* some time in silence, but tiring of it, I requested George to play his flute; which, by the way, as a memento of his residence on Ascension, he had taken care to keep with him. Accordingly he struck up St. Patrick's Day in the Morning, Garry Owen, and divers other merry Irish tunes, to the astonishment and edification of the boatmen, and, after a while, to the amusement even of the officers in the stern sheets. We were pulled in this way alongside half a dozen vessels which had just entered the harbor, and endured the gratification of being pointed out to their crews as felons;—a story we took every opportunity to contradict. The feelings of the sailors were, of course, with us, and their half-expressed and doubtful sympathy was grateful, when all the rest of the world were disposed to frown.

After being paraded in this way about the harbor for half a day, we were landed, and marched with military honors up the street. We did not pay so much attention to our conductors as the honor they were paying us merited, for, after a half dozen years' absence from every thing like a town, George and I had enough to do to look about us at the buildings, the carriages, foot passengers, and other, to us, novel objects in a city.

We had reached a church—were famished with hunger, having eaten nothing since morning, and faint with exposure to the heat of a broiling sun. "Is it vespers you are taking us to? Well, prayer after fasting." The captain of our escort pointed to the opposite side of the street, and there, fronting the church, stood a less agreeable resort for sinners; one, like the church, not always sought voluntarily,—the calabozo.

They had the impoliteness to fasten the door at our backs when we entered.

CHAPTER XVIII

Upon entering we found ourselves in a sort of reception room, more convenient for its purposes than genteel or elegantly furnished. It was separated from the rest of the prison by an iron grating, through which the friends of the prisoners conversed with them. Through this grating we saw a large hall, tenanted by prisoners, but were ourselves passed up a flight of stone steps, communicating with the second story. Here, with Chinese, Malays, Spaniards and Creoles, we were locked up. At the end of the room opposite the entrance was an altar and crucifix; and we were curious as to what was coming when we were led towards it. The marvel ceased, however, when a door near the crucifix was opened, and we were ushered into the jailor's office, and requested to favor him with our autographs in his album. This done, we were returned into the common hall, and an allowance of rice served out to us.

All this time we had no precise knowledge of the charges made against us, although we knew it was something in which Captain Knight had a hand. Upon the next day the interpreter, who, by the way, had honored us with his company until he saw the key safely turned upon us, paid us a visit. From him we learned what the reader has already been informed, that there were three distinct charges, either of which was sufficient to authorize the affectionate care taken of us; namely, piracy, escape from Botany Bay, and mutinous conduct. We inquired whether we should have a trial, and how soon, to which he replied that we probably should. Of Captain Knight we saw nothing after leaving him at the landing; except, one day, when he passed the prison, and I took the liberty to hail him by name, adding sundry expletives and titles, more applicable and graphic than melodious and beautiful. Days passed, and, as a sort of desperate amusement, I commenced writing letters of complaint, and sending them out, directed to any English or American resident whose name I could learn. The rial a day, which was allowed us from some source, I never could precisely learn what, to provide our proven, was, after a while, taken off, and we were served with rice daily, and once or twice a week, beef and fish.

Sailors, many of whom visited us, were in the frequent practice of making us small presents. With the money thus obtained we sent and purchased bread and meat, but the eyes of Argus were necessary to prevent too frequent verification of the proverb, "many a slip 'twixt cup and lip." Even after our bit of meat was in the pot with the rice and we were superintending its cooking, some dexterous Chinese thief would whip it out with his chopsticks, if our eye strayed from it one moment. Each of the prisoners is obliged to prepare his own food, in a portion of the prison set apart for that purpose.

All sorts of ingenious modes of punishment were practised upon the prisoners for misdeeds while there. It would almost seem the Chinese ingenuity of torture, tempered by a little more regard for humanity than the officers of his Celestial Majesty possess. Stocks, confining the culprit in all sorts of positions, many of which were as ludicrous as uncomfortable, clogs, irons, and collars, and devices the description of which would tire, were in continual exercise. Flogging was going on all day, but the poor devils of Chinese came in for more than a proportionate share of it, and the blows were laid on with more hearty good will, as they were heretics.

To give variety to our life, we had an occasional opportunity of seeing a tenant in the pillory, opposite the prison. Here, too, during the time we lay in jail, we saw two or three executions, done in a manner to which the Turkish bowstring is tender mercy. I shall spare the reader the description of a method of strangulation the most horrible possible; only remarking that in a country where the office of the executioner is so directly instrumental to the death of the criminal, and his duty so cruel and protracted, it is no wonder that even criminals the most debased despise the hangman.

At the rear of the prison ran a river or canal. On the opposite bank stood a church, and near this lay what appeared to us a pile of human bones. When I tired of watching the passengers in the street in front, I looked out upon the church, and noted that no Catholics passed it without making a genuflexion. At night the spot was marked by a taper burning before the image of some saint, and I found myself frequently looking toward that church. I wondered if, among the bones there preserved upon consecrated ground, there lay the relics of any person so much the sport of fortune as myself, who had fallen, unwept and unattended, in a strange land. During no period of my residence upon the Carolines had I felt so utterly dispirited and forsaken, as I did at times in the prison at Manilla. I had made repeated applications for trial, besieged every person whose address I could learn with letters; the only effect of which was to bring two English merchants to the prison, to tell us that, as we came in an American vessel, as part of her crew, they could do nothing for us. The American consul, and Mr. Sturgis, an American resident, visited us in about a week after our committal. To the latter gentleman I feel much indebted, and cheerfully take this opportunity to acknowledge his kindness to two friendless mariners, a kindness which was dictated by pure benevolence alone.

We were not without amusement. George had brought his violin and flute, of course, and I had not forgotten the exercise of my heels. Then in the various assemblage there was ample amusement in watching the different disposal of time, according to character. The Chinese were most of them merchants, in a small way, vending tobacco, betel, and other "notions," as a Yankee would say; and there is no better word in the world. Stock in trade was not wanting, while there was a chance to exercise their expert fingers in tricks of sleight of hand. Others would operate as barbers, tailors,—they had a thousand resources for busy idleness. Spanish blood showed itself in games of chance —cards, draughts, dominoes; and the parties would sit as gravely and intently engaged as if they had been recreating in the palace of a grandee. An occasional industrious one wove hats; and cooking their pilau was the periodical occupation of all hands.

I indulged in an occasional game of draughts with one of my fellow-prisoners, a Spaniard. It did very well, till, one day, he tried to cheat me out of the game. The stake was not worth quarrelling about, but it was the point of pride. We wrangled, I collared him, and was reported. As a punishment I was ordered into the lower prison, and George, my shadow, was moved with me. This apartment, sacred to the lowest rogues, was by no means so light and pleasant as the upper one. There is a choice even in prisons.

Here I resumed the amusement of despatching letters; continuing it until, one day, the deputy jailor came to me with orders to put me in close confinement. I resisted, and in the scuffle was severely bruised, and my rigging dismantled. Preparatory to my solitude, and to give me food for reflection during its continuance, I was seized down to a bench and beaten with cowhides. Upon entering the cell which was to be my temporary residence, I found that the happiness of entire solitude was to be denied me, and was compelled to accept the society of a Spanish officer, who was waiting transportation to Cadiz, and trial for murder upon his own confession.

Previous to my committal to the cell, two attempts were made to compel me to ship on board vessels, one of which was the Dash, an American brig or barque, I have forgotten which. She was bound to the Fejees; but, as I had already had enough of the Pacific Ocean, I peremptorily refused to sign articles, and was remanded to prison. The other was a Spanish vessel, and I declined, in terms more positive than polite, to go in her. The American consul gave me a rating for annoying the residents with letters, and for refusing to go away by the opportunities he provided for me. After these adventures I was confined in the cell, as before stated, and could not, in my own mind, avoid connecting them as, at least, partial cause and effect.

The burden of my complaint had been the delay of a trial. Why was no attempt made to substantiate the charges made against me? Why no opportunity given me to disprove them? The treatment I endured would have been adequate punishment for any crime short of wilful murder. Beaten, half starved, and, worse than all, thrust, ironed, into a noisome cell with a murderer; a portion of the time bolted to the floor of that cell, and upon three successive Sabbaths paraded with my room-mate to prayers before all the prisoners, who classed me with the murderer; and all this without the show of any reason, or the pretence of it. No *formal* charge was ever made, or, if made, was ever prosecuted. Upon our egress from the prison Mr. Sturgis gave George and me five dollars, and the consul procured us a passage to Macao in a Spanish ship.

The reader will bear me witness that I have not unnecessarily dwelt on the gloomy passages of my life. Intending the work as a compilation of facts upon portions of the world comparatively little known, I have identified myself with it only so far as was necessary to give it the interest of a narrative. I shall be pardoned for dwelling somewhat at length upon my personal sufferings in a prison which a Howard never visited, and in a remote settlement, where the business of the better portion of the residents was too engrossing, and their stay too limited, to admit of a turning of their attention to the forgotten inmates of a prison. It was a miniature Pandemonium—a little hell, where the worst passions and propensities of the brutal officers who managed it had license unrestrained. I have been fastened in a position painful of itself, my legs extended, and arms confined, while two brutes administered flagellation with heavy cowhides. In the struggle which preceded my being thrust into the dungeon, my body was so completely denuded of clothing, that, in the cold, damp cell, I was fain thankfully to accept the comfort of a portion of the mat of the miserable felon who was the occupant of the cell with me. Even the sorry privilege of perambulation about my narrow quarters was, during a portion of the time, denied me. Heavy irons upon my feet, bolting them about three feet apart, were connected with a chain to my left arm, compelling me to keep the arm straight by my side when I stood erect. The bolt between my legs was, during about a week of the three I spent in the cell, fastened to a ring-bolt in the floor. The food served me there was a miserable pittance of half boiled rice, floating in three times the quantity of water necessary to cook it. This, with two small broiled fish, was barely sufficient to sustain my miserable existence. Never during my life did I so utterly despair as when confined in this horrid hole, seeing no person except my convict companion, save when upon the Sabbath I walked in my irons to the altar, to see the institutions of religion profaned in a place where its dictates were utterly set at naught. For all this decency would seem to require, at least, the form of an examination upon the charges preferred by Capt. Knight; but no such form, to give my confinement a color of justice, ever took place. Upon my liberation, the Spy had been sold, and Capt. Knight had left Manilla. His unsupported word had been sufficient to throw me into the power of these demons, and, careless of my fate, he left me there.

The inquiry may be made, why, if my confinement was so irksome, I did not gladly embrace the first opportunity to escape from it. To this I answer, that the worst part of my punishment did not take place till after I had so refused, and that my principal reason for refusing was my unwillingness to leave George, unfriended, in a prison. We had been together so long, and had become so endeared to each other by a participation in good and ill fortune, that to separate was even more painful than to endure the worst that the prison would inflict. I knew that no constitution, even the most iron, could long bear up under the hard usage and scanty food; the records were before me in the names of British and American citizens carved on the guard-bed. Under many of these survivors had written the date of the death of the persons who cut them there; and the mate of the Spanish vessel in which I left Manilla, who was an American, and had

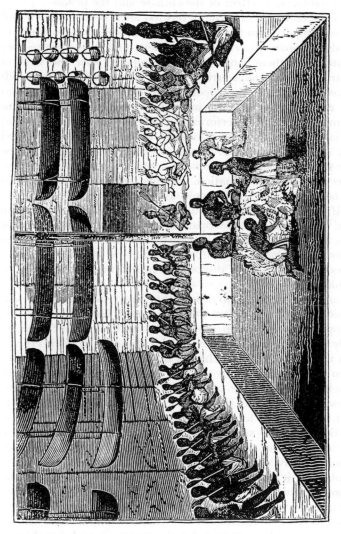

Fig. 10 Inside of a canoe house on Ponape, showing preparation of a roasted dog

himself been a prisoner in Manilla, informed me that he had known many instances where foreign sailors had fallen victims to the combined ill effect of the climate and the prison.

The appointment of a consul has too often been made without sufficient inquiry into the character and fitness of the incumbent. The discretionary power vested in them, and the influence they acquire, gives them more absolute command over the weal of the straggling—perhaps erring—sailor, than is safe in the hands of many who obtain the appointment. To this add the fact that their remuneration is often inadequate, and an insufficient inducement to careful performance of duty, and the fact that association with masters of vessels makes them a prejudiced party against the mariner. I know not that these causes operated more strongly upon the American consul at Manilla than upon others in the same situation. He had probably had his ears poisoned against me, and would allow me no chance to defend myself. When I remonstrated against his compelling me to go on board the Dash and the Spanish ship as a sailor, urging my rights as a British subject, he called me a factious fellow, a sea lawyer, and other hard names, affecting to consider my own wishes in regard to the disposal of myself the last thing to be consulted.

I am not prepared to assert that my cruel treatment was occasioned by direct orders from the consul, but I do know that he approved of it, when even the Spanish corregidor's son severely reprimanded the jailor and his deputies for their cruelty. Firm in innocence of the charges made against me, and appealing to the fact that there was not even circumstantial evidence enough to warrant the bare form of a trial, I hope that my representation of the character of the prison at Manilla, to which many other foreign prisons are similar, may lead to an investigation of the subject. Power to commit to such a prison is equivalent to the power of life and death; and where such committals may be made under cover of suspicion, and the party complaining is not bound even to attempt to substantiate his charges, it gives an undue scope for the gratification of petty revenge, and for imprisoning and treating a man like a felon for the mere convenience of a tyrannical ship-master. In our case, the corregidor was probably the means of our being shipped for Macao; for he had threatened to discharge us from the prison, and the consul did not care to have so troublesome a person as I should prove bruiting the story of my abuse about town.

The mate of the Spanish vessel in which we were sent to Macao was a Bostonian, who had been many years in India. Deep as my obligations to him are, and tenacious of names as my memory is generally, I regret that I cannot recollect his. During the passage he was very kind to us, and on leaving the ship at Macao he presented us with ten dollars from his own pocket. To Mr. Sturgis, a brother of the resident at Manilla, and to the English consul at Macao, we are also much indebted for their kind and friendly treatment.

Arrived at Macao, we were thence sent to Canton. At Canton we were objects of curiosity, and were visited by merchants and others connected with the English Factory; our tattooing examined, and our story of shipwreck and residence on the Carolines was repeated two or three times a day during the week we remained there. Through those gentlemen the owners and others interested in the John Bull probably heard of the loss of that vessel, if it had not before been published by our shipmates who took the other boats. Of the fate of any except those who escaped in the boat with us I have never heard a syllable. It may be that they found their way to other islands in the Pacific, and it may be that they perished at sea. It were an enterprise worth the munificence of the English or American governments to send some one of their cruisers to Ascension, to establish the geographical position and commercial advantages of many of these islands, which are comparatively little known, and to take off the four Englishmen we left there, or as many of them as survive.

At Canton George and myself agreed to accompany a caravan from Pekin to Constantinople. We were forwarded to Pekin in a Chinese junk, the passage occupying about ten days. Upon arrival at Pekin we found the caravan encamped outside the walls, in two or three divisions, packing their goods and preparing for their departure. There were beside us three Americans and one Englishman who had engaged to accompany the caravan, and conversation respecting the perils and fatigue of the journey disheartened me, and gave me a distaste for it. I was, beside, in extremely ill health; and these considerations combined decided me to attempt an escape. This after a few days we effected, taking our departure in the daytime, so little was such an intention suspected. I cannot say whether we were pursued or not.

We were about two months working our way back to Canton, shaping our course by the sea-side cities and towns, and getting an occasional lift in junks. We were once arrested and detained two days in prison, unable to understand our captors, or be understood by them. Nothing appearing about the "foreign barbarians" which augured ill intent, we were permitted to go again. Our baggage was simple enough, being only a spare shirt or two, and George's flute and fiddle. We gave the Chinese villagers tunes on these, in exchange for their fish and rice;—a trade they would never agree to till they had satisfied themselves we had nothing else. I had no adventures worth recording, and was, from my short stay and utter ignorance of their language, unable to make any observation worth preserving, except, perhaps, that the practice of cramping the feet is by no means so universal among the Chinese as that of painting is among the American ladies.

In about twelve weeks from the time of leaving them I stood again before my friends in Canton. They were astonished at the apparition, but I did not long haunt them with it. We were fortunate enough to ship in the Elizabeth, Capt. Rudkin, for Halifax; at which port we arrived in September, 1835. We had a pleasant passage, George's flute and fiddle enlivening the dog watches, and, to complete the band, I manufactured a drum out of a half barrel, by stretching a sheepskin over one head.

Arrived at Halifax, we found the cholera raging. Capt. Rudkin wished Keenan and myself to remain with the vessel. She was bound to Quebec, and thence to England. But we had a mind to travel the United States, and therefore declined. To get away from Halifax was the next consideration. To go by water would subject us to quarantine at the next port;—a delay we had no fancy for. Shoving our baggage on board a vessel bound to St. John, N. B., George and I boarded our land tacks for a pedestrian tour to that place. As the fates seemed long before to have settled that no journey of ours was to be prosecuted without interruption, we were not at all surprised when we were arrested by the military about fifteen miles from Halifax, and carried back to that place as deserters. We had been too well accustomed to petty vexations to consider this adventure worth more than a laugh, and after our discharge at Halifax started anew to recover our lost ground, and arrived at St. John before the vessel. Upon her arrival I applied at the health office for permission to take out my baggage, in order to proceed to the United States.

"Your baggage? where are you from?"

"Halifax."

"You are!" (retreating;) "and how did you get here?"

"By land."

"Stand back! back! The cholera is raging there, and you may have caught the infection!"

Questions upon questions followed, while I was compelled to keep at a safe distance. I saw my blunder, and was bothered completely. The scene ended by my being ordered to go to the hospital or leave the town, as I chose. "I staid no farther question," but made my escape upon the first opportunity. I was traced to my boarding-house, where chloride of lime, whitewash brushes, and other cleansing apparatus followed me forthwith. There again the women beset me, upon hearing the fact that I had brought the cholera in my pocket from Halifax. We were driven to an attic room, which, as an extreme act of grace, we were allowed to occupy, while the rest of the house underwent such a cleansing process as, I'll be sworn, nothing but the cholera and the health officers could have caused. Poor George, however, being taken ill, was immediately sent to the hospital on suspicion, though his symptoms were as little similar to those of cholera as can be imagined. There I left him, and, fearful of similar detention, shipped on board an American schooner, and arrived in New York late in the fall of 1835.

Here endeth my narration. Every man is possessed of the importance of the events which have ruled his fortune, and in love with his own history. Mine has been checkered enough; and the interest with which portions of it were listened to, and the advice of personal friends, has induced me to lay it before the reader. He will be his own judge whether it is worth that pains or not, but if he have followed it to this concluding paragraph, that attention is presumptive evidence, at least, in my favor.

APPENDIX

We present the reader with an imperfect glossary of the language of the Carolines—we mean that dialect spoken by the Bonabeeans.[1] Not being a written language, its history is of course lost, or can only be assisted by the resemblance of some words, in their sounds, to other languages, particularly to the Spanish. This may be accounted for by the early visits of the Spaniards to the Islands, and their possession of the Philippines, from which group many emigrants may have reached the Carolines. The Jesuits say that some negro slaves were left upon the islands at an early date; upon what part of the long chain we are not able to state. But for the glossary, to commence with the numerals.

[1] The first column is as O'Connell gives it; in the second column the words are given in the standard Ponapean orthography developed by Dr Paul Garvin, which has been used with some modifications in Ponapean schools and by government offices. That orthography is as follows:
1. Vowels are roughly as in Spanish except for the digraph *oa*, a low back vowel.

One, *ad.*   *ehd*
Two, *arree.*   *are*
Three, *agil'.* *   *esil*
Four, *abung'.*   *epeng*
Five, *alim'.*   *alim*
Six, *ah-awl.*   *awon*
Seven, *ah-aitch'.*   *eis*
Eight, *ah-well'.*   *ewel*
Nine, *adu'.*   *edu*
Ten, *codthinghowl'.*   *kedingoul*

For twelve to twenty, *amun* (?) seems to be substituted for *codthinghowl'* (*kedingoul*).

Eleven, *ad-ata.*   *ehd(e)te* = 'it is only one'
Twelve, *arree'-amun.*(?)
Thirteen, *agil'-amun.*(?)
Fourteen, *abung'-amun.*(?)
Fifteen, *alim'-amun.*(?)
Sixteen, *ah-awl'-amun.*(?)
Seventeen, *ah-aitch'-amun.*(?)
Eighteen, *awell'-amun.*(?)
Nineteen, *adu-'amet.*   *edu met* = 'this is nine'.

---

2. Consonants are approximately as in English except that there is generally no aspiration and presence or absence of voicing is of no phonemic significance. The exceptions are:
    a. *t* is a retroflex alveolar stop;
    b. *d* approximates English *t*;
    c. *ng* is a digraph for a velar nasal;
    d. *s* is about midway between English *s* and *sh*, and is sometimes heard as English *ch*, *ts*, and almost *j*;
    e. *pw* and *mw* each represent single phonemes, pronounced approximately as written but with lip rounding beginning before closure.
3. *h* represents no phoneme and is used only as a sign of phonemic length of the vowel preceding it.
4. Those consonants that can occur doubled (*m, mw, n, ng, l, r*) are written by repeating them, except for double *mw*, which is written *mmw*, and double *ll*, which is written *nl* when this is its etymological derivation.

Wherever nothing can be made by the present editor of one of O'Connell's words he has inserted a question mark.

* *G always hard in this glossary.*

Q

For twenty they say *arree-amun-codthinghowl* (*are . . . kedingoul*). This would seem literally to mean *twelve-ten*; but as custom has established it otherwise, the arbitrary arrangement, or rather disarrangement, answers very well for their limited business. Thirty is *agil'-amun-codthinghowl*; forty, *abung'-amun-codthinghowl*; and so to one hundred, which is expressed by repeating *codthinghowl* once or twice, and showing the ten digits. For two hundred, the open hands are lifted twice; for three, three times; and so on. For thousand they have no term, and seldom have occasion to count beyond fifty.[2]

The language is guttural, the number of words small, and many bear so close a resemblance in sound that it is necessary to be very distinct in enunciation, and to assist language by continual gesture. There are many words which are slightly varied to express things different, but of the same general class. Take the following as instances.

Window,		*wenihmw*
Light,	*ya hour'a.*(?)	*marain*
Clouds,		*depwek*
Cold, or windy, *mahour'a.*(?)		*lemwilemwir*
Day, *hour'a-hour'a.*(?)		*rahn*
Eyebrows, *agour'a.*(?)		*padi*
Thunder, *ya hour'a-mah.*(?)		*nahnsapwe*

But *kid'jinny* (*kisin*, a frequent diminutive) appears to be a more universal prefix than any other.

Cord, or twine, *puale*.	*pwel*
Sling, *kid'jinny puale*.	*kisin pwel* = 'bit of string'. Properly *peii*
Yam, *kid'jinny kiup*.	*kisin kehp* = 'bit of yam'
Bamboo, *puala*.(?)	*ahlek*
Bamboo knife, *kiup-et*, or *kid'jinny-puala*.	*kapit*
Fire, *kid'jinny-ai*.	*kisin iei*
Lightning, *kid'jinny-ai-moonjob*.(?)	*kisin iei mwohnsapw* = 'chiefly bit of fire'. Properly *lioal*.

[2] There are some nine series of numbers for the numbers 1 to 9 in Ponapean. Choice of one series or another during speech depends upon the class of object to which the numbers are to be applied. Classes include animate objects, fruits and small globular objects, stick-like objects, strings of small objects, etc. The series for 1 to 9 that O'Connell gives

Hair, *mung-ai.*	*moangei* = 'my head'. *Moang* = 'head' is often used for 'hair', which is more correctly *piten moang*.
Eyes, *ickn-ai.** (?)	*mese*
Smoke, *kid'jinny-ung.* (?)	Perhaps *kisinieng* = 'wind'? Smoke = *ediniei.*

---

are the basic numbers, used in counting aloud without reference to particular objects.

But the form O'Connell gives for the number 11 means literally 'it is only "one"'. In the case of number 19 he is saying 'this is "nine"'. And the forms for 12 to 18 are suffixed by *amun*, which is unrecognisable in modern Ponapean.

It may be that O'Connell is confused about the use of one of the nine series of numbers, that which applies to animate objects, in which the suffix applied to the elementary numbers 1 to 9 is *emen*. However, Dr John L. Fischer has suggested a different explanation for *amun*. In using the counting-aloud series Ponapeans repeat the same numerals in each series of ten, the only change being at twenty, at thirty, etc. It is conceivable that O'Connell, in learning the numbers, lined up a number of similar objects in a row and asked people to count them. When he got to the eleventh in the row he would have elicited the number *ehd*, 'one', again. If he did not accept this the teacher might finally have said *ehdete*, 'it is only one', and O'Connell might then have taken this to mean 'eleven'. Similarly, O'Connell's word for 'nineteen' contains the suffix *met*, 'this', the whole word meaning 'this is nine', as though the teacher had finally come to the end of the row. Dr Fischer points out that although *amun*, used by O'Connell for the suffix in numbers 12 to 18, has no meaning in modern Ponapean, in the language of the next major island to the west, Truk, there is a demonstrative form *eemwuun*, 'that'. Perhaps *amun* is a cognate but obsolete demonstrative in Ponapean. In that case the word for twelve as O'Connell gives it would mean 'that is two', thirteen would be 'that is three', etc., as the teacher pointed to successive objects in the row. This would also explain the use of *met*, 'this', instead of 'that' for the last in the row. And *arree-amun-codthinghowl* (*are . . . kedingoul*) would mean not 'twelve-ten' as O'Connell has it but 'that is the second ten'.

As for the absence of a term for 1,000, O'Connell is wrong. Andrew Cheyne gives numbers up to 10,990 in the early 1840s, only a decade after O'Connell, and another ten years later Luther H. Gulick recorded words for 10,000 also. There are terms, at least in modern Ponapean, for numbers into the thousands of millions.

* *Is the* ai *in* mung-ai *a particle borrowed from the resemblance of flame to the hair?—and is the same particle in the word for eyes traceable to the same source for their light, or fire?*

Bread-fruit, *kid'jinny-mai.* — *kisin mai* = 'bit of breadfruit'

Rat, *kitty-ticatic* (literally, little dog).(?) — *kitik*

Fresh water, *kid'jinny-nianpeel.*(?) — *kisin nanpihl* = 'bit of at-the-water'? Properly *pihl.*

Salt water, *nan'chate.* — *nansed*

Plantain, *kid'jinny bana'na.* (?) — Obviously *uht*

Banana, *kid'jinny banee'na.* — English *uht*

Tortoise, *kid'jinny-but.* — *kisin pwet* = 'piece of turtle shell'. *Wehi* = generic term for turtle; *kalahp* = green turtle; *sapwake* = hawksbill.

Tattooing, *kid'jinny-ding.* — *kisin inting*

And, *an.* — *a*

My, mine, near connections, friends, *ni, eni,* or *ni-a-met.* — *nei* = 'my (child)' *nei met* = 'it is mine'

Bread-fruit preserved in the earth, *kid'jinny-mah.* — *kisin mahr*

Fish, *maam.* — *mwahmw*

„ for food, *kid'jinny-maam.* — *kisin mwomw* = 'a little fish' or 'piece of fish'

Cocoa-nut, *kid'jinny-but.*(?) — *nih, ering, mwangas, uhpw,* etc. = coconut at different stages of growth

Dog, *kitty,* and *kid'jinny-kitty.* — *kidi, kisin kidi*

No, *cho'.* — *soh*

There (with the finger pointing to the place intended), *met.* — *met* = 'here'; *mwo* = 'there'

What? *tham?* — *da*

Yes, *aye.* — *ehi*

Here, *met.* — *met*

Some of the principal adjectives are:

Good, or handsome, *maco'jalale.* — *me kaselel*

Bad, *mid'jiwid.* — *me suwed*

Brave, *ma coo'mot.* — *me kommwoad*

cowardly, *mucha-purk'.* — *masapwehk*

Pleasant to the smell, *pour-mow*.
pwoh-mwau

Pleasant to the taste, *ma-kow'a.*(?)
song-mwau

Hot, *mahor'ragorra.*
me karakar

Sick, *jo'mow.*
soumwau

Well (literally, not sick), *cho'-jomow.*
soh soumwau

Dead, *midjila.*(?)
melahr is the modern word, but since Cheyne gives a similar form, *mejilaar*, O'Connell's word is acceptable as obsolete.

Large, *lapalap.*
lapalap

Small, *ticatic.*
tikitik

Straight, *mara'ra.*
marahra = 'light, swift'. Properly *ihnen* or *wahsak*

Long and straight (applied to trees, or deep to water), *miri'ri.*
me reirei = 'tall'

Crooked, *mawu'ka.*(?)
me epu, or *pirok*

White, *but'abut.*
pwetepwet

Red, *whyta'ta.*
weitahta

Black, green, any dark color, *maton'-dawl.*
me toantoal

Wet, *peel'amet.*
pihl met = 'this is water'. Properly *wisekisek*

Dry, *lee'amet.*(?)
matakong

Old, *mow'nawee.*(?)
me laud, or *memir*

Many, much, or all, *toto.*
tohto

Names of things

House, *nannaim'.**
nan-ihmw = 'at the house'

Mat, for bed, *loach.*
lohs

„ „ man's clothing, *call.*
koahl

„ „ woman's clothing, *lagow.*
likou

Sash, *wy'wy.*
weiwei

Hat, *lajor'rob.*
lisoarop

* *Spelt* nanname *in the body of this book.*

Tree, *too'ga.* — *tuhke*

Flowers, *ellan too'ga.* The same word is also used for beads, and other ornaments. — *elin tuhke*

Paddle, *paddel'.* — *padil*

Milk, *lecha.*(?) — Obviously Spanish. *pil-en dihdi.*

Canoe, *wah.* — *wahr*

War-canoe, *wah-en-wye.* — *wer-en waii* = 'foreign canoe'. No special war-canoe exists; there is a chief's canoe = *warasapw*

Ship, *wah-en-wye lapalap.* — *wer-en waii lapalap* = 'large foreign canoe'

Stone, *tockye.* — *takai*

Spear, or any other war implement, *cod jic.* — *kesik*

Calabash, *ajurk.* — *isek*

Whale, *maam lapalap.* — *mwahmw lapalap* = 'big fish'. Properly *rohsa.*

Shark, *maam majorhowi.* — *mwahmw me sarawi* = 'sacred fish'. Properly *pako.*

Sand, *cha'va.*(?) — *pihk*

Forest, *toogas-toto.* — *tuhke tohto* = 'many trees'. Properly *wel.*

Mosquito, *mas'wah.* — *amwise*

Reef, *nan'chete toky'ah.* — *nansed takai* = 'sea stone'. Properly *mmad.*

Parts of the body

Head, *magun'gong.*(?) — *moange*

Hair, *mungai'.* — *moangei* = 'my head'. *Moange* can also mean 'hair' but is *piten moange* in full.

Mouth, *shabagou'la.*(?) — *awa*

Eyes, *icknai.*(?) — *mese*

Eyebrows, *agour'ah.*(?) — *padi*

Nose, *canoup'.*(?) — *timwe*; possibly is the honorific form *kaunuhni*

Cheek, *marock a'rock.*(?) — *sepe*

Ears, *paroof.*(?) — *salenge*

Breast, *de'-de*.	*dihdi*
Stomach, *mowauk'*. (?)	*kapehdi*
Arms, Hands, } *gorah'*. (?)	*pehi*
fingers, *pammah'*. (?)	*sendin pehi*
finger-nails, *ve'nah*. (?)	*kikin pehi*
Back, *ah'vah*. (?)	*tihnseu*
Leg, *purong'*. (?)	*nehi*
Feet, *noup*. (?)	*nehi*
Toes, *purvath'*. (?)	*sendin nehi*
Tongue, Speech, } *laky'a*.	*lokaia*
Teeth, *gurh*. (?)	*ngih*
Blood, *mahru'nah*. (?)	*nta*
Heart, *mahvi'tah*. (?)	*moahngioang*
Breath, *arung'*. (?)	*ang en awa*
Hearing, *iningah'ry*. (?)	*rong*
Eating, *nam'anam*.	*neminem*
Smelling, *varen'*. (?)	*ned*
Seeing, *iningah'*. (?)	*kilang*
Man, *awl'aman*.	*ohl emen* = 'a man'
Woman, *ley'aman*.	*lih emen* = 'a woman'
Crowd, or army, *awl'aman toto*, or *har'ramatch*.	*ohl emen tohto* = ungrammatically 'a man, many'; *aramas* = 'people'
Infant boy, *jere awl'aman*.	*seri-wol emen* = 'a male child'; *seri-mwahn* = 'boy'; the common form, at least today, is *pwutak*.
„ girl, „ *ley'aman*.	*seri-li emen* = 'a female child'; common form is *seripein*.
Husband or wife, *ambode*.	*omw pwoud* = 'your spouse', or perhaps it is *omw pwoud e* = 'this spouse of yours'.

A complete grammar of the language we cannot, of course, attempt; nor would it repay the labor. With a few more of the principal words, with their English meanings arranged alphabetically, we shall close.

Bone, *tey*.	*tih*

Bone needle, *tey-gong'*.   *dikek*

Bird, *parrut'*.   *paret* = a species of tern; generic word for bird = *menpihr*.

Children, *ee'ni*.   *ih nei*

Chief, *aroche*.   Obsolete. See p. 151 n. 64.

Come, *gowthou*.   *kohdo*

Darkness, or night, *neebung'*.   *nihpwong*

To drink, *nimpeel a-met*, (?) or *jagow a-met*. (?)   *nimpil* . . . *sakau* (= 'kava') . . .

Drunk, *jagowlo*.   *sakaula*

Dancing, *gur'lic*.   *kahlek*, one type of dance

Father, *ba'ba*.   *pahpa*

Fish-hook, *kroh*. (?)   *kehs*

   „   net, *kerruk*. (?)   *uhk* = 'seine'

Fly, *marah*. (?)   *pihr*

Go, *kit-ai'*. (?)   *kohla*

Grass, *mowee*. (?)   *dihpw, reh*

Give, *gi'tui*.   *kihdo*

Hungry, *mung-ata'*.   *men mwengehda*

Kill, *codjic midjila'* (?) (literally spear dead).   *kesik* (= 'spear') . . . Modern word is *kemehla*.

Land, *lan'job*.   *nansapw*

Laugh, *hara'hara*. (?)   *kouruhr*

Leaf, *tan*.   *tehn* = 'leaf of'. *Teh* = 'leaf'.

Lizard, *ler'vah*. (?)   *lamwer* = 'gecko', *li-meni-menin-seri* = Perocheirus, and other species.

Liquor, from *piper methysticum jagow*.   *sakau*

Madiah, satisfied with food.   *medila*

Marriage, *ambodge'*.   *omw pwoud* = 'your spouse'

Mind, spirit, ghost, *a'niman*.   *enih-men*

Mother, *no'no*.   *nohno*

Moon, *jow'naboo*.   *sounpwong*

Noise, *agou'la*. (?)   *katairong*

Priest, *e'diomet*. (?)   *samworou, leiap*

Rain, *codhow*.   *keteu*

Rough skin, *kilanwy'*.   *kilin waii* = 'foreign skin', ringworm

Sky, or visible heavens, *moon-*   *mwohnsapw* = 'first of the *job.*(?)

land', a chiefly rank; sky = *lahng*

Sun, *cod'ripin.*   *ketipin*
Sit down, *moondie.*   *mwohndi*
Singing, *cockholt.*   *kokoal*
To-morrow, *lockup.*   *lakapw*
You, *cow'ay.*   *kowe*
Washing, *doo doo'.*   *duhdu* = 'bathe'

INDEX

230

Dr S. H. Riesenberg is Curator of Pacific Ethnography at the Smithsonian Institution in Washington. In the course of a distinguished academic career he has spent several years engaged in anthropological field work in the Pacific islands, particularly on Ponape in the Caroline Islands, the locale of much of O'Connell's narrative. It was here that Dr Riesenberg's interest in O'Connell's book was first aroused, and he devoted much time to tracking down O'Connell's background. From his personal knowledge of the Caroline Islands, he was able to check many of the Irishman's facts.

Dr Riesenberg is the author of *The Native Polity of Ponape*.

Designed by Philippa Walker
Text set in 10 pt Intertype Baskerville
and printed on 85 gsm Burnie English Finish paper
by Halstead Press Pty Ltd, Sydney

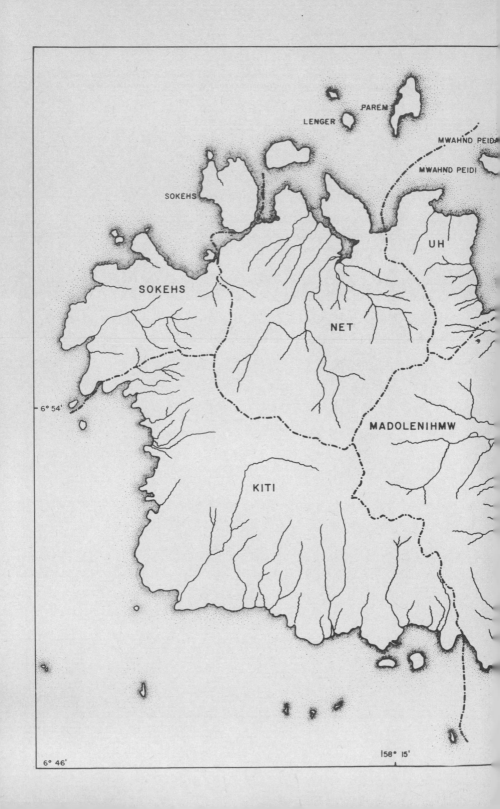